OREGON
FOR THE
CURIOUS

by

Ralph Friedman

Photographs by Phoebe L. Friedman
(except as individually noted)

The CAXTON PRINTERS, Ltd.
Caldwell, Idaho
1993

First printing, Third Revised Edition, October, 1972
Second printing, Third Revised Edition, March, 1973
Third printing, Third Revised Edition, April, 1974
Fourth printing, Third Revised Edition, October, 1976
Fifth printing, Third Revised Edition, February, 1979
Sixth printing, Third Revised Edition, February, 1982
Seventh printing, Third Revised Edition, November, 1987
Eighth printing, Third Revised Edition, May, 1993

International Standard Book Number 0-87004-222-X

Library of Congress Catalog Card Number 7-151057

Lithographed and bound in the United States of America
157338

Table of Contents

List of Illustrations

List of Abbreviations

m	mile or miles
E	east or eastern
W	west or western
S	south or southern
N	north or northern
L	left
R	right
O	Oregon (road designation)
CB	covered bridge
SP	state park
FS	U.S. Forest Service
BLM	U.S. Bureau of Land Management
CG	campground
PG	picnic ground
Mtn.	mountain
H-T	historical tour
PO	post office
Jct.	junction
Rec.	recreation
Res.	reservoir
station	service station
*	off the main road

Other abbreviations are readily identifiable.

The Latch-String

Oregon for the Curious has been amazing to everyone who has had an acquaintanceship with the history of the book. It has been particularly awesome to my wife and me who, ourselves, published the first two editions.

Our first printing in 1965 was 7000 copies——and after the books arrived, we wondered what madness had prompted us to order so many. We thought it would take at least two years to sell them. We knew very few booksellers, or even where they were, and possessed no publishing experience. But within four months, the 7000 books were sold.

From the beginning we underestimated the popularity of *Oregon for the Curious*. We always ordered or reordered too few, and sometimes several months passed between reprintings. I must say, my wife was the optimistic one, and if I had listened to her, we might have sold another five or ten thousand books.

In addition, we did little to promote our product, having neither the time nor the money to do so. Despite all negative factors—the fumbling of amateurs—35,000 copies of *Oregon for the Curious* were sold in the first two editions. The book has been purchased by persons in every state of the nation and in about a dozen countries. At least a score of books have gone to Viet Nam.

Most of this sales performance has been accomplished by word of mouth, the very best kind of promotion. We have many letters bearing such comments as: "I've sold about 25 books for you"; "I sent your book out to all our friends and relatives"; "Please mail me five more copies of *Oregon for the Curious*, everybody who comes to the house and sees it wants a copy"; "I talk up your book wherever I go." And all these letters from strangers.

"Many folk coming through our area use your book as their Bible for traveling and seeing Oregon," wrote the postmaster and storekeeper of Ashwood, Roberta Symons. Wherever we go we find people with the book in hand or by their side—a Lake Oswego couple looking for Oregon Trail ruts above Echo Junction, a Port Orford man camped in Succor Creek Canyon, a Portland woman photographing the Darlingtonia bogs, a Jordan Valley rancher at Shaniko, a retired schoolteacher from Jackson County strolling through Cornucopia . . . I could go on for a page or two.

In this edition—the third—the book has practically been rewritten and is much, much larger than the second edition (1966). Places no longer existent have been eliminated and several hundred new specific places added. Almost all the photos are new—and there are many more of them than appeared in the second edition.

In response to reader interest, we have added a great deal more on fishing than we presented before, and much information for boaters and campers (including trailerists). Rockhounds will find this edition quite profitable, we believe, because of the detailed data. Indeed, the index carries an entry on rockhounding, with an abundance of sites listed.

Let me repeat what I stated in the introduction to the previous editions:

Although comprehensive, this book clearly emphasizes the off-the-beaten-path places. For information on the well-publicized places, you can obtain free literature by the pound. Most of it will not be very accurate or well written, but there will be enough virtue in both instances to meet most needs.

If, however, you want to know about the places which are rarely or never mentioned in the free, or other, literature, this book will be a text of discovery. You might be surprised at the number of travel information agencies—from national to local, including public and private—who use *Oregon for the Curious* to direct persons to off-the-beaten-path places or who recommend the book to tourists.

This book is not concerned with tourist facilities except in such areas where readers might wonder if any services at all are available.

Since the only obligation this book has is to the reader, it can afford to be honest. Many readers have complimented us upon the book's candor; some chambers of commerce and some merchants and local patriots have been disappointed.

Prices are not listed because, in general, they are unstable. A museum that is free today could charge a fee tomorrow, and vice versa.

The great majority of travel guides list mileage on a cumulative basis: that is, starting with 0 at Town A and adding mileage between towns to the mileage before, so that when you come to Town Z the mileage may be 200, or 300, or 400.

This system is simply not practical for ordinary travelers, let alone those bent on straying off the main roads. In this book, all mileage is on a point-to-point basis.

It will soon be evident to you that mileage variations arise. We have learned that an odometer is an extremely imprecise and inconsistent instrument. Let me cite an experiment we tried. We traveled a stretch of road in three cars, making three trips. Each car not only registered a different mileage, but each car showed a distance variation in the return to the starting point. We then checked with three official road departments. Each gave us a different figure—for that same stretch of road. However, you will not find the variations large enough to give you concern and, by following the simple directions, you should find any place listed in the book without difficulty.

A word of caution: The state is constantly changing. ("Current" maps are out of date before they are released.) Houses are torn down, ranches sold, tourist facilities increase or decrease. But, in the main, this book will prove to be an invaluable guide. It contains, based upon personal travel and research, the most contemporary information available.

As for format, this book has been arranged in the simplest, yet most exact form possible—by section and road. There is also a comprehensive index.

The areas off the main roads are indented and are preceded by an asterisk(*). When the specific indented section ends, you are back on the key road. In addition, phrase guides have been inserted, at many returns to the main roads, to guard you from any confusion.

So—where shall we go exploring? To thunderous Cascade Head, which no road touches? To Lost Forest, where you cannot find water? To the virgin oaks on the Big Muddy? To the soul-stirring panoramas of Joseph Viewpoint or Mascall Overlook? To abandoned gold mines reached only by dim rutted traces? To a Wilderness few people have penetrated, or even approached? To ghost towns deep in the desert?

Open the book—and a new world of Oregon is yours to discover.

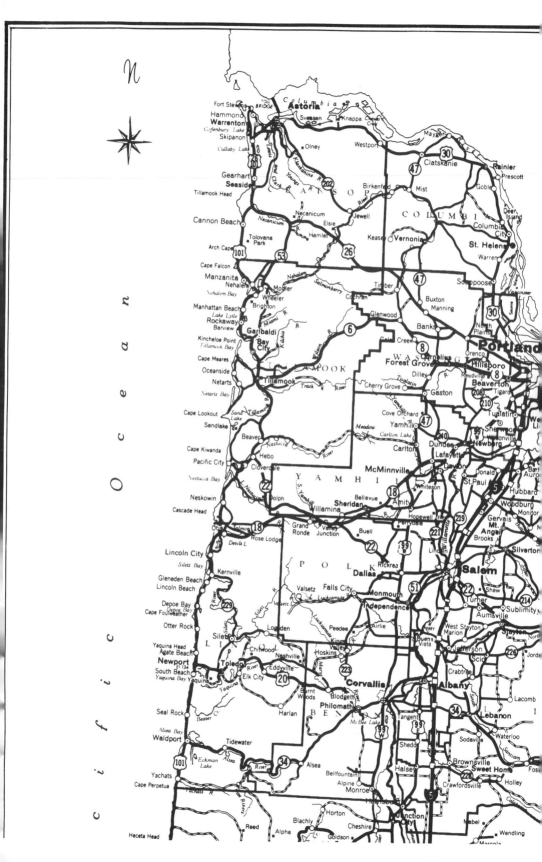

Northwest Oregon

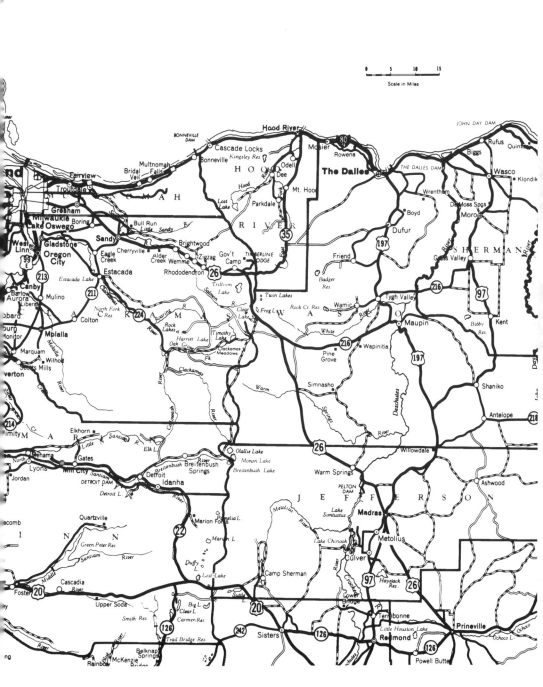

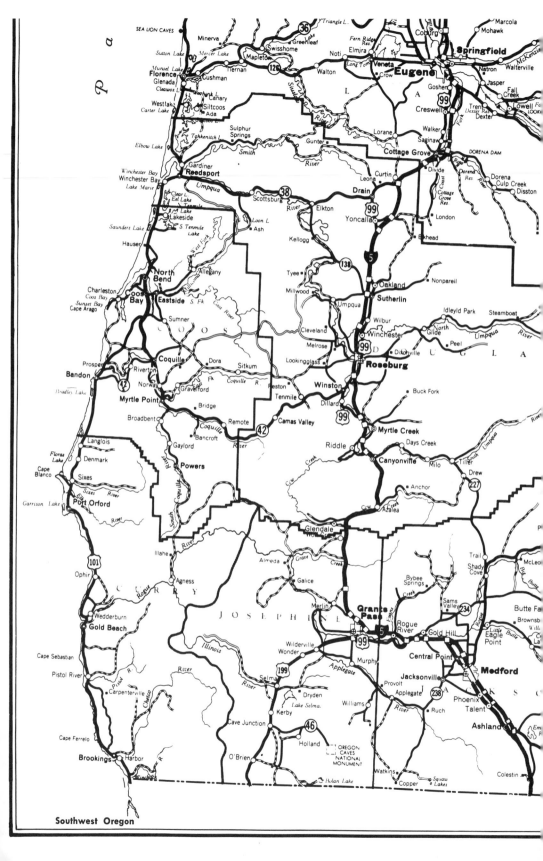

Southwest Oregon

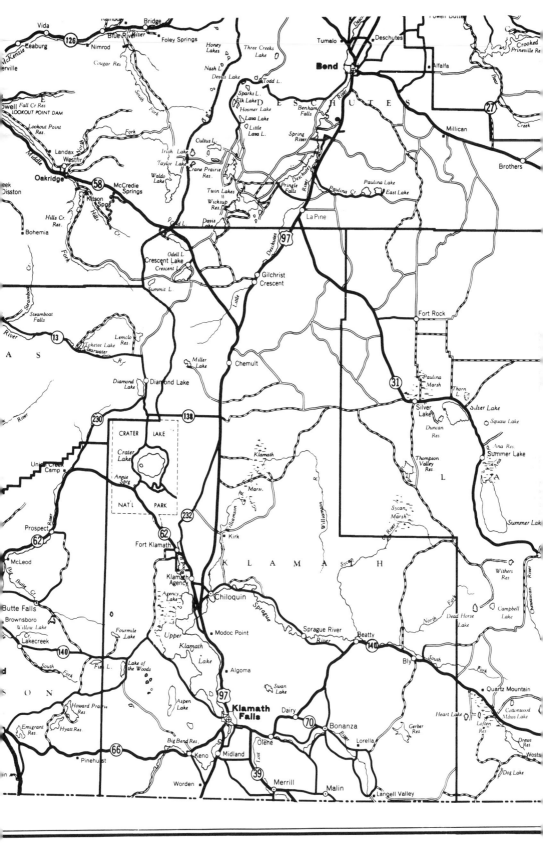

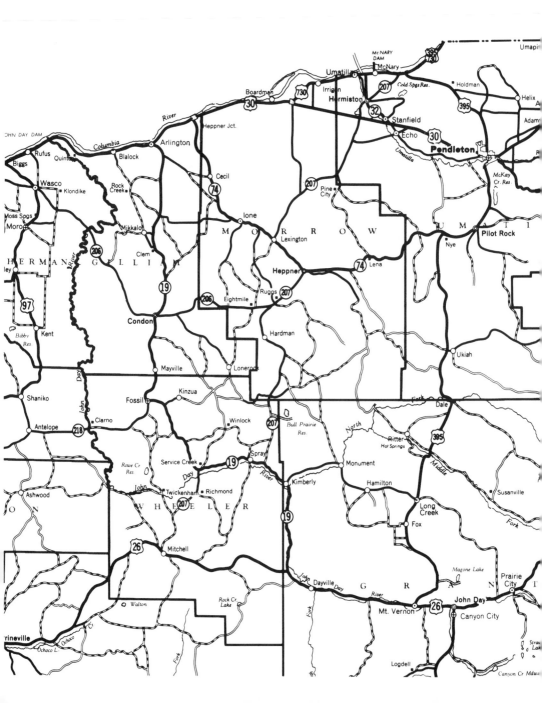

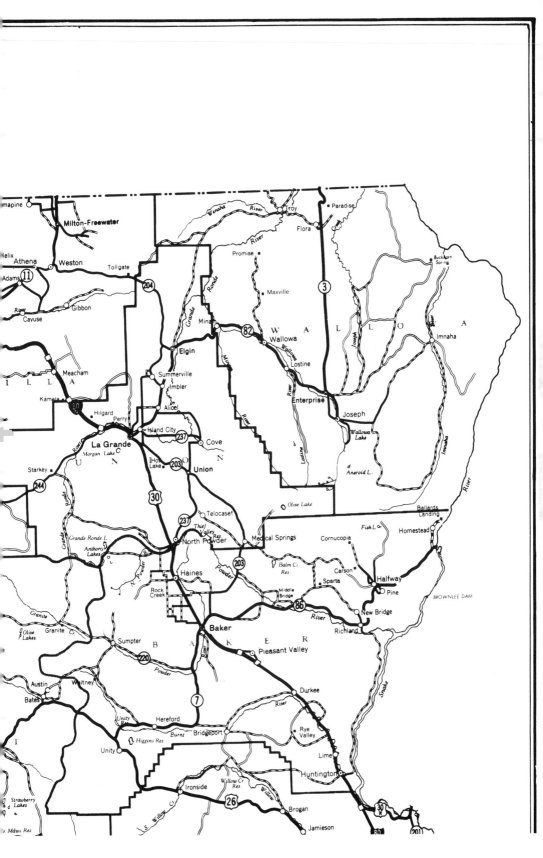

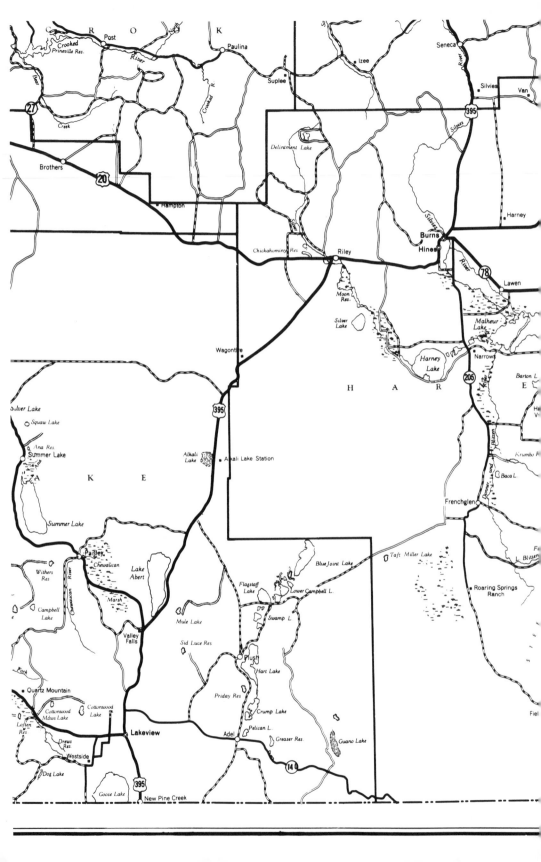

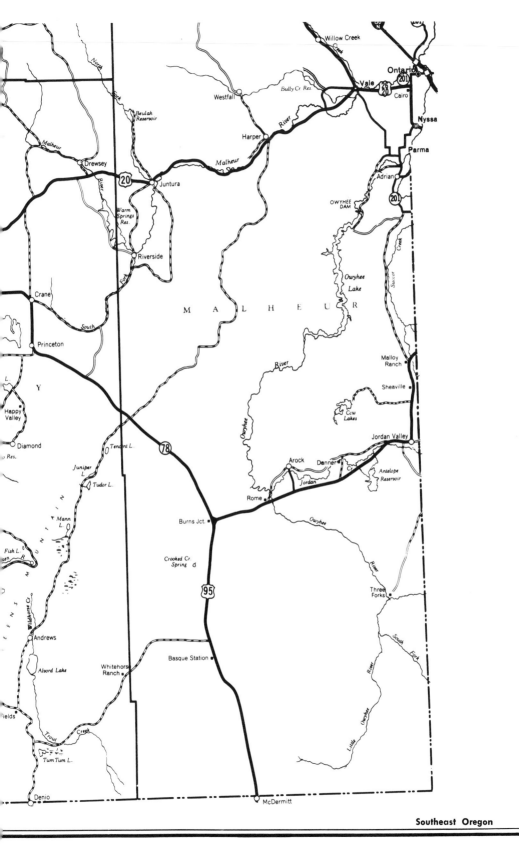

Southeast Oregon

OREGON FOR THE CURIOUS

The Oregon Coast

US 101 enters Oregon at **Astoria** from Washington on a 4-m.-long bridge that spans the Columbia River. A few miles westward, the first known white men to touch the NW tip of Oregon landed from Captain Robert Gray's fully-rigged windjammer—the first white mariners to find the river Gray named after his vessel. The date was May 11, 1792.

The first white settlement in Oregon was founded in late 1805, near present Astoria, with construction of Ft. Clatsop by the Lewis and Clark party. A few months later the stockade was abandoned.

A more durable American settlement was established at Ft. Astoria in 1811 and lasted until 1813, when the British took over. Nominal control was returned to the Americans in 1818, but the British continued their dominating presence here for some years.

In late 1844 the first overland emigrants arrived on the Clatsop Plains, to the SW. Soon thereafter the first permanent white settlers came to the site of today's Astoria. By then there was scarcely a vestige of Ft. Clatsop and not much more of Ft. Astoria. In 1847 Astoria became the first U.S. PO W of the Rockies and two years later the first American Customs House in the W was established.

Much of Astoria's history is emblazoned on a 525-ft. spiral frieze of the 125-ft.-high **Astoria Column** atop Coxcomb Hill (see front cover for illustra-

Columbia River bridge, from Astoria

tion). Inside the tube a circular stairway of 166 steps climbs to a viewpoint platform. The vistas encompass sea, rivers, forests, hills, towns and farms on both sides of the Columbia. Fringing the parking area is a memorial to Chief Concomly, friend of Lewis and Clark. Part of the memorial "arch" is a replica of an Indian burial canoe. Also at the edge of a paved lot is a giant slab of a 600-year-old Sitka spruce. Clatsop County once had many immense forests—but everyone was in a hurry for quick profits.

Astoria Column is 1.2 m. up 16th St. from Marine Dr. Between 16th & 17th, off Marine Dr., is parking area for **Lightship No. 88**, the *Columbia*, moored two blocks from the **Columbia River Maritime Museum**, at 16th & Exchange. The vessel came 'round the Horn in 1909 and served as lightship for 52 years. It is the largest artifact of the museum, one of the best of its kind in the nation.

Astoria's fishing fleet is the largest in the state. Boats tie up at West Mooring Basin (Fishermen's Dock). There is a happy hum in the air when large catches of Royal Chinook salmon are unloaded.

The site representing Ft. Astoria is at 15th & Exchange. The handsome city library, 10th & Exchange, was a gift of British descendants of John Jacob Astor, who sought to establish a fur empire here and after whom the town is named.

Astoria is dotted with old and interesting houses, with many of the dwellings having been tastefully remodeled. Best known structure is the **Flavel House**, Duane & 8th, cupola-topped, 3-story Victorian mansion put up in 1883 and now the museum of the Clatsop County Historical Society.

For examples of architecturally exciting 19th-century homes, see the Ben Young House (1883) at 3652 Duane and the Gust Holmes House (1889) at 682 34th. Other historic homes are at 1687 Grand (1870), 690 17th (1883), 836 15th (1880), 788 Franklin (1869), 469 Bond (1863), 765 Exchange (1863), 1337 Franklin (1854), 1393 Franklin (1879), 1585 Exchange (1880), 1524 Jerome, 1711 Grand, 1243 Franklin.

All these homes are private and not for interior public inspection—but there is no prohibition of outside viewing.

1.3 m., jct., O 202—to Mist. (See *Cross-Coast Range Roads.*)

2.6 m., Warrenton Jct.

* Turn R. *1.2 m.*, **Warrenton**, charter boat center for salmon fishing at mouth of Columbia. Warren House (1884), across road from boat basin, is ghostly mansion of baronial days. *3.1 m.*, **Hammond**. First schoolhouse, built in 1901, is now a dwelling, and two stories shorter than in its teaching days. Gymnasium, in rear, is now also used as a dwelling. Schoolhouse is two blocks up Harrietta St. Catholic church, Boone & Harrison, long abandoned, has grass growing out of cracks on bottom stair. In its ravaged state this church bldg. holds far more beauty than most contemporary church structures. *0.6 m.*, **Ft. Stevens**. Established in 1864 and terminated as military post in 1946, fort was only U.S. mainland fortification shelled during WW II—by Japanese sub. Old coast

Warren House, Warrenton   Abandoned Catholic church, Hammond

artillery guns lacked the range to reply. Post grounds today, with most bldgs. still in good shape (occupied by civilians), comprise picturesque setting. *1 m.*—take R fork—**Battery Russell,** emplacements for the removed "big guns." Return to Willow St.-Seaside Rd. at E edge of Hammond. Turn R.

1.1 m., **Ft. Stevens SP,** one of Oregon's most patronized parks. Freshwater Coffenbury Lake is only short walk from ocean surf, where waders frolic around the diminishing remains of the *Peter Iredale,* a British bark stranded on the beach during a heavy storm in the autumn of 1906. *3.2 m.,* US 101. Turn R.

0.6 m.—from Warrenton Jct. on 101—turnoff L for **Ft. Clatsop National Memorial.**

* *3.1 m.* to replica of Ft. Clatsop, built in the soggy wilderness by the Lewis and Clark party for their stay through the winter of 1805–06. Graphic displays and audio-visual presentations dramatize epic of the trailblazers. Return to 101. Turn L.

3.5 m., on R—and reached by very narrow lane—Gray Memorial Chapel, better known as **Clatsop Plains Pioneer Church,** because bldg. is on site of the first Presbyterian church, erected in 1850 as outgrowth of Presbyterian Society organized in 1846. Congregation, whose early members included William H. Gray, pioneer missionary, compatriot of Marcus Whitman, and author of probably the most controversial history of Oregon, claims to be

Remains of the "Wreck of the Peter Iredale," Fort Stevens State Park

oldest continuing Presbyterian church W of the Rockies. Present bldg. has original 1850 pulpit.

6.8 m., Gearhart Jct.

  * Gearhart was for a long time the prime convention host of the Coast because of the hotel and golf links.

2.2 m., **Seaside.** Oregon's "Coney Island," with state's longest boardwalk and most used swimming beach. Seaside Aquarium has lively seal shows— but after watching seals compete for fish food hour after hour, one begins to wish they could escape their small, crowded prison. Reconstructed salt cairn, on Lewis and Clark Way, near S end of promenade, marks location of the plant built by the Lewis and Clark party to obtain salt by boiling sea water. Levi Coffman House, 616 N Holladay, was built in 1853.

3.9 m., Jct., US 26. (See *Cross-Coast Range Roads.*)

3.1 m., turnoff for Ecola SP and Cannon Beach.

  * *0.4 m.,* turnoff R for Ecola SP. *2.2 m.,* picnic area, **Ecola SP.** The views from Tillamook Head dance before the startled eye. One is reminded of the observation made by the British mariner, Captain John Meares, in 1788: "Many beautiful spots, covered with verdure, solicited our attention: and the land rose in a very gradual ascent to the distant mountains, skirted by a white sand beach to the sea. . . ." Less than a mile offsore is sea lion rookery. That dot far out at sea that looks like a lighthouse is one, or was one. The abandoned, crumbling structure rises 41 ft. on an isolated rock, often swept in winter by gales of hurricane force. The base of the lighthouse is only 91 ft. above the water, so the keeper must have had some chill moments in strong blows and lashing waves. Within the park, tame deer and elk roam freely.

Return to Cannon Beach Rd. *0.3 m.,* **Cannon Beach,** famed for its offshore Haystack Rock. During low tide, the pools around the rock swarm with jellyfish, small crabs, starfish, sea anemones and other marine specimens swept in by the tides. (Do not try to climb the rock!)

2.8 m., 101. Turn R.

On US 101. *3.2 m.*—from Ecola SP-Cannon Beach turnoff—to S end of Beach Loop.

2.3 m., turnoff R to Hug Point SP. Parking for access to long, clean beach.

1.5 m., Arch Cape. Just a store now, but certain to be developed. Plenty of trees to cut down for houses, motels, stores, etc.

4 m., Short Sands SP. Picnicking in a virgin forest or on a dazzling beach.

0.3 m., **Oswald West SP**, named for a maverick governor who fought to preserve the coastal strip as a public heritage. CG *0.5 m.*, by trail; wooden wheelbarrows available for lugging in gear.

1.3 m., **Neahkahnie Mtn. lookouts**. The heart rises to the drama of the boiling, pounding surf and to headlands beset by vagrant winds. There are still so many exhilarating scenes along the Oregon Coast, and as exciting as when Warren Vaughn wrote in 1852: "It is a grand sight when the ocean is rough to see those monstrous waves chasing each other shoreward in wild confusion and dashing themselves against those huge rocks and throwing their foam high in the air. It is indeed a sight worth beholding."

The Tillamook Indians called Neahkahnie Mtn. "The Place of the Fire Spirit" and showed it reverence—but whites have a different view. Since pioneer days, there have been frequent searches for a treasure supposedly buried on a slope by the crew of a wrecked Spanish galleon. And a few be-

Fort Clatsop

lieve that the first European colony—probably Spanish—on the Pacific Coast was established here.

2.2 *m.*, turnoff for Neahkahnie Beach.

   * 0.9 *m.*, quiet, small beach with high driftwood bank.

0.3 *m.*, Manzanita Jct.

   * 0.5 *m.*, Manzanita, in the midst of 7 m. of sand. Continue 2 *m.*, following signs, to Nehalem Bay SP, a sand spit between Nehalem Bay and the ocean.

1.8 *m.*, **Nehalem.** Still has the appearance of a sea-scoured fishing village, though it is giving way to the arty and touristy. The Nehalem River, which completes its journey here, is the first sizeable salmon stream S of the Columbia. Fishing all by trolling.

US 101 follows Nehalem Bay, so full of the pastel colors of a Maine fish harbor.

2 *m.*, **Wheeler.** Once a gusty fish-packing town, Wheeler is now best known for its Rinehart Hospital, specializing in arthritis therapy.

7.7 *m.*, **Rockaway.** One of the least expensive and unpretentious coastal "bedroom" towns. Twin Rocks, seen clearly from the beach, looks like a Roman arch of antiquity, through which a seafaring Caesar would pass in tri-

Clatsop Plains Pioneer Church   **Haystack Rock, Cannon Beach**

Sunset at Rockaway

umph. The Duck pond behind the Standard Oil station is a trace of Walden Pond off the highway.

3 m., Jct., **Barview Jetty County Park.**

* *0.2 m.* Fishing from rocks at N jetty of Tillamook Bay. Some fishermen swear this is best place for deep-sea jetty fishing in state.

0.5 m., tree growing out of offshore rock; one of the many unusual bits of scenery on the Coast.

1.2 m., **Garibaldi.** Fishing fleet at boat basin is romantic forest of masts. *Morning Star II*, permanently moored, is replica of pioneer sailing vessel.

1.2 m., Jct., Miami River. Dikes along the river gave the district the name of Little Holland.

3.4 m., Bay City Jct.

* *0.2 m.*, Bay City Methodist Church, said to be oldest church in Tillamook County.

3.6 m., on L, Tillamook Cheese Factory. Samples.

2 m., **Tillamook**, cheese capital of Oregon. **Pioneer Museum** has finest wildlife exhibits in state, the art of curator Alex Walker.

Jct., O 6. (See *Cross-Coast Range Roads.*)

Probably the most kaleidoscopic side trip on the Oregon Coast begins at Tillamook.

* Turn R, or W, at 3d St. *1.8 m.*, Cape Meares Jct. Turn R. *5.4 m.*, turn L toward lighthouse & Oceanside. *2 m.*, Cape Meares SP. Turn R. *0.6 m.*, parking. Trails lead to lighthouse (no longer occupied) and to **Octopus Tree**, giant Sitka spruce whose massive trunk is the base of fantastic candelabra branching. Return to Oceanside Rd. Turn R. *2.5 m.*, Oceanside Jct. Turn R. *0.2 m.*, Oceanside, a breeze-filtered hamlet facing out to **Three Arch Rocks National Wildlife Refuge.** During nesting

Barview Jetty

"Octopus Tree"

Replica of old sailing vessel at Garibaldi

season, rocks are inhabited by swarms of sea birds—including murres, gulls, cormorants, puffins, petrels and guillemots—and become one of largest "bird cities" on continent. Rocks also permanent home of large herd of northern sea lions.

Return to jct. Continue straight, toward Netarts. *2.1 m.*, Netarts, modest beach village. *0.4 m.*, turn toward Cape Lookout SP. *6.2 m.*, **Cape Lookout SP** parking. Golden sands below a headland projecting 1.5 m. into the sea. Sizeable stand of virgin Sitka spruce. Sea bird rookery, with huge flocks of California murres in nesting season. SP a magnificent place to camp or picnic.

Backtrack *0.4 m.* to Sand Lake Jct. Turn R. *1.2 m.*, **Anderson's View Point.** Sweeping vista of Three Arch Rocks, miles of sunburst beach, Cape Lookout and the expansive Pacific.

Now the road winds through logged-off hills, thick banks of wild shrubbery, tall beach grass, and dune ridges and past overlooks, beaches and camping and picnic grounds. The mood of this stretch of road extends from the gloomy moors of 19th-century British novelists to barnyards out of Iowa. The road swings around the E rim of Netarts Bay. The W side, Netarts Peninsula, reached from the S end of the bay, has more than 5 m. of beach.

9.8 m., **Cape Kiwanda.** A sculptured headland cave flanking a sprightly cove, shimmery beach and Haystack Rock, second so named on the

Coast. *1.5 m.*, Pacific City. The barn-like store bldg. here was once a stagecoach inn and later, reputedly, a hideout for rum runners.

(South of Pacific City lies **Nestucca Spit,** a "sand wall" for Nestucca Bay. Only in the N part is there human habitation. The rest—3.5 m. long —belongs to nature, and no part of the Coast is so unspoiled, though highway engineers dream of rerouting 101 over it. Dunes topped by waves of beach grass roll back from the sea to heights of 40 ft. in the narrow part of the spit; in the widest part, a higher, naked "traveling dune" is pushed back and forth by fickle winds. Those who hike the beach in winter find Japanese glass floats, sand dollars and charming bits of driftwood.

At Pacific City, turn R. *2.8 m.*, US 101. Turn R.

From Tillamook—on US 101: *7.1 m.*, turnoff L for Munson Creek Falls County Park.

* *1.1 m.*, turn L into park. *0.5 m.*, through rain forest, parking. *0.5 m.* trail climb to **Munson Falls,** at 319 ft. the highest falls in the Coast Range. Flow is heaviest in winter and spring. The park—a darkling mass of old-growth firs, maples, alders, cedars, spruce and hemlock—is a suggestion of what much of the Coast looked like before frenetic logging began. *0.3 m.*, Pleasant Valley. Just an old-fashioned country store.

7.2 m., Beaver. Meadow Lake Jct. (Meadow Lake Rd. to Carlton. See *Cross-Coast Range Roads.*)

4.6 m., Hebo. Jct., O 22—to Salem. (See *Cross-Coast Range Roads.*)

Many fishermen consider the Nestucca River, near Hebo, the finest fishing stream in the state. Some Chinook are taken, but the catch is chiefly silver salmon.

2.5 m., Cloverdale, burly roadside town on a spinning portion of US 101.

2.9 m., jct., S end of Pacific City-Cape Meares-Tillamook Loop Rd.

7.4 m., **Neskowin,** an affluent resort community bordering a splendid bit of the sea-battered beach.

Cape Lookout from Anderson's View Point

* At S end of Neskowin, turnoff L for an 11-m. scenic forest drive, ending at O 18, near US 101. If you have the time and love trees and plants, you will not mind the many crooks in the road. The finest forest trip on the Oregon Coast.

6.3 m., Three Rocks Rd.

* Turn R for Cascade Head. *3 m.,* forks. Take Lower Salmon River branch to end of road, at Cascade Head Ranch. The SW-most portion of **Cascade Head,** a 1400-ft. promontory jutting out in the Pacific, was purchased late in 1969 by The Nature Conservancy for preservation as a natural area. The 300-acre Cascade Head natural area includes high meadows, rainforest areas with coniferous trees up to 200 ft. in height, and steep rocky cliffs down which waterfalls plunge into the reaching sea. Accessible only by trail.

1.3 m., jct., O 18—to McMinnville. (See *Cross-Coast Range Roads.*)

2.7 m., on R, Lincoln City Information Center. The beginning of Lincoln City, made up of five small once-independent towns in the "20 Miracle Miles." (The miracle will be if the Coast survives the excessive commercialization.)

0.4 m., on L, Lacey's Doll House, doll museum.

0.7 m., turn L at traffic light for Abraham Lincoln Memorial.

Haystack Rock, Cape Kiwanda

"Lincoln on the Prairie," Lincoln City

Depoe Bay

Devil's Punch Bowl

* 1 block, turn L. *0.1 m.*, on R, 14-ft. bronze statue, **"Lincoln on the Prairie."** The lank lawyer, in his saddle, reads pensively while his horse grazes.

0.7 m., turnoff L for **Devil's Lake SP.** Anglers find catfish weighing up to 20 lbs., as well as rainbows more than 2 ft. long, and large bass. The wild, white swans which cruise the placid lake are accommodating photographic subjects. The overnight camping area is within walking distance of the ocean beach where the first white vacationers on the Oregon Coast camped in 1837. Early missionaries Jason Lee and Cyrus Shepard, guided by Joe Gervais, the old voyageur, came with their brides to honeymoon on the whispering sands. Legend records that, in the week the ardent missionaries were here, they "cured themselves of malaria and evangelized the Salmon River Indians." Neither the malaria nor the Indians could have been serious.

0.2 m., "D" River, one of several streams in the state hailed as the "World's Shortest River."

4.3 m., Drift Creek Rd.

* Turn L for **Drift Creek CB,** one of few remaining in coastal area. *1.6 m.*, turn R. *0.5 m.* The bridge is typical of the flaring board-and-batten sides, curved portals and shingled roofs of the covered spans in Lincoln County. Most of them, if ever painted, have lost their paint and are as weathered and weary looking—which contributes to their backwoodsy

charm—as this bridge at Drift Creek. The CB was built here in 1914, which makes it one of the oldest of its species in the state.

1.1 m., Kernville, at the S end of Siletz Bay. The Siletz River, which empties here, is a popular salmon stream, especially for Chinooks in Aug. and Sept. and silvers in Oct. and Nov.

 * O 229, which begins at Kernville and runs S 31 m. to US 20 near Toledo, with only one town—Siletz—along the way, randomly follows the Siletz, and there are many places along the river for trolling.

1.2 m., on L, Salishan Lodge, the innkeeper's Taj Mahal of the Oregon Coast. Fine collection of coastal art.

1.1 m., turnoff for Gleneden SP. Day-use area for enjoyment of delightful beach.

2.4 m., Fogarty Creek SP. The sheltered creek trickling into the sea below seagrass bluffs splits a swath of well-trod beach, creating a most cheerful and photogenic setting. A very lively place when the summer sun shines.

1.3 m., Boiler Bay SP. A wayside offering an unbroken view of the ocean adjoining a bay named for a boiler that was the last remains of a small freighter lost here in 1910.

1.3 m., **Depoe Bay.** Geographically the most exciting town on the Oregon seaboard. The rockbound bay and colorful harbor, with its amphitheater setting, tingles with flair. Through a restaurant window, above the cove, you can look down on deep-sea trollers. From a sidewalk adjoining US 101, you can see the Spouting Horn, a gap in the rocks through which the tide races upward in a geyser of spray. The aquarium, near the cove, specializes in clowning seals and has one of the best shell shops in the Pacific NW.

2 m., Rocky Creek SP. A wayside in an area of meadow and stunted tree growth. The view of the scalloped sea wall is worth a pause. Also fishing, picnic facilities.

0.3 m., turnoff R for Otter Crest Loop.

 * *1.9 m.*, **Otter Crest Viewpoint** on Cape Foulweather (see front cover for illustration). The superb view of miles of rugged coastline quickly brings out cameras; it is the Coast's most photographed seascape. The cape was given its dismal name by Captain James Cook, the celebrated British sea dog, on a nasty March day in 1778. Sea otters once dwelt on shallow rocks about 0.5 m. offshore. Gone now, their place has been taken by a herd of gray sea lions and seals. The larger rock is a sea bird rookery. *1.3 m.*, town of Otter Crest, small and placid. Turn R. *0.5 m.*, **Devil's Punch Bowl,** a wave-worn, bowl-shaped rock where incoming tides pour through openings in the deep, round cauldron to boil up, then retreat. Return to Otter Crest Loop. *0.4 m.*, Jct., US 101.

1.5 m., turnoff for **Otter Crest Viewpoint.**

1.2 m., Otter Rock Jct. Turnoff R for **Devil's Punch Bowl SP.**

0.5 m., S end of Otter Crest Loop.

1.1 m., turnoff to Beverly Beach SP. Camping in a heavily vegetated area drained by Spencer Creek. Excellent facilities. The broad, sandy beach is great for casual strolling or vigorous hiking. Finds of Miocene marine fossils, including the bones of whales and sea lions, as well as shells, have been made in the cliffs of the park.

3.6 m., turn R onto Lighthouse Rd.

* 1 m., **Yaquina Head Light Station,** whose 96-ft. tower is the highest of all Coast lighthouses. The station was built by mistake, the designated site being Otter Crest. The original lenses, manufactured in Paris, France, in 1868, are still in use. Actually, the most stirring (and chilling) scenery here is to the R, or E, of the tower. Cliffs plunge to rocky caves that are tumultuous with the wild agitation of the lunging waves. Even in summer the wind bites with cold teeth—and the fall is long. So beware, beware.

0.1 m., Agate Beach, for many years the home of the late, great composer Ernest Bloch, who died in 1959. Many of his grandest works were created in his studio above his garage. The bldg. stands at the first turnoff on the road to a motel, off the W side of US 101.

2.7 m., **Newport.** Garlanded around Yaquina Bay, Newport was once the social lion of the Oregon Coast. Today its picturesqueness is found chiefly in its Bay Front, an irridescent buttery oyster stew of sea food restaurants, pubs, wharfside bldgs. and fishing boats nodding at rest, like plow horses after a hard day's pulling. Sunset at Yaquina Bay, when the fishing fleet rides at anchor, is a color symphony of vivid orange, yellow, red and saffron, muted by a subtle range of pastels.

(Bay Rd. follows Yaquina Bay and then the Yaquina River to Toledo, 13 m. from Yaquina Bay Fish Co. A century ago there stood along this road the

Yaquina Bay Bridge from Bay Front, Newport

boom towns of Yaquina City and Oysterville and the homestead of George Luther Boone, great-grandson of Daniel. But these are remembered only in plaques now—and much that is along the road seems to be in slumber.)

Across the bay the peripatetic Phil Sheridan, only a few years from Civil War fame, built a blockhouse in 1856. No trace of it remains.

Undersea Gardens, 267 Bay Blvd., is the finest indoor marine life show on the Coast. Stick around to watch a scuba diver wrestle with an octopus—or would you rather the octopus were not bothered?

Newport is the center of the rocky beaches of the central Oregon Coast. Along these beaches are found a rich variety of seashore life, including limpets, mussels, clams, sea slugs, snails, chitons, sculpins, sea lettuce, surf grass, squirts, barnacles, sea palm, sea urchins, sea cucumbers, sea stars, sea anemones, sponges and crabs. (Newport calls itself the "Dungeness Crab Capital of the World.")

The city is as well known for its sports as its commercial fishing. Deep-sea boats on the prowl for salmon make regular or chartered trips from May through Sept. Aug. brings swarms of fishermen to the bay and the river, their hopes high for Chinooks and silvers.

Jct., US 20—to Corvallis. (See *Cross-Coast Range Roads.*)

Lincoln County Historical Museum, in log bldg. back of Visitors Information Center, at 555 SW Coast Highway, is ambitious undertaking in collection of regional artifacts. Across street—US 101—is Wax Museum with some interesting figures. One block N of Wax Museum—and just off W side of US 101—Bateman Funeral Chapel bldg. is Victorian-style house with eight-sided cupola on one side. Owner says house was built as dwelling in 1860, later was used as boarding hotel; has been funeral home since 1926.

0.4 m.—from Visitors Information Center—turnoff for Yaquina Bay SP. **Old Yaquina Bay Lighthouse,** established in 1871, is no longer active but, somewhat restored, is museum now.

0.5 m.—across Yaquina Bay bridge—turnoff for Marine Science Center of Oregon State University.

  * *0.8 m.,* **Marine Science Center.** Museum and aquarium designed to key viewers to an awareness of the beauty and frailty of the ocean.

1.2 m., turnoff R to South Newport SP. Climb a sand dune for a sweeping vista of the ocean or, closer to the eye, behold the varied botanical species.

3.9 m., turnoff R to Lost Creek SP. Picnic above a drifting beach in the cool Pacific breeze.

1.8 m., turnoff R to Ona Beach SP. One of the best equipped of the lesser known, day-use coastal SPs; it even has a boat ramp—to Beaver Creek. The beach, close by, attracts fishermen and waders.

5.1 m., Waldport, on the S shore of Alsea Bay. Small boats perch at the ocean's lip, where the fishing is supposed to be good; a stone's throw away, the sea waves lash at the driftwood beaches. The finest beaches, wild and thinly peopled, are N of the bay. Cross the bridge and take the first road L. Sunsets here are gorgeous: in its last moment of visibility, the great solar ava-

tar kisses the brow of its earth child and leaves in its wake cerise and pome-
granate pools.

Jct., O 34—to Corvallis. (See *Cross-Coast Range Roads.*)

1.2 m., turnoff R to Governor Patterson SP. A trim, landscaped, seashore
area by a sandy beach.

2.2 m., turnoff R to Beachside SP. Camping, picnicking near a generally
smooth beach which was once, before US 101 was completed, part of the
only road between Newport and Yachats.

5 m., Yachats (Ya-hots), Indian for "at the foot of the mountain." The
town, on namesake river, is popular resort for salmon fishermen, but surf fishing and clam digging also attract visitors. Yachats SP, bordering the river as it
enters the sea, is scenic picnic stop.

2.7 m., turnoff R for Devil's Churn. The 0.5 m. Trail of the Restless
Waters leads through a variety of coastal vegetation and views of the many-
splendored coastline, with tidepools etched in the rocky shelf, to **Devil's
Churn,** a deep-wrought fissure where the sea rushes in like a wounded whale
and spouts furiously. Volcanic action created a fracture in the earth's surface,
and eons of water erosion have done the rest.

A self-conducted auto tour starts at the Devil's Churn parking area and
winds 22 m. through arboreal hills and valleys, returning to US 101 at
Yachats. Woodland animals sometimes seen include blacktailed deer, raccoons and bears.

0.1 m., turnoff L for **Cape Perpetua Viewpoint.**

* A tolerable road climbs 2 m. to the top of Cape Perpetua, 800 ft.
above the sea. The cape was named by Capt. Cook, for St. Perpetua, who
was martyred for professing her Christian faith in Carthage exactly 1575
years before Cook sighted the massive headland, on March 7, 1778. The
view from the aerie of Cape Perpetua is truly spellbinding: a breath-
taking vista of wave-fringed beaches broken by headlands and offshore
rocks strewn below the green-clad hills.

0.3 m., turnoff for **Cape Perpetua Visitor Center.**

* A movie, "Forces of Nature," and a dramatic diorama introduce the
interested to the "living museum" that is the Oregon Coast. Trails from
the Center lead to Cape Creek (lush coastal forest and fern-lined
stream); Cook's Chasm (spouting horns, rock fishing, and ancient shell
mounds); Cape and Good Fortune Coves; Devil's Churn; and, through
spruce giants, to the cap of Cape Perpetua.

1.1 m., turnoff to Neptune SP. At Cook's Chasm, on the N, the sea
charges in on roars of vengeance and, in retreat, leaves pullulating foam. Trees
stunted and bent by banshee winds shrink against slopes shrubbed by evergreen huckleberry. Surf fishing from the rocks for rock fish, perch and
greenling.

7.6 m., Washburne SP. A pleasant place to picnic, browse, wade in the
ocean surf, romp on the beach or fish.

Darlingtonia Botanical Wayside

2.9 m., Devil's Elbow SP. Although many come to relax on the spongy beach, the most striking sight is **Heceta** (Heh-see-ta) **Head Lighthouse,** standing since 1894 on a spectacular headland rising sheer above the ocean. Devil's Elbow Tunnel, within the SP, is a 600-ft. bore through a jutting promontory. US 101 swings around a cliff far above the Pacific, affording a startling view of land and sea.

1.1 m., Sea Lion Caves, a huge marine cavern inhabited by varying numbers of huge sea lions. Probably the most popular commercial tourist attraction on the Coast.

5.2 m., Sutton Lake, a small, lovely body of clear water in the Siuslaw National Forest. FS CG.

0.8 m., turn L for **Darlingtonia Botanical Wayside.**

* 0.5 m. nature walk leads through bog clusters of the carnivorous, fly-catching pitcher plants, the Darlingtonia, also known as "cobra lily," perhaps because they look like cobras poised to strike. Insects that crawl into the hood-like leaves are caught and devoured. The plants need these minerals as their small root systems cannot supply them with necessary nutrition.

0.6 m., on L, Indian Forest, a commercial "Indian village," including replicas of a birch-bark wigwam, Mandan earth lodge, Plains tipi and Hupa cedar plank house, set in a coastal forest.

1.5 m., on R, Heceta Jct.

* *2 m.,* **Heceta Beach,** secluded nook on the littoral. A favorite journeying point for sophisticated driftwood collectors.

Jct., O 36-O 126—to Junction City and Eugene. (See *Cross-Coast Range Roads.*)

0.2 m., center of **Florence,** a Siuslaw River-mouth fishing town and a trading post for farmers of the narrow Siuslaw Valley. In spring and early summer, rhododendrons run riot over hills and lowlands and are celebrated in the showy Rhododendron Festival held the latter part of May. Sand dunes rise to heights of 100 ft. between Florence and the ocean. Harbor Vista Park, on Rhododendron Drive, 4 m. from turnoff downtown, has commanding view of Siuslaw River giving itself to the Pacific.

3.1 m., turnoff R for Honeyman SP, one of Oregon's most developed and popular SPs. The 522-acre tract includes a dense forest, Cleawox Lake and part of Woahink (Indian for "clear water") Lake. Trails lead from the park into the cool, resilient woods or to bizarre sand dunes.

Turnoff L from US 101 for the E side of Siltcoos Lake.

* An 18-m. road wambles around the N end of Woahink Lake, scuffs past Canary, finds the E shore of Siltcoos Lake at Siltcoos, slips by Ada, jogs down Fivemile Creek, and nudges the SE corner of Tahkenitch Lake before ending its green and never-dull ramble at US 101, 2 m. N of Gardiner.

1.1 m., Sand Dunes Frontier, largest of sand-buggy tours in the 45-m. long dunes area stretching between Florence and North Bend. Mounds in "Oregon's Sahara" rise to heights of more than 250 ft. The sand seems to be constantly shifting, moved by the winds, so that a hill today can be a hollow

Cleawox Lake, Honeyman State Park

Dunes Pacific Railway

next week and a small knob one day can be a soaring peak by the next morning. Commercial sand buggies—motorized vehicles from jeep to bus size—push up 45-degree slopes and perch on the brink of seemingly precipitous cliffs. At such moments, screams of fright are not uncommon. But the buggies crawl safely down.

0.8 m., turnoff to Woahink Lake.

1 m., Dunes Pacific Railway. A miniature RR winds through a border of a vast sand dunes area.

2.2 m., turnoff L for FS CG on Siltcoos Lake, largest of Oregon's coastal lakes.

0.7 m., turnoff R to Carter Lake FS CG. Boating in the golden shadows of the dunes.

3.7 m., Tahkenitch Lake, a jewel in a cup of the emerald hills. FS CGs.

1.4 m., Elbow Lake, which looks more like a sleepy lagoon. At sunset it could be taken for a watercolor painting.

5.3 m., Gardiner, a mill town not completely odorless.

Jct., Sulphur Springs-Smith River Rd.—to Willamette Valley. (See *Cross-Coast Range Roads.*)

1.1 m., Smith River, named for a great mountain man, whose life was as lonely and as uneven as the stream. He was Jedediah Smith, the first white man to cross the Sierra Nevada and the first to travel up the Pacific Coast from the Mexican province of California to the Columbia. In July 1828, while camped just W of here on the bank of the Umpqua, into which the Smith empties at this point, Jedediah's party was attacked by Indians, who helped themselves to all the furs the group had accumulated. Fortunately for Smith, he and two other men were away from the camp. Only one of the 17 men in camp escaped with his life, and eventually he reached Ft. Vancouver, a day before Smith did. Through the intervention of Dr. John McLoughlin, head of the Hudson's Bay Co. post, Smith got his furs back and promptly sold them, at no discount, to his benefactor. Less than three years later, Jedediah Smith was killed on the Cimarron River, far away, by Comanches. He had lived to be all of 33 years old, no small achievement for a bold trailblazer.

1.2 m., across Umpqua River bridge, Reedsport, a crisp lumber town and gateway to fine salmon fishing.

Jct., O 38—to Drain, US 99. (See *Cross-Coast Range Roads.*)

4.2 m., Winchester Bay, a vigorous fishing town. Turnoff R for Salmon Harbor.

* 0.2 m., **Salmon Harbor.** Gulls wheel low over the bobbing rows of boats in the sheltered basin, and the wind spices the blown spray with the aroma of salmon. One of the finest sports fishing moorages on the Coast, with many boats catering to tourists. During July, Aug. and Sept., silvers and Chinooks are caught by trolling (mostly herring).

0.9 m., turnoff R for Umpqua Lighthouse SP.

* 0.9 m., **Umpqua Lighthouse.** A long and wide view of ocean-rim scablands and driftwood beaches from the lighthouse road. The SP touches the mouth of the Umpqua River and ribbons the seashore for 2.5 m. Sand dunes in this area are claimed to be highest in U.S. Spring turns much of the SP into a gorgeous rhododendron display.

0.5 m., Winchester Bay Viewpoint. A forest of coastal shrub provides a

Salmon Harbor, Winchester Bay

deep and vari-tinted foreground to the Pacific spectacle. On a calm day the sea seems to be woven of sheets of glass here and there pitted and cracked.

1 m., Clear Lake, just an indentation where the forest meets the dunes, but elsewhere a winding between fjord-like formations in the mossy woods, where the lake hides the secrets of its gossamer coves.

3.2 m., turnoff to Tugman SP, named for a gutty newspaperman. Smack in the coastal lake region, it has paved boat ramp to Eel Lake.

0.6 m., jct., Lakeside-Ten Mile Lakes Recreation Area.

    * *1.2 m.,* Lakeside, a growing village at the marriage of N Ten and S Ten Mile Lakes, which comprise a sizable and uncluttered recreationland. Few roads of any kind approach these lakes, so boatmen feel the touch of adventure here.

0.4 m., turnoff R to Eel Creek FS CG. A good place to explore sand dunes.

4 m., turnoff to Saunders Lake, whose charm lies chiefly in its chameleonic topography.

2.7 m., The Dune Scooters, sand-excursion enterprise.

4.6 m., 1-m.-long McCullogh Bridge, spanning Coos Bay Channel. Longest of Oregon's coastal bridges.

0.3 m. from S end of bridge, **Coos-Curry Museum,** a well-administered collection of pioneer mementos.

0.2 m., on R, Bayview Myrtle Shop, one of largest myrtlewood factories and retail outlets in state. There are many myrtlewood plants and gift shops on this part of the Coast, probably because the beautifully grained myrtle trees grow around here. They form the basis of a unique hand-craft industry. There are, however, increasing signs that the myrtle has been overexploited and some people in this area fear that private myrtle groves may be extinct within a decade or two. Another reason for the state to preserve its myrtle trees.

0.4 m., turnoff to downtown **North Bend,** a lumber town whose most distinguished architecture is the Pony Village shopping center.

1.6 m., **Coos Bay,** one of the world's largest lumber export ports and the center of striped bass fishing in Oregon. The bay, once tingling with the romance of shipping, now stands in danger of being poisoned by pulp mill sulfite waste. Several species of fish, which brought many sportsmen into the bay, may be wiped out.

For one of the most joyous coastal scenic trips, turn R on Commercial Ave. from US 101.

    * *9.1 m.,* **Charleston,** a salty fishing burg with a gusty nautical atmosphere.

0.7 m., Jct., Bandon-Seven Devils Rd.

(On Bandon-Seven Devils Rd.: *6.5 m.,* turnoff to Sacchi Beach (2 m.). *3.1 m.,* turnoff to Agate Beach (0.5 m.). *1.6 m.,* turnoff to Merchant's Beach (0.5 m.). *1.7 m.,* turnoff to **Whiskey Run** (1.4 m.). Pacific vistas here are superb. During the Coos County gold rush of 1853-55, there was some pretty feverish activity (including drinking) along Whiskey Run (hence the name), and people still pan for gold here. Whiskey Run and the beaches N of it—Merchant's, Agate and Sacchi—contain not only agates, agatized myrtlewood and jasper but are rich in clams. *3 m.*, jct., US 101. *5.1 m.*, Bandon.

1.6 m.—from jct., Bandon-Seven Devils Rd.—turnoff for **Cape Arago Lighthouse** (0.3 m.). The promontory on which the lighthouse stands was initially called (by whites, that is) Cape Gregory, because our fellow traveler, Capt. Cook, sighted it on March 12, 1778, and named it after the saint of that day. He knew well the pantheon of Christianity. Had he as good ritualistic knowledge of the Polynesians he encountered in the Hawaiian Islands, he might have come out of there alive. About 1850 the name of the cape was changed to honor a French geographer, Dominique Francois Jean Arago.

0.8 m., turnoff to **Sunset Bay SP.** Wind-shorn and wave-battered cliffs and offshore rocks provide for memorable photo views, especially at sunset. *1 m.*, **Shore Acres SP.** S and N, the coastal bluffs appear as desert formations, with miniature sand dunes plastered into whorls on some of the rocks. Waves break against the rocks and plume into vertical streamers. To the S, a chain of rocks, perhaps 0.5 m. out to sea, looks at dusk—or in the shroud of fog—like a bit of the Maine Coast displaced, or, on a gloomier day, like the remnant of a lost continent. And the eye returns to the cliffs and the massive openings, appearing as tunnel entrances, gouged by giants and hollowed by demon serpents. The park was once an

View from Sunset Bay State Park

View from Shore Acres State Park   Simpson Reef

estate famed for its splendid botanical gardens, with flowering trees, shrubs and plants brought from many parts of the world by fast-sailing clipper ships and schooners. The luxurious gardens now belong to the state. *1.4 m.*, turnoff to **Cape Arago SP.** A long, wide view of the sea and the curving cliffcoast from a high promontory bulging 0.5 m. into the Pacific. Bring out your field glasses for spotting sea lions on Shell Island and Simpson Reef.

Another rewarding scenic trip from Coos Bay leads to two unusual SPs.

* *2.3 m.*, Eastside. Cross Coos River bridge. *13 m.*, the huddled hamlet of Allegany. *4.1 m.*, the 15-acre Millicoma Myrtle Grove SP, showing off the glossy-leafed evergreen in true brightness and poetic symmetry. *5.9 m.*, **Golden and Silver Falls SP,** with two waterfalls, each dropping about 200 ft. down a brow of the Coast Range—Golden fans out over a circular cliff—into the shining Glenn Valley. Picnicking at the confluence of Millicoma River and Glenn Creek. You have to bring your own drinking water, which is like carrying coal to Newcastle.

* Still another exhilarating exploration stemming from Eastside: take county rd. *5.9 m.* to Sumner. *8.1 m.*, Fairview. Turn N up N fork of the Coquille. *5 m.*, **Laverne County Park.** Camp amidst huge myrtle trees. Return to Fairview. Turn E. *17.8 m.*, **Maria Jackson SP.** A virgin myrtle stand, complemented by maples and alders, along Brummit Creek.

6 m.—from US 101 and N Commercial, in Coos Bay—jct., O 42—to Winston. (See *Cross-Coast Range Roads.*)

13.2 m., jct., Seven Devils Rd. (The short way from US 101 to Whiskey Run.)

2 m., turnoff for Bullards Beach SP.

* Follow road *2.8 m.* to abandoned lighthouse (see back cover for illustration) at N jetty of Coquille River. From mid-Sept. into Nov., the river is aswarm with boated fishermen hot for silvers. Jetty fishing yields perch, sea trout, ling cod and snappers.

2.3 m., jct., O 42S. (To O 42, at Coquille, 17 m.)

* *1.5 m.* E on O 42S, Oregon State Fish Hatchery. Trout and salmon.

0.8 m., **Bandon.** Because of the many cranberry bogs in the area, the city calls itself the "Cranberry Capital of Oregon." Like many coastal communities, Bandon has two business districts, one in old town, down by the water—in this case the Coquille River—and one on the highway. Old Town is the more interesting because of its grainy atmosphere.

A pleasurable side trip out of Bandon is the Beach Loop, starting at Old Town.

* 1.8 m., **Face Rock Viewpoint.** One of the largest and weirdest array of offshore rocks to be seen anywhere on the Oregon Coast. They look like deserted monoliths turned back eons ago into an ancient sea. Below the viewpoint a small beach, slicked by tides, adds incongruity to the scene. To the S, you can see for miles—more odd-shaped, odd-colored rocks, a long beach and the serrated waves of the Coast Range crests.
3.5 m.—past Bandon Beach SP—jct., US 101.

7.6 m.—from Bandon—on R, **West Coast Deer Park.** Deer and goats and sheep that eat out of your hand, plus an American bison, a South American water buffalo, four-horned rams from Scotland, peacocks, a nursery trail with fun-learning exhibits and much more. Wisely managed to create a warm, informal atmosphere.

Face Rock

West Coast Deer Park

6.1 m., Langlois, a run-down burg that in its better days had two cooperage plants which supplied the coastal towns around with tubs for preserving fish. It also had sawmills and was a dairymen's trading center. It seems odd that, on the Oregon Coast where "progress" is busting out all over, there should be some declining towns like Langlois, but there are.

1.1 m., turnoff R for Floras Lake.

* *2.8 m.*, **Floras Lake**, a short walk from the Pacific. Boat ramp, CG, fishing for salmon, trout, catfish, yellow perch, large-mouth bass and carp. It seems hard to believe, but a city once sat on the shore of the lake. Speculators promoted madly, ballyhooing that a canal could be built between the lake and the sea, making the town (first called Lakeport and then Pacific City) a great shipping port. The push started in 1908 and soon thousands of lots were sold, a three-story hotel constructed, and a newspaper started. When the first breeze of sanity returned, some citizens began asking each other what would be the economic base for the city. None, they agreed, and pulled up stakes. The rest of the populace followed. On Nov. 6, 1909, the hotel clerk scrawled the final entry in the register: "Not a damn sole." It was the town's epitaph.

1.6 m., Denmark, founded by Danes, who developed a profitable dairying industry in the area. But the vast improvement of US 101 reduced Denmark's business section to a local gas stop.

5.2 m., Sixes. Store. Jct., FS rd. 322.

* The road follows the Sixes River, known to astute fishermen for its salmon, steelhead and cutthroat trout. *4.5 m.,* Edson Creek CG, distinguished by a grove of giant myrtle trees at the entrance. Wild blackberries grow in profusion, ripening in late summer. *6.5 m.,* Sixes River Rec. Site. CG on the whispering Sixes.

0.9 m., Cape Blanco Jct.

* *5.6 m.,* **Cape Blanco Lighthouse,** built in 1870 on the most westerly point of Oregon. Coast Guardsmen conduct tours through lighthouse.

1.5 m., on L, jct., FS rd. 325.

* A forest road clings to the twisty path of the Elk River, renowned for its superb fishing for chinooks and steelhead as well as for cutthroat trout and coho salmon. *6.8 m.,* **Elk River Salmon Hatchery,** only one of its kind on the S Oregon Coast. The road E of the hatchery is bounded on one side by the Elk River and on the other by lofty stands of Douglas fir, with small prairies opening at unexpected places. *2.7 m.,* turnoff for McGribble FS CG.

(*2 m.,* CG. Tall firs and Port Orford cedar look down on a grassy meadow licked by the cool waters of Bald Mtn. Creek. Only a few campsites and picnic tables. Good fishing and hiking in this primitive area.)

6.5 m.—from McGribble turnoff—Panther Creek FS CG. *1.5 m.,* **Butler Bar FS CG,** in a glorious stand of Douglas fir sheltering a few shy maples. None of the CGs have trailer space. All are sited in woods ablaze with wildflowers and thick with shrubs and ferns. Especially lovely is dogwood, which brightens every corner it touches.

Cape Blanco Lighthouse   **Lindberg House, Port Orford**

2.6 m., **Port Orford**, founded by William Tichenor, a sea captain. On June 9, 1851, Tichenor brought his small sailing vessel, the *Sea Gull*, into waters S of here, landed nine men, and sailed away. The next day the local Indians, who resented white intrusion, attacked and forced the newcomers onto a large rock. The whites held off several charges, thanks to their cannon, and when the Indians had relaxed their vigilance, the whites fled N to Umpqua City, W of where Reedsport now stands. Tichenor returned on July 4 with a sizeable body of well-armed men, built a blockhouse, and began laying out a town. After he left the sea he retired to Port Orford, where he became a local celebrity and a teller of salty tales. He lies in the Tichenor Family Cemetery, located on a hill overlooking the city, Garrison Lake, and the ocean. Take 9th St. W.

The freshwater Garrison Lake, separated from ocean beaches by a narrow strip of land, is partly within the city. All year trout fishing. Take 14th St. W.

Five generations of Lindbergs have lived in the 1892-built house at 9th & Washington. Redwood shingles exterior provides compelling look. Architectural style was described by pioneer as "Queen Anne story-and-a-half cottage."

Battle Rock SP, at S end of town, is where Capt. Tichenor's valiants sought refuge. The rock is a cautious but not difficult climb, and the view from the top is well worth the effort. Some people picnic here—but it is no place to let tots run free.

In the summer of 1970, 30 wild sea otters were airlifted from Alaska's Aleutian Amchitka Island to Port Orford and released in the offshore kelp beds. North American Pacific waters were once alive with sea otter, but they were slaughtered for profit and vanity and almost became extinct. Now there is an attempt to "reseed" these waters with the rare, dark-furred animals. They may sometimes be seen around the rocks S of Battle Rock.

* For more than a century, on and off, scientists and adventurers have sought the "Lost Port Orford Meteorite," reported in 1859 by a government geologist, Dr. John Evans, who estimated the rock to weigh 11 tons. Supposedly, by his account, it lies 40 m. E of Port Orford. However, hard evidence for the find has always been lacking and some competent geologists now suggest that the meteorite is a myth.

5.7 m.—from Battle Rock SP—turnoff for Humbug Mtn. SP.

* 0.2 m., entrance to **Humbug Mtn. SP CG.** (Just before the entrance to the park, a R turn will take you up a mtn. road that leads 3.7 m. to McGribble FS CG.)

A 3-m. trail from the SP reaches the top of 1750-ft. Humbug Mtn. The climb is not recommended for those not in good condition.

Humbug Mtn. SP CG is a joy: myrtles, alders and maples; an old apple orchard nearby; a trout stream at hand; and only a short stroll to sweeping sea views and breezy sand beach.

The beach here, as ought to be said of all the coastal beaches of S Oregon—and, indeed, the entire length of the Coast—is remarkable for what can be seen, heard and found. Whales—up to 50 ft. in length—and sea lions (and now sea otters) provide sights and sounds most pleasurable to the hearts of those who believe these animals have as much right as we to inhabit this pale, frail, precious tiny star which is the only home any of us will ever know. Japanese glass floats washed ashore are treasured items. They come in an amazing variety of color: every shade of blue and green, oranges, yellows, smoke, white, pinks; and when you find that special one purple, a spindle of glass through the center, sand blasted, and with distinctive markings, you know you hold in your hand a thing of exotic kinship and beauty. (The beachcombers of Curry County say the best time of year to go hunting for glass floats is from late Dec. through early May, and the best time of day before dawn, when other beachcombers ought to be asleep.) Finds also include driftwood in every conceivable form, Oregon "jade," jasper, petrified wood, agate, marine fossils, rare shells, beeswax, kegs, bamboo and bottles. And undoubtedly there is more. The serious beachcomber carries a plastic bucket, rock hammer and small garden rake.

0.8 m.—from turnoff for Humbug Mtn. SP CG—Humbug Mtn. SP picnic area.

5.6 m., Prehistoric Gardens, a "lost world" of life-size replicas of the dinosaurs and other prehistoric animals that roamed in these parts.

9.1 m., Geisel Monument SP, commemorating John Geisel and sons, who were slain by Indians on Washington's birthday in 1856. (Where are the monuments for Indians who were slain by whites?) A four-acre wayside shaded by spruce, alder, fir and Port Orford cedar.

5.2 m., turnoff L to Wedderburn, a mini-town on the N bank of the Rogue. Turnoff for boat trips up the Rogue River.

* 0.4 m., boat docks for white water excursions. Most publicized are the 64-m., round-trip runs to Agness. Two lodges serve lunch. More thrilling is the 104-m. round-trip on the untamed Rogue to Paradise Bar Lodge.

0.2 m., jct., Rogue River Rd.—to Agness, Galice and Grants Pass. (See *Cross-Coast Range Roads*.)

0.5 m., Gold Beach, a typical coastal roadside community, pale in design to all the wondrous beauty around it. Like other towns in Curry County, its population declined from 1960 to 1970. One wonders why: the climate is very good, the scenery grand.

* (One of the most delightful "suburbs" of any coastal community is the Little Botany Hills district, across Hunter Creek, S of town. Here, with the Hunter Creek store as the hub, are found lupine, dogwood nuzzling out of ferns and moss, sand verbena, shooting stars, snake lilies, rose lavenders stretching their heads on moss-covered logs, Oregon fairy bell, azaleas in a wide range of colors, the creamy white feathery bloom of ocean spray, beach asters, ox-eyed daisies, white yarrow and a host of others.)

6.1 m.—from Gold Beach—turnoff for Cape Sebastian SP.

* *1 m.,* **Cape Sebastian,** a 700-ft.-high precipitous headland commanding a far visual reach of the rocky sea wall.

1.7 m., viewpoint. A jumble of gigantic offshore rocks, including one that has the outlines of a sheer-cliffed island. On a foggy day they appear as monsters risen from the deep.

0.9 m., viewpoint. Another observation of those incredible rock formations. The one straight ahead suggests the image of the horns of a rhinoceros hung above a grotto.

1.9 m., Pistol River SP. Sand dunes between US 101 and the ocean beach are flowered by fragrant native yellow lupine.

2.8 m., **Mack Arch,** a 325-ft.-high offshore monolith. A child said it looks like a shoe—which is the way the child will remember it.

2.9 m., turnoff for Arch Rock Point of Boardman SP. (0.4 m.) More than a great arched rock: clumps of trees grow out of the tops of rocks; broken shells of cliffs are boiling pots for waves; the bulky, green-thorned face of the seawall is a mask of eternity.

0.3 m., Spruce Island viewpoint. A rocky isle topped by spruce.

0.9 m., **Natural Bridge Viewpoint.** The portraiture is as dramatic as any Oregon coastview. Above the natural bridge, which spans a current appearing as a river, is a great island rock erupting from the roof of a grotto. The stream flows past the cove, through the arch of the bridge, past a smaller cove, through another arch and returns to the ocean.

0.8 m., viewpoint. A headland facing a scatter of rocks that are wrinkled pebbles compared to the sea massifs directly N.

0.4 m., 350-ft. **Thomas Creek Bridge,** highest in Oregon.

0.9 m., **Indian Sands Trail Viewpoint,** an abundant sight of the forest plunging down to the sea. A trail flanked by toadstools of brilliant orange and yellow polka-dots, descends to where trees and wildflowers are halted by rocks, sand and thundering waves.

0.8 m., turnoff for **Whalehead Beach** (0.2 m.). The offshore rock formation resembles a whale spouting.

Arch Rock   Natural Bridge

0.5 m., **Whalehead Trail Viewpoint.** A more graphic picture of the odd-shaped "spouting rock."

1.6 m., turnoff for House Rock Viewpoint (0.3 m.). Monument on crest honors Samuel H. Boardman, "Father of Oregon State Parks." The view is of a choppy, battered, green and sand-faced coast.

0.8 m., **Cape Ferrelo Viewpoint.** A touch of Scotland: sweet-smelling thistled hills softly rolling down to a mauve-toned beach facing a hundred rocks, most of them small.

0.7 m., turnoff for Lone Ranch Beach (0.2 m.). A curve of beach between two minor headlands; stacks of driftwood; and clusters of offshore boulders.

2 m., turnoff for Harris Beach SP.

    * *0.5 m.* All year SP, with complete facilities. Thick shrubs and firs provide privacy for each campsite. The vista from **Harris Butte** encompasses 24 m. of curving coastline, from Point St. George in Calif., around Pelican Bay, and N to Cape Ferrelo.

0.9 m., **Brookings,** which probably enjoys the most temperate climate of any city in Oregon, is home of Azalea SP, and calls itself "Easter Lily Capital of the World." About 90% of the pot lilies used in the U.S. come from a 500-acre area here. Azalea SP is a botanical glory. Spring pushes up wild strawberry blossoms, purple and yellow violets, and wild cherry and crabapple blooms, partitioned by bushes of five varieties of native azaleas. Swarms of butterflies, bees and hummingbirds feed on the plants, within a wing flap of fir and spruce housing finch, robin, jay and killdeer colonies. Eat off hand-hewn myrtlewood tables, each weighing more than 200 lbs.

Brookings lies at the mouth of the Chetco River, the best known salmon and steelhead stream S of the Rogue.

    * From Brookings a road up the N bank of the Chetco meanders 7.6 m. to Loeb SP. Camp near old, giant myrtle trees. *5.7 m.,* Little Redwood FS CG. No redwoods here, but the tall Douglas firs, wild flowers and berries compensate.

1.7 m.—from Brookings—Harbor, a sport and industrial fishing port. Fields of commercially grown daffodil bulbs spread out from the settlement.

4 m., California line. *17 m.,* jct., US 199 to Grants Pass. (See *Cross-Coast Range Roads.*)

Cross-Coast Range Roads

US 30—Astoria to Portland

For many years US 30 was the most important and heavily used of all Cross-Coast Range roads. Following the sinuous Columbia, US 30 twisted so convulsively that the drive from Astoria to Portland was a hard half-day's work. And when the fog moved in on the narrow road, it was like trying to follow the outlines of a pretzel floating in a murky basin after someone had turned the lights off. Now, except for a few short stretches, US 30 is rather straight. It has been broadened, too, and is a breeze to drive, especially in summer.

15 m., Knappa, an up-to-date roadside settlement, with its own telephone company.

7 m., **Clatsop Crest.** A marvelous overview of the Columbia—if the smog, industrial fumes and truck vapors permit.

5.1 m., **Westport,** a soggy burg right out of a musty sawmill album.

  * L *500 yds.* to ferry landing—toll ferry to Cathlamet, Wash. Even if you don't cross the river, the picture is fascinating. The scene, with the ferry rounding a bend, has a Mississippi River flavor.

Entrance to Cathlamet Ferry at Westport on the Columbia

All that is left of Mayger on the Columbia

9.2 *m.*, **Clatskanie.**

Jct., O 47—to Mist.

* *12 m.* The road spins like a top. Few houses and no stores on this hilly, green-bordered asphalt thread.

Turn R in Clatskanie onto Nehalem St. *0.3 m.*, turn R on 7th. *1 block,* turn R on Tichenor. At 620 Tichenor, oldest and most intriguing house in town, locally known as "The Palace" because of its twin cupolas, gingerbread balcony and other conspicuous symbols of affluence. From the sidewalk, a refreshing panorama of US 30 sweeping grandly up a forested hill.

Return to Nehalem Ave. & US 30. Turn R for Rainier—*15 m.*

* For an off-the-beaten-path route to Rainier, cross US 30 and continue straight on Nehalem through downtown Clatskanie to W 5th. Turn L toward Mayger.

The view N, on this backcountry road, is of a broad, deep meadow, emerald and dotted with many barns, lowland hay and dairy farms. So flat and in such sharp contrast to the rugged hills just a few miles S.

5.4 m., turn L at rd. marked Port Westward. *1.2 m.*, through open farm terrain—cows and red barns and a few fruit trees—to Port Westward, a minor point of Columbia commerce. Return to Mayger Rd. Turn L.

The road rolls on in nostalgia: wooden schoolhouses that were calling children to class at least 50 years ago; barns and houses as aged. A drowsy, slightly musty atmosphere. With the river so close, you can almost hear the whistle of a steamboat coming 'round the bend.

2.2 m., forks in road; take L fork. *0.2 m.*, all that remains of **Mayger—**

Caples House, Columbia City   Columbia County Courthouse, St. Helens

the crumbling bldgs. of a once-busy river dock. Outside of that, only a few houses scattered about. Return to forks. Turn L.

After Mayger the road leaves behind the open farm country and bobs through woods that block the view of what is behind them, except for glimpses of stump ranches, a few "suburban" homes, and flashes of Longview, Wash.

6.5 m., Alston. Store. Turn L. *0.2 m.*, US 30. Turn L. *3.7 m.*, turnoff to bridge spanning Columbia to Longview. *1.8 m.*, **Rainier**.

Turn L *0.1 m. to* "downtown" Rainier, on the Columbia. All the early river cities were built against the stream and the main rd. ran right through the business sections. Now there is more business "uptown," or away from the river, and US 30 does not touch any of the first hearts of these settlements.

Return to US 30. Turn L.

12.4 m., on L, marker at Deer Island. The island, in the Columbia, not where the marker or hamlet is, was named by the Lewis and Clark expedition which camped there in early Nov. 1805 on its way downstream.

3.7 m., turn L to Columbia City on I St. *0.2 m.*, **Caples House** (1870). Now that it has been restored by the DAR, which has opened it as a museum, it is one of the most beautiful 19th century houses along the river. Tool shed and carriage house, as old as the mansion, have also been restored, and "country store" added. One of the largest and most aesthetic museum complexes in the NW. The house overlooks a particularly attractive bit of the Columbia. On some days as many as 50 boats, large and small, pass by.

Return to US 30. Turn L. *2.2 m.*, Columbia Blvd., in **St. Helens.**

Turn L. *1.1 m.*, through new business section, to S 4th. Turn R. At 155 S 4th, **Knighton House,** oldest structure in St. Helens. Built by town founder Henry Knighton in 1847. Its original site was on S 1st, near courthouse. Despite some changes in bldg. materials, original shape has been maintained.

Straight to corner, St. Helens St. Turn L. 3 *blocks,* S 1st, old business section. Turn R. *1 block,* Courthouse Square, a tintype of the steamboat past. Columbia County Courthouse (1906), built of stone from a nearby quarry, has clocktower charm. Stroll to the rear for a canvas-look at the Columbia River and Mt. St. Helens.

Return to US 30. Turn L. 3.6 *m.,* on R, a striking rural scene—an 1890 water tower. Windmill (1926) next to it is one of few of its kind in W Oregon. Mr. and Mrs. Sam Dahlgren have received many offers to sell the windmill. Behind it are two barns constructed before 1895.

4.2 *m.,* Scappoose, Indian for "gravelly plain." Hudson's Bay Co. had farm and trading post around here in the 1830s; nothing very colorful has happened since then.

10.1 *m.,* turnoff to Sauvie Island. (See *The Great Heartland, Sauvie Island.*)

2.5 *m.,* Linnton. Now part of Portland, Linnton was laid out in 1843, a couple of years before anyone thought that what is now central Portland was a good enough place to put up a cabin. Peter Burnett, co-founder of Linnton, prophesied: "I have no doubt that this place will be the great commercial town of the territory." Burnett later moved to California, where he was elected that state's first governor. Linnton today looks like a run-down river town.

8 *m.,* Portland.

O 202—*Astoria to Mist.* O 47—*Mist to US 26*

The least known national or state road from the Coast, and one of the most delightful. A fine alternative on crowded summer weekends when US 26 and US 30 are jammed. Traffic is sparse and the terrain zestful.

Dahlgren water tower and windmill near St. Helens   **Business district of Mist**

At Olney Jct., *9.5 m.* SE of Astoria, a secondary arterial bends SW on Young's River Loop, a scenic drive which returns to Astoria.

2.2 m. beyond Olney Jct., Klaskanine River Salmon Hatchery.

12.8 m., **Fishhawk Falls.** The white waters of Fishhawk Creek cascade down a 75-ft. cliff. Here, 20 crow-fly m. from the Pacific, is a divide point between the coastal hemlock and spruce rain forests to the W and the drier Douglas fir belt to the E.

4.4 m., Jewell, in a Y between Fishhawk and Beneke creeks. Beer, gas.

Beyond Jewell the road enters the Nehalem Valley, a placid setting of serene meadows and modest farmsteads.

12 m., Birkenfeld. Store, garage, cafe. A wide spot in an earthy country where life is still sociable and relaxed. But the developers are moving in.

5.3 m., **Mist.** The Mist Store has been open since 1874. It is the center of village trade, gossip, decisionmaking, occasional haircutting and snacks (lunch counter.) Mist is the kind of place where it seems perfectly natural for an elderly woman to be dressed in levis and flannel shirt and grumble about a pet deer having chewed on her roses.

At Mist, O 202 surrenders to O 47.

The road to Vernonia winds and winds, gallumphing through a cool arboreal corridor as though it doesn't know where it's going and doesn't really care. At stretches the trees reach across the road to form a tunnel. Where the trees have been cleared, there are rural signs of a slower, less hysterical period.

8.2 m.—from Mist—**Big Eddy Park.** Camping under fir and maple. Fishing in Nehalem River.

7.6 m., on L, **Columbia County Historical Society Museum.** Folksy collection of early-day artifacts, with emphasis on logging. Museum was built in 1922 as office bldg. for Oregon American Lumber Co.

0.6 m., corner of Adams & Bridge, **Vernonia**, open-air transportation museum. Steam locomotive, fire-hose cart, wooden wagons, etc.

Vernonia was a buzzing lumber town until the mill shut down in 1957. The town sagged downhill for a few years, but is reviving. It kicks up its heels the last week in June, at Friendship Jamboree. Logging competition recalls memories of the robust timber days.

15 m., US 26. *32 m.,* Portland.

US 26—Seaside Jct. to Portland

Most people traveling from Astoria prefer US 26 as the fastest route to Portland because it encounters no towns or stop lights to hinder progress.

2 m.—from Seaside-Cannon Beach Jct.—**Klootchy Creek Park.** Giant firs and spruce tower as hoary monsters of a dim age. Mammoth trees, with twined roots above ground, seem to belong in an ancient art museum. Look for world's tallest Sitka spruce, more than 195 ft. high and almost 16 ft. in diameter. It was more than 300 years old when Columbus landed in the New World. CG.

7.4 m., jct., O 53.

Sitka spruce, Klootchy Creek Park

* R on O 53: 0.7 m., Hamlet Jct. (Turn L. 6 m., Hamlet, a spread-out, rural settlement down to a faded community hall, once a school-house, and a cemetery that hasn't had a burial for almost two genera-tions.) Continue on O 53. 19.5 m., through a microcosm of a rain forest and then stump ranch dairy country, to Wheeler, on US 101.

0.8 m., jct., Saddle Mtn. SP.

* L, 7 m. to **Saddle Mtn. SP** parking area (see back cover for illustra-tion). 4 m. trail to top—elevation, 3283 ft. Inexperienced climbers require about four hours for round trip. Along the trail you brush surges of wild-flowers and are likely to encounter insects, birds and some deer. At the top, the eye is nourished by views such as the mouth of the Columbia, beaches and breakers, and the spine of the Coast Range.

9.3 m., Elsie, one of the best known roadside stops in Oregon.

0.2 m., turnoff R for Spruce Run Park.

* 5.3 m., **Spruce Run Park.** This forested CG on the Nehalem is touted by some folks as the finest county park in the state. Clean, restful, scenic, far from traffic.

56 m., Portland.

O 6—Tillamook to Portland

Also known as the Wilson River highway, a large portion of the route winds through the Tillamook Burn, a sickening char of the wilderness that is slowly being reborn. Oregon's worst forest fires occurred here; one, in 1933, swept over 290,000 acres of woodland.

37.3 m., turnoff L for **Trolley Park,** an open, live museum of old-time trolleys and RR passenger cars. Fun for everyone. PG.

1.6 m., Glenwood, roadside village for the outer suburbanites.

2.9 m., jct., O 8.

Trolley Park near Glenwood

* O 8 was the old road to Tillamook, and though some of it has been abandoned, the section from here to Portland remains. O 8 to Portland is slower than staying on O 6, but it is less frenetic and more interesting. 2.5 m., Gales Creek, pioneer settlement that ought to be a juicy morsel for tract developers. 7.8 m., Forest Grove, seat of Pacific University. 6 m., Hillsboro, gateway to several historic areas. (For details on these and other towns and places on and back of O 8, see pertinent sections of *The Great Heartland—Short Trips out of Portland*.) 16 m., Portland.

6.9 m., jct. O 47— turnoff for Vernonia and Mist to N, and Forest Grove to S.

3 m., O 6 merges with US 26.

19.5 m., Portland.

Meadow Lake Road—Beaver to Carlton, O 47

The 48-m. road does not pass a single settlement worthy of the name. It is generally little traveled and, therefore, relatively free of gas vapor pollution. On the whole, a pleasant drive, though not high speed. The first half of the road, through the Siuslaw National Forest, follows the Nestucca River, a favorite haunt of fishermen. Don't look for anything aquatic at Meadow Lake; it has more dust than water. Public CGs 14 and 15 m. E of Beaver.

O 22—Hebo to Salem, US 99E and Int. 5

A slow road, lightly traveled, that puffs and staggers through rude farm-land scratched out of the woods until it emerges from the Coast Range.

5 m., Castle Rock FS CG, on Three Rivers. Small, quiet retreat for casual anglers.

20 m., Valley Junction, where O 18 is met. Site of Ft. Yamhill, established in 1856 and long gone. The old blockhouse is now in Dayton. Phil Sheridan, then a lieutenant, served as post commander for several months, chafing at being isolated from the action across the nation. When he finally received orders to join the Civil War, he told his troops: "I am going into this war to win a captain's spurs, or to die with my boots on." He became a general and lived until 1888. By the time he departed Oregon he had been in the state (and Ft. Vancouver) for six years. Grand Ronde Agency, also of the dim past, stood about 3 m. W of Valley Junction, as HQ of Indian Reservation discontinued in 1908. Some farmers in this area are descendants of the reservation Indians.

O 22 and O 18 are as one for 4.2 m., then part. *4.1 m.* from parting, Buell Store.

* Turn L at Buell onto paved county rd, and follow rd. that parallels O 22. *0.4 m.* to old Buell and **Buell County Park**. All that remains of old Buell are grange hall, no-longer-used rustic schoolhouse, and abandoned church bldg. Buell Park, hacked out of a primeval valley forest, is lovely spot for eating and resting. Playground equipment for children. *0.2 m.*, county rd. rejoins O 22. Turn L.

0.9 m.—from Buell Store—L at edge of narrow dirt lane, giant white oak locally claimed to be largest on Pacific Coast. Sculptured into painful and triumphant shapes by its struggles with other trees for sun and by wind attacks, the oak is an anguish of beauty. Owners say tree surrounded by poison ivy.

7.7 m., jct., O 223. (R for Dallas.)

3.5 m., Rickreall—US 99W.

10.5 m., Salem.

O 18—Otis Jct. to US 99W, McMinnville and Dundee

The shortest and easiest route between the Coast and the Willamette Valley.

0.6 m., Pixieland, a wan touch of Disneyland.

8.4 m., **Van Duzer Forest Corridor Wayside.** Magnificent grove of firs, hemlock and spruce in the cool, green Van Duzer Corridor.

11.3 m., Grand Ronde, a former trading post, but not the original, of the Grand Ronde Indian Reservation.

1.9 m., Valley Junction, the major roadside hamlet on O 18.

3.8 m., turnoff for Willamina.

* *2.3 m.*, Willamina, an earthy lumber town hurt by the bypassing new highway, but stoutly hanging on.

White oak at Buell

5.8 m., turnoff for Sheridan.

* *0.9 m.,* Sheridan, straddling the S Yamhill River. Another town built on timber. **Sheridan Inn,** 238 S Bridge, built in 1913, recalls days when passenger trains brought traveling salesmen to town and hostelry.

5.5 m., turnoff L at drive-in for Glacial Erratic Rock.

* *0.8 m.* up county rd. to footpath on L. *0.5 m.* uphill trail to **Glacial Erratic Rock.** Rafted from far up Columbia River by iceberg at twilight of ice age. Erratics are so called because they are unrelated to local rocks. Bonus of climb is vast gob of scenery—plains and mountains—from knoll.

5.6 m., McMinnville Jct. (*2 m.,* McMinnville.)

7.4 m., Dayton Jct., O 221. (*2 m.,* Dayton.)

1.3 m., US 99W.

(*3.8 m.,* N on 99W, Dundee.)

US 20—Newport to Corvallis, US 99W

5.6 m., Toledo Jct.

* *1.2 m.,* **Toledo,** an unpretentious mill town tacked onto a hill. (From Toledo a road plods 10 m. along the Yaquina River to Elk City. The river looks like a dozing dragon which wakes up just long enough to yawn before it returns to slumber. Not a spectacular trip, but holding some backriver country atmosphere.)

0.2 m., jct., O 229.

  * *7.4 m.*, Siletz, former HQ for an Indian reservation. *24 m.*, Kernville, at the jct. of US 101. O 229 plays hopscotch with the Siletz River.

  (At Siletz, turn E onto Logsden Rd. *0.2 m.*, on L, gravel turnoff to Siletz Indian cemetery, *0.5 m.* up gravel trace. *4.6 m.*, on R, Sam's Creek CB, an old-timer in these parts. *3.2 m.*, through waves of fern hills and past tucked-away farmsteads, Logsden. Store. *15 m.*, Nashville. Store. *2 m.*, Summit, on the crest of the watershed between the Willamette and Yaquina Rivers. Just a few houses. *5 m.*, Blodgett, jct., US 20.)

7.3 m.—from O 229 Jct.—on R, Elk City Jct.

  * *5 m.*, **Elk City.** The first town platted in Lincoln County, back in 1868, and named for the great herds of elk roaming the area. The settlement was started as a depot for the Corvallis and Yaquina Bay Wagon Road Co., builders of pioneer road from Willamette Valley to Coast, and later became port for small boats on Yaquina River. Mail and stage routes from Corvallis terminated here and rest of way, to Yaquina Bay where Newport stands, was by boat. Still later, Elk City was key point on Oregon Pacific RR. That's all in the past, of course. Elk City now is down to a very rustic general store, a few homes, a charming CB, which reaches 100 ft. across the Yaquina, and a leafy county park.

  1.2 m., on R, Thornton Creek CB. At one time the road beyond the bridge was a well-traveled pike to Elk City; now it leads only to a few houses.

  1.2 m., on R, **Chitwood.** There was a snappy little RR settlement here once and enough remains to bear out that impression. Drive or walk through the sturdy CB; there's always something exciting going on at Chitwood, whether it's a goat trying to butt down the mailboxes, kittens playing

Glacial Erratic Rock off O 18

tag on the tracks, or some amateur painters finding a touch of the "real" Oregon.

5.1 m., jct. Nashville, *12 m.*; Summit, *14 m.*

0.3 m., Eddyville. Though burg has dwindled to a couple of gas pumps, schools (high and grade) have enrollment of about 200 students.

8.6 m., Ellmaker SP, shady picnic spot along Tumtum Creek.

0.8 m., Burnt Woods. Just a store at a crossroad to Harlan, 8m. S, and there's nothing much at Harlan. (But if you want to get away from traffic, on a lean lane jogging through burly landscape, try the 21 m. from Harlan to Elk City, along Elk Creek.)

(Observations spoken into a tape recorder at Burnt River: For a national highway, US 20 sure does a lot of winding. Many of the curves are 30 and 25 and 20 miles an hour. The road doesn't seem to have been altered in many years. It winds around meadows and small groves and some stump ranches that grew into half-way prosperous farms and tired-looking little hills and even wearier-looking little barns. It's a road that definitely is not in a hurry to go anywhere. It seems to stop and say Hello to every cow, tree and house.)

Rear of Elk City's general store
Ralph Friedman

Philomath College, Philomath

6.9 m., Blodgett, a single-store hamlet on the banks of Marys River. (Jct. Summit, 5 m.; Nashville, 7 m.)

5.5 m., jct., O 223. (See *The Great Heartland, West Side Shunpiking.*)

5.3 m., **Philomath**, named after Philomath College, started in the mid-1860s by the United Brethren Church and discontinued in 1929. The New Englandish brick bldg. is now part of the Evangelical United Brethren Church and as attractive as it was a century ago.

6 m., Corvallis, US 99W. (See *The Great Heartland.*) 13.6 m., Albany. (See *The Great Heartland.*)

O 34—Waldport to Corvallis, US 99W

In its W portion, O 34 companions the Alsea River, a popular stream boasting ample runs of blueback, cutthroat, silvers, Chinooks and steelhead.

2.4 m., Nelson Wayside, on Eckmann Lake, a blue-ruffled slough fringing the hems of gently contoured hills of green. Across the road the Alsea River is, by contrast, rugged and workaday, a market ground for fishers.

7.8 m., **Tidewater**. Store-gas. The Alsea flows mistily below, creeping between apple trees, rushes of corn, tawny slopes, pilings, and the back porches of solidly built wooden homes.

0.6 m., on R, shallow turnout for view of **"Little Switzerland,"** a gorgeous green setting that reminds one briefly of a lower Alpine scene from "The Sound of Music." At the bottom of the tangled hillside is the Alsea and across it, cows munch in a neatly trimmed vale. The river curves around the elliptical meadow and the last you see of it is a sheaf of white ripples between overhanging boughs. Above the meadow, the wooded hills rise in waves, as on a musical scale, and at the crest, the leafy crowns of a line of erect trees foam in the breeze, as though waving in triumph. The only sound in this idyllic scene is the occasional putt-putt of an outboard motor.

4.5 m., Slide FS CG, across the road from where the Alsea curls through rocky islands and shore outcrops.

2.6 m., Blackberry FS CG, on the Alsea. Well patronized by shore anglers.

2.4 m., on R, Five Rivers Rd. Jct.

* A bouncy drive to a colorful CB. At 3.2 m., take R fork. L fork leads to Lobster Valley, a backwash of small farms. R fork, 6.3 m., **Fisher CB**, across Five Rivers, so named because of the five creeks—Alder, Couger, Buck, Crab and Cherry—that make up the stream. So young is this country that, when the bridge was built, in 1927, lumber for it had to be floated 7 m. downstream from the Paris Ranch, which had the first sawmill in the valley. Across the bridge stands the Fisher school, looking neat and modern, but the children are hauled elsewhere, and the school is now used only as a sometime community hall. The general store, a creaky ghost, appears ready to collapse. The Grange hall was torn down. So all that is still functioning of the old Fisher settlement is the CB—used about as often by deer as by people.

Fisher covered bridge   *Ralph Friedman*

6.7 m.—from Five Rivers Rd. Jct.—turnoff L for Alsea River Salmon Hatchery.

　* *2.4 m.* Far more captivating than the hatchery is the scenery along the narrow, fidgety road. Fall Creek, on L, with its mossy air and thick-leafed alder canopy, looks at times like a bayou lifted out of Louisiana. And, at other places, its delicate stone island configurations and flower arrangements seem imported from Japan. A lovely watercolor few pause to observe.

13.1 m., **Alsea,** at a crook in the highway. The quaintness of nature and town give Alsea a storybook flavor that calls for a second look.

3.3 m., turnoff L for Alsea Fish Hatchery.

　* *0.7 m.,* for steelhead raising. Rearing ponds set in a greensward shaded by red cedars.

4.3 m., turnoff L for Marys Peak (4097 ft.), one of the highest mountains in the coastal cordillera.

　* *11.2 m.,* summit. On a clear day, the eye may roam as far W as the Pacific and as far E as the spires of the Cascades.

9.6 m., jct., US 20.

0.8 m., Philomath. (See US 20, preceding.)

6 m., Corvallis. *7 m.,* US 99E. *2 m.,* Int. 5. (See *The Great Heartland.*)

O 36—*Florence to US 99, near Junction City*

From Florence to Mapleton, O 36 is the same as O 126. (See O 126, following.)

Beyond Mapleton, O 36 is a far slower, narower and more difficult road than O 126, which explains why O 36 is relatively quiet. But O 36 has more things for the curious to investigate than does O 126.

8.3 m.—beyond Mapleton—Swisshome. The full opening of "Route F"—O 126—dealt a severe blow to Swisshome and reduced it from a charming tourist village, with alpine touches, to a splotch of hollowness on the highway.

4.8 m., Deadwood. Store-gas.

4.7 m., on R, Nelson Mtn. Rd.

  * *0.1 m.*, CB over Lake Creek. Red house, on L, just before bridge, is turn-of-century farmhome.

0.6 m., Greenleaf. The PO bldg. surely must be one of the smallest in the state. *8.4 m.*, Triangle Lake, whose popularity as a sunporch and aquatic subdivision of Eugene has diminished in recent years.

2.2 m., on L, round barn, one of the very few of its kind in Oregon.

2 m., Blachly. Store. *7.7 m.*, Alderwood SP, a heavily timbered wayside along Long Tom River.

7.9 m., Elmira Jct.

  * *8.5 m.*, Elmira. A refreshing drive along W side of Fern Ridge Reservoir, with a SP halfway between the jct. and Elmira. *1.5 m.*, Monroe Jct.

  * Cutoff for US 99W. *9 m.*, Monroe. (See *The Great Heartland, US 99W.*)

Post Office, Greenleaf

Round barn on O 36 near Triangle Lake

3.6 m., on R, C. A. Pitney home. Private collection of pioneer artifacts owned by Century Farm occupant. Visits upon appointment.

0.8 m., US 99. N on US 99, *1.8 m.,* Junction City.

O 126—*Florence to Eugene, US 99 and Int. 5*

The highway keeps company with the Siuslaw River to Mapleton. The river is alive with small fishing craft, which seem to proliferate in the rain, and log rafts, which lie on the water like soaked beaver skins.

3 m.—from Florence—Cushman. Store. RR turn-bridge, which opens to permit ocean-going barges to negotiate the Siuslaw to a lumber plant at Mapleton.

11.5 m., Mapleton, a one-block roadside community that lost its key attraction when its CB was removed.

3.1 m., Archie Knowles FS CG. Good news for trailerists—especially those with rod and reel—on the banks of Knowles Creek.

15.3 m., Walton, serene on the green E slope of the Coast Range.

5.8 m., L, on rise, Lester Hale house, built circa 1870.

0.2 m., L, on knoll, Farmer Hale house, built about 1860 and one of the oldest homes in this part of state. Octogenarians in the area remember it as a well-known stagecoach inn.

3.2 m., Noti. Store, station. *5.2 m.,* Elmira, on the W shore of the multi-recreational Fern Ridge Reservoir.

0.9 m., Veneta Jct.

  * *4.8 m.,* Crow, named not for the bird but for first postmaster, Andy Crow. Continue toward Lorane. *1.9 m.,* at Battle Creek Rd., turn R. *0.1 m.,* CB across Coyote Creek (see back cover for illustration). Farmstead at forks beyond CB makes pretty picture. (12 m. from Battle Creek Rd., Lorane. See *The Great Heartland, US 99.*)

0.2 m.—from Veneta Jct.—Veneta, which has grown from a no-place nameplace to a thriving Eugene suburb.

3.1 m., Perkins Peninsula SP, on S shore of Fern Ridge Reservoir.
10.3 m., Eugene. (See *The Great Heartland, US 99.*)

Smith River Road—Gardiner to Cottage Grove, US 99

The road adherese to the contours of the twisty Smith River, which slithers through the bottoms of rugged hills until the dizzy motorist swears he is following the trace of a dodging snake. *8.8 m.,* Noel Ranch FS CG, with boat ramp on the Smith. *9.2 m.,* Sulphur Springs, where the early settlers came for the cold mineral water and which until 1920 had a PO. *6.7 m.,* near Smith River Falls, BLM CG and picnic site. *4.7 m.,* picnicking and swimming at the mouth of Vincent Creek—an enchanting setting. *11.6 m.,* at forks of road, International Paper Co. CG in Twin Sister Creek area. From the forks, the branch to the R continues to chase the squirmy Smith, ending its reeling adventure 42 m. later, at US 99, 2 m. N of Drain. It passes only one map point, Gunter, which is easy to overlook. You may be surprised to learn it had a PO once. The branch straight ahead from the forks finds clearings, and in 14 m. reaches the Siuslaw River. Here a road enters from the NW. Following the Siuslaw upstream, it has come 25 m. from O 126, 12 m. E of Mapleton. The branch straight ahead continues for another 2 m., where it forks. The NE fork goes 12 m. to Crow, 15 m. W of Eugene; the SE fork stays with the Siuslaw to Lorane, 18 m., and terminates at Cottage Grove, US 99, in another 13 m. The road from the Siuslaw to Crow is in tame contrast to the road to Lorane, and both are conservative in topography compared to the roads to Gunter and O 126, but the greatest variety of scenery is in the first 41 m. out of Gardiner.

O 38—Reedsport to Drain, US 99

For almost the entire route to Drain, O 38 follows the Umpqua River, a full stream that seems to breathe pure peace as it flows through a low cut in the Coast Range. Douglas fir, hemlock, Sitka spruce and some Port Orford cedar on the wavy hills to the W add both strength and softness to the river scenes.

0.4 m.—from US 101—**Reedsport** business district.

8.9 m., Umpqua SP, a picnic facility wayside with boat ramp to the Umpqua.

3.9 m., Loon Lake Jct.

* 9.1 m., Loon Lake rec. area. *2.9 m.,* Ash. CB spans Lake Creek just W of Ash.

2.5 m., Scottsburg Park. A restful green above the honeyed Umpqua.

1.1 m., **Scottsburg.** Not a trace remains of the days when Scottsburg was the metropolis of S Oregon. As head of tidewater on the Umpqua, it became the distributing and shipping point for the gold mines. Its glory lasted only a few years. Nearer and better ports and more efficient methods of transportation than pack-horse trains spelled Scottsburg's doom. The town began to decline some years before the disastrous flood of 1861 just about did it in.

Since then Scottsburg has been little more than a pretty tintype of a sleepy hamlet.

19.3 m., **Elkton.** Long before Oregon was even a Territory, Hudson's Bay Co. operated a fur trading post at the confluence of the Umpqua River and Elk Creek. Events then may have been livelier than they are in Elkton now, which has about 150 people, most of whom wish the town would stay as it is.

0.3 m., jct., O 138. (Roseburg, *40 m.*)

7.4 m., on R, and partially hidden from road by bldg. that was a roadside restaurant, CB across Elk Creek. The bridge is used only by a dairyman and is not open to the public, but you can take photos from the shoulder of the road.

6.7 m., Drain. (See *The Great Heartland, US 99.*)

O 42—Coos Bay Jct. to Winston, US 99

Coos Bay Jct. is 6.8 m. S of downtown Coos Bay on US 101.

A few years back, this was such a charming road. But now it is heavily traveled, especially by logging trucks, and somehow most of the sweet and gentle nuances have drifted from the land. Still, O 42 is the direct route between Coos Bay and the Umpqua Valley, sprawled around Roseburg.

10.1 m.—from jct.—on L, The Myrtle Bowl, which has been producing handcrafted giftware since 1907.

1 m., Coquille, a virile logging town.

5.9 m., Norway. Settled by Norwegians—but most of their offspring migrated to the bright lights. Just a wide place in the road.

2.9 m., **Myrtle Point.** Round bldg., at E edge of downtown and one block S of O 42, was built around turn of century as Russian Orthodox church. An old-timer described the architecture as "Byzantine, with Coos County modifications." Has not been used as a church for five decades.

3.2 m., Powers Jct.

This road leads to some of the most pristine and scenically exhilarating terrain in W Oregon. Until recently it has been almost the exclusive preserve of sportsmen.

    * *10.3 m.,* Coquille Myrtle Grove SP, a natural stand of myrtles on the S Fork of the Coquille. *8.5 m.,* Powers, a grainy lumber town. Wagner House (1867) is oldest in this part of state. *16 m.*—dotted with FS CGs and picnic sites along Coquille—forks. E fork, *58 m.,* Galice. S fork, more FS camping in *14.5 m.* to Illahe, on the Rogue. Lodges. FS CG. *4.5 m.,* Agness. Store-gas. 31 m., Gold Beach, on US 101; or Galice, 38 m. (See *Rogue River Road* below.)

7 m.—from Powers Jct.—Bridge. Store, cafe, tavern, station. The place was named for a CB, which isn't any more.

2.3 m., white house on L was a stagecoach stop.

4.3 m., on L, Sandy Creek Rd.

    * *0.1 m.,* Sandy Creek CB. Old schoolhouse across rd. from bridge.

0.4 m., Remote. House W of Remote Store—which just about makes up the settlement—was built in 1884. Some mossy old orchards sleep on, shaking off rain and wind to slumber deep, though sometimes tremulously, like an

Originally a church, Myrtle Point

Covered bridge over Elk Creek west of Drain   Sandy Creek covered bridge near Remote

aged dog, and they seem to take on apples like the old dog takes on dandruff.

16.5 m.—the road winds and winds and winds, and be respectful of boom-down logging trucks—Camas Valley. Indians used to come to this vale to pick the nourishing sweet-fleshed bulbs of the blue-flowered Camassia. If any Indians came these days to pick whatever "Lakamass" grows, they'd probably be arrested for trespassing.

17.5 m., Winston, US 99. At W and E ends of Winston are roads leading to Lookingglass.

* 6.5 m., **Lookingglass**, the latest of Oregon's local oddities. Community of less than 50 persons, spread around a pioneer general store, has attracted wide attention with a parking meter, telephone booth, manhole cover and a few other "big city" gadgets. There is also a hitching post and water trough, for the horses the farmchildren ride into "town." The Lookingglass Valley received its name in 1846 from a wanderer with a poetic eye, who noted that the shining green grass reflected the light. Being an old-fashioned soul, he did not name the valley Mirror.

3.4 m., Int. 5.

Rogue River Road—Gold Beach to Grants Pass, Int. 5

Someday this road may be the main link between the S Oregon Coast and the Int. 5 valley. Presently it is chiefly a passage for logging trucks and sportsmen.

View of Rogue River Canyon on road to Agness

The road begins at the N end of Gold Beach, (at the S end of the Rogue River bridge).

27 m. up the Rogue River to the Illinois River bridge, where the Illinois enters the Rogue. The road from Gold Beach winds above the Rogue River canyon, but there are few turnouts for viewing the impressive gorge.

2 m., jct.—FS Rds. 333 and 3400. This point is also known as Shasta Costa Jct. because Shasta Costa Creek empties into the Rogue here.

* For a lunch stop at Agness, take FS Rd. 333 across Rogue River bridge and backtrack 2 m. down Rogue. County park at Agness.

From Agness a forest rd. follows the Rogue upstream 4.5 m. to Illahe, a jumpoff point for sportsmen. Illahe FS CG along Rogue. Lodges. 14.5 m., jct. E, 51 m., passing BLM CGs, Grave Creek bridge. 7.3 m., Galice. The rough terrain between the jct. and Grave Creek bridge is highly mineralized and years ago quite a few prospectors beat the bush along this trail in hopes of striking it rich. Most of the cabins they built have tumbled down, decayed by time and nibbled to kindling wood by the elements. After the prospectors and hermits departed, a silence covered the mist-green hillsides and the moon-filtered gaps, but now the road, and others that straggle in this web-eyed backcountry, are filled by vacationers. (For details on Grave Creek bridge and road from Galice to Grants Pass, see *The Great Heartland, US 99.*) From jct., where E road started, 16 m. N to Powers. (See O 42, preceding.)

At Shasta Costa Jct., take FS rd. 3400, also known as Shasta Costa Rd. and Bear Camp Rd. *36 m.*, Galice, without any store or station between. The road rises to an elevation of 3000 ft., passes through heavily timbered woods, sweeps up and down slopes, and meets emerald pastures. *18 m.*, Grants Pass. (For further information on E section of this road, see *The Great Heartland, US 99.*)

US 199—Jct., US 101 to Grants Pass,
US 99 and Int. 5

US 199 enters Oregon 40 m. NE of its jct. with US 101 and 44 m. from Crescent City, Calif. The grandest scenery of US 199 is in Calif., where redwood forests turn the road into an aisle of a vast, majestic arboreal cathedral.

People from Brookings who want to visit Grants Pass and Medford have to drive 57 m. through Calif. before touching Oregon again.

5.4 m.—N of Calif. border—O'Brien. Store, gas, cafe. There was a lot more activity around here more than a century ago, when the Illinois Valley was in the grip of a gold-mining fever. Most of the gold camps in the area lie under weeds. Finding them is difficult, when you get there, there isn't anything to see.

5.8 m., **Woodland Deer Park**, which has become somewhat formalized in the last few years. But deer still bound up to anyone carrying cones of food and eat out of the hand without nibbling or biting the fingers. With so many other animals inside, the park has become a zoo.

0.8 m., Illinois River SP, at the confluence of the E and W forks of the stream. A relaxing place to picnic, throw out a line or take a dip.

0.7 m., jct., O 46.

* *20 m.*, **Oregon Caves National Monument**, "The Marble Halls of Oregon." Pioneer settler Elijah Davidson "discovered" the caves—the Indians must have known about them—in 1874, while chasing a bear that seemed to vanish into the mountainside. A labyrinth of weird and beautiful caverns in a 7000-ft. limestone and marble formation in the Siskiyou Range. The chambers, corridors and passageways would seem as remote as the moon—or the River Styx—if the place weren't so crowded with tourists. The Chateau, blending with the forest mosaic and moss-covered ledges, looms six stories above the canyon floor. The falls of a mountain stream splash into the Chateau, roll across it, tumble out the other side, and continue toward the sea.

0.2 m., downtown Cave Junction, the largest town between Crescent City and Grants Pass, with all its 350 or 400 people. In recent years an influx of communal settlers has created tension in the town. If you're going to wear long hair in Cave Junction, at least put on shoes. It will keep the locals' blood pressure down.

2.1 m., Kerby. Back in the 1850s, when the town was known as Kerbyville, it was the seat of Josephine County, the only Oregon county to be named for a woman—Josephine Rollins, daughter of a pioneer gold miner and the first white woman in these parts. For a spell the settlement was officially designated as Napoleon, at the insistence of a doctor who had bought up a big chunk of the real estate. After a political wrangle, the issue was put in the hands of the state senate judiciary committee—which hasn't yet tackled the problem. Anyway, the town is Kerby now, honoring early farmer-merchant Jim Kerby, who also spelled his last name as Kerbey. **Kerbyville Museum,** at E end of town, occupies house built in 1878, with second story added later; balconied structure was restored in 1959. Log schoolhouse on grounds was built in 1898 at base of Elijah Mtn., holding Oregon Caves. It was taken apart, log by log, and reassembled here. Kerby Market Bldg., across the road and just E of the museum, was built in 1886 as the local IOOF hall. Masonic Temple, nearby, was put up in 1907.

2.1 m.—from museum—Kerbyville Ghost Town, a boardwalk and dirt street setting designed to capitalize on TV Western popularity.

0.4 m., on L, turnoff for **Kalmiopsis Natural Area.**

* 17 m. to boundary of one of the least known wilderness areas on the Pacific Coast and to some of the most rugged and inaccessible terrain in Oregon. Deep, harsh canyons, swift and dangerous streams (including the Chetco), red-rocked peaks, and granite outcrops form a bristling and sometimes terrifying contrast to the gem-like lakes, the wide variety of conifers, and the rare plants, including several species of orchids, genetians, the darlingtonia, and odd members of the lily family. Rarest is the Kalmiopsis, a small shrub that calls to mind a delicate rhododendron. Foresters regard it as a "living fossil" because it is a relic of the Tertiary Age. No part of the plant may be collected without a written permit; to the FS rangers it is more precious than gold. Almost as rare is the Brewer or weeping spruce—also a pre-ice age relic—which bears resemblance, except for its slender and drooping branchlets, to the Engelmann spruce. Botanically, the area is regarded as the most interesting in the Pacific NW. Perhaps the most fascinating section is the Babyfoot Lake Botan-

Log schoolhouse at Josephine
County Museum, Kerbyville

Babyfoot Lake, Kalmiopsis Wilderness
Courtesy U.S. Forest Service

ical Area, at the E edge of the wilderness, with half the 350 acres inside it. (From wilderness gate at end of road to trail, 0.5 m.; trail to lake, 0.5 m.) The deep-blue, translucent Babyfoot Lake is rewarding in cut-throat trout for anglers who come this way. Wildlife is also abundant in the Kalmiopsis—but beware of rattlesnakes, yellowjackets and hornets, as well as poison oak, and come prepared to cope medically with possible bites and rashes. The trails are too rough for horses and so lonely you will probably not see another human all the time you are in the wilderness. Don't go alone, let it be known when you started and from what point— and check with the FS at Cave Junction for road conditions. If you want to explore the roads rimming the wilderness, you're better off in a four-wheel drive. Probably the easiest place to reach and the safest to browse around is at Babyfoot Lake.

15 m.—from Kalmiopsis Jct.—Wilderville. Murphy Jct.

* The scenic, breezy way to Medford, through the lilting Applegate Valley, kept in tune by the Applegate River humming below soft green hills. The road meanders like an old gossip past rail fences, pungent hay-stacks, full-bossomed barns, wildberry vines, pumpkin patches, breathing meadows, cows feeding lazily on rich grass, horses that never seem to stop scenting the wind, and folksy hamlets that catnap from morning to night, when they go to sleep.

7 m., O 238, 0.2 m., Murphy, near Missouri Flats, a serene green-drenched, smoke-whisped vale that is the nostalgic picture of an early Oregon setting. 8 m., Provolt, just a store at the jct. to Williams. (Williams, 6 m. S, is near the dim scene of an 1857 gold rush, as short-lived as it was frenetic, but the Williamsburg of the Argonauts passed into oblivion long ago.) 4.3 m., Applegate, at a refreshing bend in the road. Named for Lindsay, one of the three famed pioneering Applegate broth-ers. Lindsay, on his way to the Calif. mines in 1848, didn't tarry here, but in those days a man didn't have to stay put to have something named after him. The Applegate and other streams in the area were meticulously panned for gold, with many Chinese miners working claims. Eventually, white hostility drove them from the valley. 5.5 m., on R, **Bosworth House**, built in 1858. One of the most picturesque and eye-warming homes in S Oregon. The barn and sheds are also vintage structures. 2.3 m., Ruch. When C. M. Ruch built a blacksmith shop and a store, in the late 1890s, he was appointed postmaster and told he could give the PO any name he chose. So, with all humility. . . . There isn't a PO or black-smith shop here any more, but there is a store, though not the one Ruch built. 7.9 m., Jacksonville, a partially restored and reconstructed town that was quite a city during the gold mining days of the last century. A living historical museum that threatens to lose its naturalness in a tide of arty profusion. (For details, see *The Great Heartland, US 99*, Medford.) 5.2 m., Medford. (See *The Great Heartland, US 99*.)

Bosworth house west of Ruch on O 238

1.7 m.—from Wilderville—Merlin Jct.

* 12 m., Merlin, on Rogue River. (See *The Great Heartland, US 99,* Grants Pass.)

7.8 m., Grants Pass. (See *The Great Heartland, US 99.*)

The Great Heartland

Lying between the Coast Range and the Cascade Mountains, this area contains far more people, industry and institutions than the remainder of Oregon combined. Think of it as a river system, with the main stream being Int. 5 and its direct US 99 links.

Portland

The best way to see the city is to follow the 50-m.-long **Scenic Drive**, starting at the Chamber of Commerce Bldg., 5th & Taylor, downtown.

The Scenic Drive carries motorists to the summits of three hills—Council Crest, Rocky Butte, Mt. Tabor—which afford sweeping views of Ore. and Wash. Clearly visible, smog permitting, are Mt. Rainier, the Fujiyama-like Mt. St. Helens and Mt. Adams, all in Wash., and the great peaks of the Oregon Cascades: Mt. Hood, Mt. Jefferson and the Three Sisters.

Other attractions in the Scenic Drive include Washington Park, with its exquisite **Japanese Garden,** where five traditional garden forms combine to mirror the mood of an ancient Japan; the Rose Test Gardens; an imaginative statue of Sacajawea, the young Indian mother of the Lewis and Clark expedition; the nearby "Smithsonian of the Northwest," **Oregon Museum of Science and Industry** (OMSI); the disputatious Portland Zoo (most fun is the midget RR ride thru Washington Park; and the Western Forestry Center, with its knowledgable "talking tree"; and, elsewhere, Reed College, renowned for its academic achievements; the opulent **Pittock Mansion** (1909–14) and the University of Portland.

A clump of cedars, looking, to the eye of history weaving, like a stalwart platoon of green-clad trailblazers, backgrounds **Commemorative Rock**, near West Hall on the U of Portland campus. Here, at Waud's Bluff, a detachment of the Lewis and Clark party arrived on April 3, 1806—the farthest known point reached by the explorers on the Willamette River. The bluff overlooks the industrial complex of Swan Island, with freighters at the docks.

In June, July and Aug., the Port of Portland conducts free bus tours of the harbor, starting at noon each Wed. from the Hilton Hotel, 921 SW 6th.

More than 100 structures have been designated as landmarks by the city's Historical Landmarks Commission. Some of the more interesting are listed below, with historic name (if available), date of constuction, and address.

The most historic grouping is spread around the Skidmore Fountain (1888), SW 1st & Ankeny. During the '90s it was the center of Portland's night life, with men, women, horses and dogs drinking from the elegantly sculptured spouts.

New Market Theater (1872), 50 SW 2d, was the city's entertainment palace and platform untl the mid-1880s. Among the great names who trod the stage: E. H. Sothern, Madam Madjeska, Henry Ward Beecher, Robert Ingersoll, John L. Sullivan.

Also in the Skidmore area: New Market Annex (1889), 58 SW 2d, (note unusual fire escapes); Smiths Block (1872), 10 SW Ash; Bickel Bldg. (1892), 208 SW Ankeny; 233 SW Front (1883–84); 28 NW 1st (1890); 81 SW Oak (1859); 224 SW 1st (1889); 235 SW 1st (1886); Poppleton Bldg. (1873), 83 SW 1st; a former livery stable (1886), 126 SW 2d; 112 SW 2d (1889); Haseltine Bldg. (1893), 133 SW 2d.

Another historical grouping is known as the "Yamhill District," because of location: 71–73 SW Yamhill (1878); 124 SW Yamhill (1885); 728 SW 1st (1878); 730 SW 1st (1878); 814 SW 1st (1878); 818 SW 1st (1878); 920–928 SW 3d (1895), originally a music hall.

Other official historic landmarks: 200 NW Davis (1885); Blagen Block (1888), 78 NW Couch; 105 NW 3d (1883); 208 SW Stark (1891); Bishop's House (1879), 219–223 SW Stark; Dekum Bldg. (1892), 519 SW 3d; Hamilton Bldg. (1893), 529 SW 3d; Pioneer Courthouse (1869–73), SW 5th & Morrison; Olds & King store (1903), 514 SW 6th, Portland's first steel frame bldg; City Hall (1895), 1220 SW 5th; Ladd Carriage House (1883), 715 SW Columbia;

Union Station (1890), end of NW 6th; U.S. Customs House (1901), 220 NW 8th; Shea residence (1892), 1809 NW Johnson; Koehler residence (1905), 723 NW 19th; Isom White residence (1905), 311 NW 20th; Captain John Brown House (1898), Couch Park, NW 20th & Glisan; Heusner Residence (1905), 333 NW 20th; MacKenzie Residence (1892), 615 NW 20th; Mills Residence (1908), 733 NW 20th; Trevitt House (1891), 2347 NW Flanders; Bates Residence (1908), 2381 NW Flanders; St. Patricks Church (1889–90), 1639 NW 19th;

Brewery (1907–08), 1133 W Burnside; Wilcox Residence (1893), 931 SW King; McCamant Residence (1899), 1046 SW King; Governor Curry Residence (1865), 1020 SW Cheltenham Ct., originally at SW 8th & College; Nicholas-Lang Residence (1884–85), 2030 NW Vista; Piggots Castle (1892), 2591 SW Buckingham Terr., at least from a distance the most bizarre-looking house in Portland;

First Presbyterian Church (1886–90), 1200 SW Alder; Portland Art Museum (1932–39), SW Park & Madison; First Congregational Church (1889–95), 126 SW Park; First Baptist Church (1894), 909 SW 11th; Calvary Presbyterian Church, now known as "The Old Church" (1882), 1422 SW 11th; Morris Marks Residence (1881–82), 1501 SW Harrison, originally at corner of SW 11th & Clay;

Freiwald Residence (1906), 1810 NE 15th; David Cole Residence (1885), 1441 N McClellan; Finnish Workers Hall (1907), 3425 N Montana; Mock Residence (1894), 4333 N Willamette; West Hall, U of Portland (1891), 5000 N Willamette; St. Johns City Hall (1907), 7214 Philadelphia; St. Johns Bridge (1931), N Syracuse & Philadelphia;

Allen Prep School (1905), 1135 SE Salmon; Burrell House (1902), 2610 SE Hawthorne; Buehner Residence (1905–06), 5511 SE Hawthorne; Reid Residence (1914), 4755 SE Stark; Kendall Homestead (1894–99), 3908 SE Taggart; Eliot Hall and old dorm block, Reed College (1912), SE 32d & Woodstock; St. Johns Episcopal Church (1851), 8039 SE Grand.

Other structures, sites and sculptory of interest: Temple Beth Israel (1927), 1931 NW Flanders; Sanctuary of Our Sorrowful Mother, with its famous Grotto, NE Sandy at 84th; Peninsula Park, with its color-splashed Sunken Rose Garden, 6400 N Albina; statute of Abraham Lincoln, SW Main & Park; the "people's fountain"—an abstraction of NW waters, at Civic Auditorium, SW 2d & Clay; Lovejoy Fountain, at S end of Portland Center Towers, SW 2d & Harrison.

Music Museum, formerly at Seaside, is now in Opera House of **Western Dairyville**, 6149 SW Shattuck Rd.

One of Portland's most genuinely interesting places is **Lone Fir Cemetery**, SE 20th, between Morrison & Stark. The great democratic burial ground of Oregon, it contains without discrimination the remains of men and women of every race, color, nationality, occupation and degree of morality who died in Portland or were carried here from the nearby hinterlands. An estimated 30,000 persons were laid to rest in the 30-acre grounds. Great names of political power and wealth sleep near modest toilers and nameless drunks. Markers

Tombstone in Lone Fir Cemetery

are inscribed in at least seven languages, and there are more colorful markers here than in all other cemeteries of Oregon combined. The markers in the area set aside for the graves of firemen, for instance, have intricate carvings of hooks, ladders, trumpets and shields, signifying the trappings and glory of early fire companies.

Portland is one of the few cities on the continent which contain within their corporate limits a "wilderness area." The 5000-acre West Hills forest and park complex contains 15 m. of inviting trails. Two good starting points are Forest Park, at the W end of Thurman St., and Macleay Park at the W end of Upshur St.

Short Trips out of Portland

Sauvie Island

For centuries this island, largest in the Columbia, and, in part, washed by the mouth of the Willamette, was a summer and autumn homeland to the Multnomah Indians, and was known later to some whites as Multnomah Island. Lewis and Clark called it Wap-pa-to and Wap-pa-too and to the early white traders and trappers it was Wapato. But by the mid-1850s the area was known as Sauvie Island, after a Hudson's Bay Co. employee named Sauve.

In recent years Sauvie Island has become a Portland suburb, a summer recreational retreat (swimming, boating and picnicking) and, above all, a game management area, designed for wintering waterfowl.

About 10,000 hunters per year use the waterfowl hunting parts of the game management area. More than 20 publicly owned waterfowl hunting areas and as many publicly owned fishing areas dot the island. In addition, some landowners lease duck ponds to hunters.

Raccoon hunting is permitted on the management area other than during waterfowl season. Almost gleefully, a brochure of the Oregon Game Commission advises that "most successful hunting of the animals is done with a pack of hounds at night. Best area is the north unit near Ruby and Millionaire Lakes." Stay away from these, raccoons.

A note to crows: the same OGC brochure states: "A stuffed owl perched in a tree about twenty feet from the ground plus judicious use of a crow call can provide the hunter with some active sport." There are no suggestions as to how crows can hunt humans.

Despite all the onslaughts of man, Sauvie Island still retains an air of pastoral beauty, except when smog covers it.

Follow US 30 to the Sauvie Island turnoff, approximately 11 m. from downtown Portland. Along the way the road passes the approach to St. Johns Bridge, the most aesthetic river span in Oregon, and Linnton, whose founding predates Portland, but which is now part of the city.

From the N end of the Sauvie Island bridge, follow Sauvie Island Rd. *1.2 m.* to Howell Park Rd. Turn R. *0.1 m.*, **Bybee-Howell House**, built in the 1850s on a donation land claim of the Bybee family. For more than a century

St. Johns Bridge, Portland

the house belonged to the Howell family, hence its name. Classic revival house, restored and now a museum place, has nine rooms and seven fireplaces. The house sits on a knoll (about 50 ft. above sea level) that is the highest point on the island. *0.5 m.,* one of the largest broadleaf maple trees in the world.

Return to Sauvie Island Rd. *1 m.,* Reeder Rd. Continue straight on Sauvie Island Rd. *1.9 m.* on L, Ft. William marker. In 1834, Nathaniel Wyeth, a Mass. ice merchant who sought his fortune in the Oregon Country, established a post at Warrior Point, on the NW "neck" of the island. The next year he moved his Ft. William to the Multnomah Channel, about 0.5 m. S of marker. There is no path to the channel and no sign at the channel to indicate the existence of the post.

0.5 m., on L, a 13-room house that is one of the oldest on the island. It has had many tenants. *0.8 m.,* Lucy Reeder Rd. Continue on Sauvie Island Rd., which follows the Multnomah Channel, a winding wash that departs from the Willamette and empties into the Columbia. The channel possesses some photogenic touches: moorages, log rafts, houseboats, fishing silhouettes and drowsy shades, where clumps of trees snooze above the lazy water. The R side of the road is a great saucer of rich farmland.

3.6 m.—and into Columbia County—end of paved road and beginning of Game Management Area.

Bybee-Howell House, Sauvie Island | Broadleaf maple on Sauvie Island

Return to Lucy Reeder Rd. and turn onto it. *1.4 m.*, through peaceful countryside, to road's end. Return to Sauvie Island Rd. Turn L. Continue to Reeder Rd. and turn L onto it. *1.2 m.*, at fork, turn L onto Oak Island Rd. *1.5 m.*, on R, moss-shrouded house with wood-shingled roof has all the characteristics of a pioneer dwelling. *2.2 m.*, Oak Island, a picnic area dominated by large oak groves and surrounded by recreational waters.

Return to Reeder Rd. Turn L. *3.1 m.*, Gillihan Rd. Continue on Reeder Rd. *6.7 m.*, past large dikes, to Walton Beach, on the Columbia. Most popular beach fishing area on island.

Return to Gillihan Rd. Turn L. This is the only road that parallels both the Columbia and the Willamette, though the rivers are hidden by dikes and meadows. Some of the largest barns on the island are seen from this road. *6.3 m.*, entrance to bridge linking island to US 30.

Columbia Gorge Tour

It is difficult for most recent Oregonians, whatever their age, to realize that not too long ago, US 30 approaching Portland from the E was for some miles a very narrow, very winding road, scary for travelers and a terror to truckers. Today the same road, free of trucks, and with the through traffic on the freeway, is a scenic trip. Spongy woods and lushly ferned hills, latticing the sunlight and shading the road, contrast with bulging cliffs and rocky brows to create pastel moods that unreel as a kaleidoscope of fluid images.

Cross Morrison Bridge and take Int. 80N. *15 m.* from Chamber of Commerce Bldg., SW 5th & Taylor, entrance to **Columbia River Scenic Highway.** *1.1 m.*, Troutdale, a Portland suburb with an old-fashioned rural business block. *0.9 m.*, turnoff to Lewis and Clark SP on Sandy River. A favorite CG and day park for Portlanders. *2.9 m.*, Dabney SP. CG; fishing, swimming on Sandy River. *5.5 m.*, **Portland Women's Forum SP.** Viewpoint of Columbia River Gorge. Crown Point, Rooster Rock and Beacon Rock are most prominent clearly visible landmarks. *0.4 m.*, turnoff for Larch Mtn. *14.5 m.*—reached through a cool forest corridor blissfully devoid of power lines—**Larch Mtn.** parking area, at 4050-ft. elevation.

The view from Larch Mtn. is enough to make your head swim. The Cascades roll eastward in a series of uneven green waves, with Mt. Hood and Mt. Adams towering above the swells of hills. Picnic area in woods above parking lot gives one an eagle's nest feeling—and, if you feel restless, there are trails to explore. But don't let small children loose; too many sharp drops.

Return to jct. At this point the scenic route really begins. *0.7 m.*, **Crown Point (Vista House).** Parking. The most celebrated view of the Columbia Gorge. *2.2 m.*, Talbot SP. Picnic under a green canopy; easy hiking trails. *0.3 m.*, **Latourell Falls,** tumbling sheer for 250 ft. from an overhanging basalt cliff. *1.3 m.*, Shepperd's Dell SP. Paths to waterfalls and odd rock formations. *1 m.*, Bridal Veil, Petticoat Junction of the Columbia Gorge. *3.1 m.*, **Wahkeena Falls.** The name is supposedly taken from the Yakimas, meaning "most beautiful." *0.6 m.*, **Multnomah Falls,** second highest in the U.S., most famous in the NW, and one of the loveliest on the continent. Set in a sylvan glen, the long white plume (620 ft. in two steps) seems a soft scarf of windblown lace against the rugged basaltic cliff of the Gorge, down which it ethereally descends.

2.2 m., **Oneonta Gorge.** A craggy, dramatic chasm. A 0.5 m. "trail" winds through the narrow cleft to Oneonta Falls, but few make it, because the "trail" is often part of the stream bed. Only when the stream is very low is there little problem—unless you wear hip boots or don't mind getting your

Columbia River Gorge from Portland Women's Forum State Park

Oneonta Gorge

feet and ankles chilled in the cold stream. You have to cross many "bridges" of slippery rocks, and at times progress is made only by inching around the cliff walls, on precarious footholds.

0.4 m., **Horsetail Falls.** The 176-ft.-high cataract was so named because it supposedly looks like a horsetail hanging down the sheer rock wall. *0.6 m.,* Ainsworth SP. CG in a fir and hemlock forest at the base of St. Peter's Dome, a 2000-ft. basalt pinnacle. *0.9 m.,* road enters Int. 80N. *4.9 m.,* turnoff to **Bonneville Dam.** Self-guided hatchery tour includes all phases of salmon raising, a pond where you can throw vending machine food to fish, and a pool where giant sturgeons prowl on the bottom, conjuring up images of submarines. Other sights: fish ladders, the dam, power house and navigational locks. *1.2 m.,* Cascade Salmon Fish Hatchery and Eagle Creek Park. FS CG on giggling stream.

1.9 m., turnoff for **Bridge of the Gods** and Cascade Locks. Toll bridge crosses Columbia at point where, according to Indian mythology, a natural rock span arched the river. (A good way back to Portland from here is to cross to the Wash. side and drive W on the N bank of the Columbia. Chief attraction on this road is **Beacon Rock,** inferior only to Gibraltar as a monolith. The view from the top, reached by trail, speaks eloquently of Columbia Gorge scenery. Beacon Rock SP has CG, boating facilities.)

0.5 m.—from turnoff—Cascade Locks, an old river town with aged wood and modern neon staring at each other. *0.2 m.,* turn L to Historical Museum. *0.1 m.,* Museum, boat locks and park.

Cascade Locks Museum (1905) was home of lockman: two houses to W are identical in design and year of construction and were also inhabited by lockmen. It seems odd that so few Portland people know of this museum. It is one of the finest small, authentically-sited historical museums in state. Upstairs bedroom has hard maple bed which was brought across the plains in 1852. Rope or rawhide was used for springs; then a tick or pad of straw or corn husks; and finally a feather tick on top. Another room contains a true replica of a fishing wheel, the kind common on the Columbia for many years. A large

Navigational locks, Bonneville Dam   **View west from Cascade Locks Park**

wheel was 30 ft. in diameter and caught as many as 3000 salmon in a single day. More than 40 wheels were operated on the Columbia in 1900; all wheels were outlawed in Oregon in 1927. Locks due N of museum were, prior to Bonneville Dam, extensively used to negotiate the Columbia here. On top of the old lock walls, fishermen toss their lines into the channels, place their poles under heavy rocks, to hold them fast, and loaf, stretching out for a snooze or lounging in lawn chairs. The river flowing through the locks sounds like a dog lapping water, which is probably soothing. Even if no steelhead are caught—and the fish are in no hurry to awaken anyone—a man can always say he tried. In front of museum stands "The Oregon Pony," first locomotive built on the Pacific Coast and first used W of the Missouri. Built in San Francisco and brought to mouth of Tanner Creek, W of salmon hatchery at Bonneville Dam, in spring of 1862. It operated for two years on 4.5-m. stretch of portage between Tanner Creek and Upper Cascades. From 1929 to 1970 it was on display at Portland Union Station. Park near museum has grassy area for camping, marina, and unblemished panorama of a rugged, contorted spur of the Cascade Range across the river. The brown-salmonish exposed strata is in striking contrast to the green below.

Return to freeway. Turn W. *12.1 m.*, turnoff to Multnomah Falls. *6.4 m.*, turnoff to Rooster Rock SP. *0.3 m.*, parking area for beach on Columbia. Return to freeway. *23 m.*, Portland.

Mt. Hood Loop

One of the most scenic and diversified one-day tours in the state, but it can be better enjoyed on a longer trip—two or three days.

Cross Morrison bridge and take Int. 80N for *15 m.*, turnoff to Troutdale and Columbia River scenic highway. (See *Columbia Gorge Tour*, preceding.) Stay on 80N.

1.1 m., Lewis and Clark SP. Not only did the famed explorers pass this way but this site was also an encampment for covered wagon emigrants who boarded river craft at The Dalles and disembarked at where the Sandy River enters the Columbia. CG.

4 m., turnoff to village of Corbett.

From here to the next listed point there are glimpses, on the S, of Vista House, atop Crown Point, best known view of the Columbia Gorge.

2.7 m., turnoff to Rooster Rock SP. The name comes from a basalt spire between the road and the Columbia. Park on summer weekends attracts thousands of swimmers, sunbathers and picnickers.

Few river highways in America are as beatiful as the Columbia River Gorge—when it is not raining, snowing, gusty, foggy, or just plain smoggy. It took quite a while for the Columbia to gnaw through the Cascades—and if it were human, it might sometimes wonder if it was worth the effort, considering all that has been done to it.

5.1 m., turnoff to Benson SP. Picnic, swim. Motor boats prohibited. *0.7 m.*, Multnomah Falls. (See *Columbia Gorge Tour*, preceding.) *2.4 m.*, view of Beacon Rock, ahead on L, across river. *1.6 m.*, turnoff to Ainsworth SP. *1.5 m.*, directly across river, Beacon Rock, one of the great monoliths of the world. *3.4 m.*, turnoff to Bonneville Dam. (See *Columbia Gorge Tour*, preceding.) *1.2 m.*, turnoff to Cascade Salmon Fish Hatchery and Eagle Creek Park. FS CG. *1.9 m.*, turnoff to Bridge of the Gods and Cascade Locks. (See *Columbia Gorge Tour*, preceding.)

10.5 m., **Starvation Creek SP** entrance. At this point—across freeway, at RR tracks—a train in 1884 was marooned for two weeks in 30-ft snowdrifts. Passengers burned all the coal, then the car seats, finally whatever else combustible they could find, to keep from freezing. A rescue party prevented starvation.

0.2 m.—off road—SP parking area. Starvation Creek pushes through a cleft in a Cascade wall and ricochets in spumes, and plumes and wind-blown waves about 60 ft. to shelf, then leaps about another 60 ft. to a jumble of rocks, and then rolls as a creek again through the park. Beautiful view of Columbia Gorge from parking area.

Return to freeway. *0.9 m.*, Viento SP. CG on Viento Creek. V*iento* is Spanish for "wind," and here the wind can throw cars around like toys when its temper is up.

7.9 m., turnoff at second exit—city center—for Hood River, largest town in and seat of Hood River County.

* *27 m.* from Hood River, via Dee, to **Lost Lake**, seemingly at the foot of Mt. Hood. A 3-m. trail of spongy-carpeted fern, cut through stands of

Falls in Starvation Creek State Park   Mt. Hood over Lost Lake

Mt. Hood from hamlet of Mt. Hood

Douglas fir, encircles the lake. On the S, narrow clearings reveal stunning views of Mt. Hood. FS CG. Store.

(You do not need to return to Hood River to reach O 35. At Dee, 15 m. from lake, turn to Parkdale, 6 m., and drive 2 m. E to O 35.)

Still on 80N: 0.5 m. beyond Hood River city center exit, turn onto O 35. 0.6 m., turn L at sign, "Panorama Point." 1.5 m., turnoff to parking lot. 0.2 m., **Panorama Point.** The grandest vista of the fruited Hood River Valley, with Mt. Hood completely dominating background to S.

Return to O 35. Turn L. 13.2 m. past apple and cherry orchards, neat farmsteads and unconcealed views of Mt. Hood: Parkdale-Cooper Spur Jct. and hamlet of Mt. Hood.

Turn R toward Parkdale. 0.7 m., Dimmick SP. Picnic in forest on E fork of Hood River. 1.1 m., Parkdale Jct. Turn R. 0.6 m., Parkdale, key market place in upper Hood River Valley. From store beyond RR tracks, continue straight, or W. Where road to Dee turns N, take other fork, Baseline Rd. 0.8 m.—from store—continue straight on Lava Bed Rd. 0.5 m., end of road and N edge of lava beds, huge mounds of most recent volcanic outpouring of Mt. Hood. Return to Parkdale and Cooper Spur Rd.

* (For old highway, turn R onto Cooper Spur Rd. 8.1 m., Cloud Cap Jct. R, or W, on gravel road, 10.6 m. to Cloud Cap Inn, a highlight of the loop trip. 2.4 m., straight on Cooper Spur to O 35. The old road is very rough and twisty and no more scenic than the new road, O 35. So Cloud Cap Inn can be reached with less preliminary difficulty. Therefore, return to O 35 from Parkdale and turn R, or S.)

8.7 m.—from Parkdale Jct. on O 35—to just below Polallie FS CG, turn R. (This is where the old road comes into O 35, as stated above.)

2.4 m., Cloud Cap Jct. Beyond E side of road is Cooper Spur Inn, a very busy place some years ago. In olden days the affluent of Portland took the overnight boat to Hood River and spent a day riding a buggy or stage on the wagon road to here. They bedded down at Cooper Spur Inn and the next day made it to Cloud Cap Inn. The gravelly, spiraling road to Cloud Cap Inn passes Inspiration Point, with its valley and mountain vistas, and, near the top, the turnoff to Tilley Jane FS CG.

Cloud Cap Inn was built in 1889 and anchored to the mountain by cables to resist winter storms. It sits on a pumice knoll surrounded by alpine phlox, lupine, pentstamen and wind-twisted black hemlock scoured by pumice sprayed by high winds. The inn is now occupied by a mountaineer and mountain rescue group; the adjacent log lodge, built about 1910, is occupied by a private group. The view from Cloud Cap Inn is pointed directly at the headwall of Mt. Hood's Eliot Glacier, with its great crevass area and, on the L, as you look up the mtn., Cooper Spur, one of the most popular climbing routes to Hood's peak.

8.8 m.—on O 35, from Cloud Cap Jct.—turn R to Hood River Meadows FS CG and Sahalie Falls. The CG, though only a stone's throw from the highway, seems many miles removed, so thickly forested and hardily rustic is it. Generally lonely during the week. Trail leads 2 m. to Umbrella Falls.

1.2 m., on turnoff road, **Sahalie Falls.** The E fork of Hood River comes tumbling down in a big, spraying splash. *0.4 m.,* turn R onto Mt. Hood Meadows Rd. *1.9 m.,* **Mt. Hood Meadows.** A day-lodge complex with frontal look

Sahalie Falls, Mt. Hood Loop   **Umbrella Falls, Mt. Hood Loop**

at Mt. Hood. From parking lot, 600-ft trail descends to closeup of **Umbrella Falls,** a white-water torrent pouring down a rocky notch in a thickly wooded hillside. One of largest, highest, most stirring Mt. Hood falls.

Return to Sahalie Falls Rd. Straight, 30 yds.—O 35. Turn R.

6.4 m., jct., US 26. Keep straight, on US 26. *2.3 m.,* Timberline Lodge Jct. Turn R. *5.5 m.,* **Timberline Lodge.** The greatest of Oregon's mountain resorts and center of the state's most popular ski slopes. Sno-cats and chair lifts carry passengers high up the mountain.

Return to US 26. Turn R. *0.2 m.,* turnoff to Government Camp, an alpine village.

Now US 26 comes scooting and sliding and barreling down Laurel Hill, paralleling the last lap and most difficult part of the Barlow Road, opened for commerce in 1846. Until then The Dalles was the end of overland travel on the Oregon Trail, and emigrants had to chance rafting the dangerous waters of the Columbia. For some emigrants, Laurel Hill was the most hazardous stretch of the entire way West, and you can appreciate their difficulty here if you realize that, steep as US 26 is, the wagon trace was much, much steeper.

8.9 m.—from Government Camp turnoff—on L, **Tollgate.** Between two maples is replica of W tollgate of Barlow Road. Zigzag River, which the prairie schooners crossed numerous times, makes a Z here.

0.6 m., Rhododendron. Pretty little hamlet that is summer home for some lucky Portlanders.

2 m., Zigzag. Turnoff R on Lolo Pass Rd. for **Ramona Falls.**

* *4.1 m.,* turn R onto FS Rd. S-25. *4.2 m.*—passing two FS CGs—end of S-25, at parking area. From here, *4.5 m.* round trip trail hike to Ramona Falls. Some rare views of Mt. Hood along trail. Ramona Falls is not only one of the most eye-filling attractions in the Mt. Hood National Forest, it is also one of the most visited.

1 m.—on US 26—Wemme. Turn L to Welches at sign. *0.9 m.,* Bowman's resort, in a green cove of the foothills. Along with usual country club facilities, resort has some interesting attractions, including a doll museum. *0.2 m.,* on R, turn-of-the-century house built by the late William Welch, son of early pioneer Sam Welch. To rear and W of home, and also painted white, is smaller house, which for 55 years was a PO.

Return to US 26. Turn L. *16.2 m.,* Sandy. *11.3 m.,* Gresham. *13 m.,* Portland.

Clackamas River-Mt. Hood National Forest Tour

From Burnside & 82d, S on O 213.

7.9 m., turn R onto O 224 ramp. *0.2 m.,* turn L toward Estacada. *4.4 m.,* Carver, site of once-famous stone quarry. Leave O 224 to angle R onto Redland-Baker Cabin Rd. Cross Clackamas River bridge. (Long ago, say those old-timers still around, the river here was so thick with salmon the farmers brought their pigs down to gorge on the fish. Then, the story continues, the pigs would have to be fed on something else, to get the fish smell out of them. There are few salmon now, less than there are fish stories.)

Turn L at end of bridge onto County Rd. 28. *0.2 m.*, turn R. *0.1 m.*, on R corner of intersection marked "Holcomb Area," plaque tells legend of **Baker Log Cabin.** Follow dirt lane N *150 yds.* to cabin, built in 1856, restored in 1939. Pioneer dwelling has high stone chimney, overhanging roof supported by timbers, and a second-story covered porch on one side. . . . Outdoor hand pump, so common in rural Oregon 50 years ago, is added touch of past. . . . On way to cabin, dirt lane passes relocated Carver Church (1895). From its opening until its closing in 1924, all services were conducted in German. After 1924 the one-room country church had much usage as a sheep barn.

Return to County Rd. 28. Turn R. *5.4 m.*, on NW corner of Harding Rd., sprawling frame house with cone-shaped cupola, spool-trimmed porch and splotches of gingerbread. A ghostly place. The way things are going, it may be torn down for a service station.

2.7 m., on L, **Clackamas Viewpoint.** A stunning panorama of a Clackamas River bend, willowy woods, slices of meadow, the Cascade foothills and Mt. Hood. An Oregon Currier & Ives.

1.1 m., turnoff to Milo McIver SP. (*1.5 m.*, McIver SP, an open green park at a mumbling, stumbling curve of the Clackamas. Site of the disputatious "Vortex I," a 1970 state-sponsored rock festival designed to draw visiting long-haired youth away from Portland during American Legion convention.)

Return to county rd. Turn L. *1.2 m.*, Estacada Jct. Continue straight. 3 *m.*, **Springwater.** Here is the functional rural trinity of store, Grange hall, church. Presbyterian Church was established in 1889; present church (1904) has modest spire and belfry.

Turn L, retracking. *0.4 m.*, Day Hill Rd. Turn R. *0.2 m.*, turn L onto O 211. *2.8 m.*, at edge of Estacada, turn R onto O 224, up the Clackamas River.

This drive winds through a forested wonderland, dotted by camp and picnic grounds, and with a hundred up-close and long-range views of the many-mooded Clackamas. One of the finest river drives in the state.

7.4 m., on R, parking area. Sign reads: "Picnic Area." Back and down from parking lot is **Small Fry Lake,** stocked by Portland General Electric Co. for children under 14. No charge. Daily limit: three fish, any size. From rear of picnic area, the Clackamas is seaweed green, with sunbeams leaping up from the water like fish surfacing to bite. The stream flows through the mossy, shrubby, fern-stained canyon walls with the silky rhythm of a big cat rippling its muscles.

10.9 m., on L, Roaring River FS CG. A tonic under the firs. Off R side of rd., Clackamas breaks into a spasm of rapids.

7.8 m., Ripplebrook Ranger Station. Friendly personnel patiently direct travelers to all parts of the upper Clackamas River vacationland.

0.6 m., Harriet Lake-Timothy Lake Jct.

* Straight, *6.8 m.* to **Austin Hot Springs.** The Clackamas current is as cold as the bankside waters, heated by the steaming springs, are hot. Fine CG. Retrace path to Riverford-Two Rivers Jct. and turn L. Where road forks beyond Pegleg Falls, take S turn. *13.8 m.*, from Austin Hot Springs,

Small Fry Lake

Pansy Lake, Bull of the Woods
Courtesy U.S. Forest Service

trail to **Bagby Hot Springs.** Hike *1.5 m.* down FS trail into Bagby. Some hot springs partisans prefer Bagby to Austin.

(The most "get-away-from-it-all" expedition in this region is **Bull of the Woods**—from the Ripplebrook Ranger Station, 19 m. by road and 3 m. via trail. Motor vehicles prohibited. The 10,200-acre area, at the far headwaters of the Clackamas, contains craggy mtns.; 12 high, small, fish-stocked (chiefly brook trout) lakes, four of which are inaccessible by trail; and some old mines. Beware of partially-concealed shafts. This is not an area for the weak or for those who are lonely away from crowds; the largest number of camp units at any lake is four at Pansy; five lakes have no camping facilities, and all facilities are primitive.

(Good roads from Ripplebrook lead to many lakes, including famed Olallie. Follow Clackamas River Rd. *8 m.* beyond Austin Hot Springs, turn onto Pinhead Creek Rd. and stay with it *6 m.* Turn R. *10 m.*, **Olallie Lake.** Or drive *7 m.* beyond Pinhead Creek Jct. to Lemiti Creek Rd.—S806. Follow it *12 m.* to Olallie Lake. The Clackamas River Rd. leads 46 m. from Ripplebrook to O 22 through dazzling forests. This is the long way—with perhaps a detour to Olallie Lake—back to Portland, via O 22 and Int. 5.)

For main tour, return to Harriet Lake-Timothy Lake Jct.

Turn E, or L, if coming from Ripplebrook Ranger Station.

15.8 m., Timothy Lake, looking naked and glossy at this end. But some fishermen like it. *3.7 m.*, turn R onto road marked Clackamas Lake CG (FS.) *0.3 m.*, turn L. *0.5 m.*, Clackamas Lake, once a respectable lake, now a marsh you can wade across. Where has all the pretty water gone?

Return to Timothy Lake Rd. Turn R, toward US 26. *8 m.*, US 26. Turn L. *1.6 m.*, on L, turnoff to **Clear Lake.** *2 m.*, Clear Lake, large highland lake with much mood appeal. FS CG. Return to US 26. Turn L. *2.6 m.*, turn R toward Frog Lake. *0.7 m.*, **Frog Lake.** At first glance no bigger than a frog pond. (A typical small Cascade lake, with typical FS CG.) But the view of Mt. Hood from the upper end is sensational. In the morning the mtn. is fully reflected in the water.

Return to US 26. Turn R. *5.2 m.*, turn L to Trillium Lake. *2 m.*, **Trillium Lake**. FS CG. Next to Lost Lake, the most photogenic view of Mt. Hood is from here. So, take off your shoes, sit on a rock, and dip your feet in the warm water for a blissful respite. Or stick your fishing pole on the bank, with the line out, and lean back in a chair under a tree until you note some activity. If the line does not twitch all afternoon, what's been lost? Some folks put out a line just as an excuse to lazy away a few hours.

Return to US 26. Turn L. *1.6 m.*, turnoff to Timberline Jct. *0.2 m.*, turnoff to Government Camp. *54 m.*, Portland. (For points of interest, see *Mt. Hood Loop*, preceding.)

Historical Tour No. 1

From Broadway & Burnside, W on Burnside *2.2 m.* Turn R onto NW Barnes. Follow signs *0.6 m.* to **Pittock Mansion**, a baronial stone castle built

Trillium Lake with Mt. Hood in background

early in the century by newspaper tycoon Henry L. Pittock. He lived only a few years to enjoy opulent elegance of mansion, now a museum. Sweeping views of river, city and verdant W suburbs.

Return to Burnside. Turn R. (Burnside soon becomes Skyline Blvd.) *1.3 m.*, on L, **Willamette Stone SP.** Path slopes 220 yds. to spot where, in early June 1851, John R. Preston, first surveyor general of Oregon, drove the "starting stake" for all land surveys in the Pacific NW. Stake replaced by the stone in July 1885. Inscription on stone: "Beginning here, the Willamette Meridian was established running north to Puget Sound and south to the California border, and the base line was established running east to the Idaho border and west to the Pacific Ocean." All the lands of Oregon were sectionized from these guidelines.

1.3 m., NW Cornell Rd. Turn L. *2.8 m.*, Cedar Mill. Suburb crossroad, with no signs of original village. *0.8 m.*, turn R onto NW 143d-West Union. *0.4 m.*, on L, Union Cemetery of Cedar Mill. Contains graves of some early settlers. *0.8 m.*, turn R onto Kaiser Rd. *0.7 m.*, **Bethany Baptist Church**, organized in 1881 as First German Baptist Church of Bethany—first church of this specific denomination on Pacific Coast. Present structure built in 1928 in modified Spanish colonial style with carillon tower. Original chapel (1881) at rear of church. *1 m.*, on L, house built in 1882 (as was barn across road) and long used as a stagecoach station. This was original site of Bethany. *0.1 m.*, corner of Kaiser & Springville, **Bethany Presbyterian Church** (1904). Across Kaiser Rd. from church are house and barn of early 1880s vintage.

Turn L, or W, onto Springville Rd. *1.6 m.*, NW 185th Ave. Turn L toward Bethany. *0.5 m.*, Bethany. Pioneer structure of feed mill. Turn R onto NW Union Rd. *1.5 m.*, West Union, food and gas crossroads. Turn L onto Cornelius Pass Rd. *1.2 m.*, on R, **Imbrie House.** Construction started about 1862, completed about 1866. Six generations of Imbries have lived and still live here. One of the most distinguished-looking century-old houses in Oregon. (Do not drive onto property.)

Willamette Stone   **West Union Baptist Church**

Village blacksmith shop, Glencoe

Return to NW Union Rd. Turn L. *0.8 m.*, **West Union Baptist Church**, oldest Baptist church W of the Rockies and oldest Protestant bldg. in Oregon. David T. Lenox, captain of first wagon train to Oregon (1843), donated land for church and cemetery from his original land grant. In mid-1844 he organized church in his log cabin, in late 1853 present church was dedicated. When Lenox passed away in 1873, he was buried in cemetery. Earlier grave markers date back to 1860s.

0.8 m., Turn R onto Helvetia Rd. (This road is lined with old houses and barns, none of them exceptional, but all soaking the road in 19th-century atmosphere.) *1.4 m.*, Helvetia. Store. All that remains Swiss is name given by early settlers. *1.1 m.*, on L, white, belfried, spired **Helvetia Community Church** (1899). A restful scene. Across road, and slightly to R, is one of the interesting houses in this area. The view from the church knoll is a green, undulating, lyrical canvas, sweet and clean and bright.

0.8 m., turn L onto Jackson Quarry Rd. *0.9 m.*, turn ahead onto NW Union Rd. *0.8 m.*, Jackson Rd. **Jackson House**, on SW corner, and **Lincoln House**, *0.1 m.* N on Jackson Rd., were famous in 1880–90s as Tualatin Valley show places.

Continue on NW Union. *1.2 m.*, on R, **Village Blacksmith Shop**. Charles Walter worked in this shop from 1890 to 1962. He retired at age 92 and died two years later. Shop is as Walter left it—a heritage of the horse and buggy days. It contains fifth wheels for buggies, forge, trip hammer which Walter made from an old anvil brought around the Horn from England, homemade vise and early tire bender. Three generations of Walters live in houses flanking shop.

This is Glencoe, which at turn of century was a right lively mercantile burg. But business section died when most inhabitants moved to the new village of North Plains, 0.5 m. SW around 1910. Only a few houses here now.

60 yds. from blacksmith shop, Glencoe Rd. Turn L. *2 m.*, Scotch Church Rd. (Old house on corner.) Turn L. *0.5 m.*, **Tualatin Plains Presbyterian Church**, known for decades as "Old Scotch Church" and now "Old Scots Church." The modest white chapel displays the excellent craftsmanship often found in early Oregon churches. The church, and the cemetery which frames it on three sides, are bordered by a grove of firs, oaks and maples. Among those who lie in the old burial ground are the pioneer Meek family, including Joe Meek, the gruff, colorful mountain man, for whom early scribes used the longest, flashiest yarn to spin their patchquilt biographies. But it wasn't all their fault. "Uncle Joe" strung the longest bow in the territory when it came to telling tales. When an innocent newcomer once asked Joe if he had seen many changes in his Oregon years, Joe snorted that, when he first arrived, Mt. Hood was just a hole in the ground. "There's no man like Joe," his Indian wife often said, and from the standpoint of writers, there wasn't. He died in 1875, two years after the Tualatin Plains congregation was organized.

Return to Glencoe-Hillsboro Rd. Turn L. *4.5 m.*, Hillsboro (1st & O 8). Turn R onto O 8. *4.8 m.*, at W end of Masonic-Eastern Star Home, turnoff R to Porter Lane. (See *H-T No. 3.*) *1 m.*, on R, Pacific University. (See *H-T No. 3.*) *0.3 m.*, downtown Forest Grove. *1.2 m.*, on R, turnoff to Kansas City. (See *H-T No. 3.*)

6.3 m., **Gales Creek.** The first settler here was Joseph Gale, mountain man, builder and master of first ship constructed in Oregon, farmer, and one of three men elected to the executive committee of the provisional government at Champoeg in 1843. By 1850 the land along the creek named after him was getting too crowded and so, at the age of 50, he moved across the state to Eagle Valley, N of Baker. There, in the cool shadows of the Wallowa Mtns., after fathering five children by his Nez Perce wife, Eliza, Gale lived to the age of 81, trapping and farming almost to the end.

First house back of food store was a stagecoach stop and hotel in the 1870–80s. House across O 8 is of 1860 vintage, remodeled. Rural station PO, in home of Mrs. Eva Sargent, is small strip of covered porch, with flowerpots on window sills, shelves and tables. Front of house built in 1890.

2.5 m., jct., O 6. *2.9 m.*, on O 6, Glenwood. Roadside hamlet. Food, gas. *1.6 m.*, on R, turnoff to Trolley Park. *0.5 m.*, **Trolley Park**, a fun place of rail vehicles from three continents, including 1905 Blackpool (England) tram and 1912 open-sided "summer breezer" from Australia. Tots and graybeards alike enjoy trolley rides. Oregon Electric Railway Historical Society, which operates park, uses old-time car barns and repair sheds of long-defunct lumber company. Picnic tables in cool grove at clear creek. Lovely place for outing.

Return to O 6. E on O 6 *11.5 m.* to O 47. Turn R.

0.1 m., turn R toward Banks. *0.8 m.*, **Banks,** which claims it is biggest strawberry town in Oregon. Folksy place, with meadows on all sides. (A touch of rural Indiana).

Return to O 6. Turn R. Portland, *22 m.*

Historical Tour No. 2

Int. 5—from 6th St. ramp of Stadium Freeway—*11.2 m.* to Tualatin exit.

Turn L at end of exit ramp. *0.4 m.*, on R, The White Buffalo, museum of Indian artifacts.

From museum driveway, turn L, or back—toward Tualatin. *0.8 m.*, turn R. *0.1 m.*, R, old brick bldg. started life as grocery store in 1912. On L, across road and RR tracks, **Sweek House** (circa 1858). Partly remodeled but still retaining original architectural composition.

Straight, *2.2 m.* Jct., 99W. Turn L. *2.8 m.*, Eddy Rd. Turn R and bear toward Scholls. The land lies soft and wavy, one upswept meadow melting into another. There is little noise, little bustle, but the spidery fingers of suburbia are relentlessly at work.

6.2 m., **Scholls.** The road runs right up to a country grocery store, the kind that stood at every Washington County crossroad five decades ago. This

Sweek house, Tualatin

one still has an old-fashioned tang to it. Turn L. *0.2 m.*, on L, Scholls Community Church, a peaceful rural center. *0.5 m.*, on R, Trotter's Store. Built as a lodge hall around 1905. Interior looks like there haven't been many changes in the last 50 years.

Turn R. The terrain now gradually becomes choppier, the houses farther apart, the surge of suburbia is slowed, and older barns and farmhouses appear. *2.4 m.*, turn L, toward Laurel. *1.4 m.*, Laurel Valley store. Owner doesn't know when store was built but says: "I'm sure it's been a heckuva long time ago, at least 1910," and store looks it.

Beyond the store, the road is slung over the bristly Chehalem Hills, deep green and prickly tangled, with the clearings belonging to deep-rooted farmsteads that, for the moment, seem fixed in time. The wind is so still you have to lip-read what it is saying, but without a moment's notice it can break its silence and roar, a hundred tongues leaping out of hollows and gullies and racing down tree-clumped knolls to shout and wail in a dozen languages.

3.2 m., turn R, toward Laurelwood. Be extra cautious here for the road is steep as it twists roughly down a burry spur of the hills. *1.5 m.*, **Laurelwood Academy,** operated by Seventh-Day Adventists. A large secondary school, founded in 1904. Its school song tells it as it is: "Laurelwood's the greatest place/ On this old earth's battered face;/ Nestled close among the hills,/ Midst Laurel shade and rippling rills;/ Far from noisy care and strife/ Here we live a sheltered life. . . . "

1.6 m., turn R. The road flows as a swift, dark river, through bunched woods and between small farms, and finally lapping the lawns of surburban-type homes.

8.9 m., Pacific Ave. (O 8), on E side of Forest Grove. (For Forest Grove, see *H-T No. 3.*) Turn R. *1.2 m.*, 4th Ave. On NE and NW corners, two houses of 1890 vintage, in traditional Tualatin Plains style. *3.9 m.*, L to city center of Hillsboro. (For Hillsboro, see *H-T No. 3.*) Continue on O 8.

5.4 m., SW 209th. Turn R, or S. *0.5 m.*, Kinnaman Rd. Turn L. *0.1 m.*, on R, 20650 Kinnaman: **Masters House.** Built in 1853 by Andrew Jackson Masters, a native of Kentucky, who came overland to Oregon in 1843, at a cost of $6000, a princely sum for those days. Masters did not enjoy luxury and comfort very long, being shot to death by a neighbor in 1856 over an argument as to land ownership. The dwelling was once a PO and local rumor has it that U. S. Grant spent a night here. House screened from road by plum, pear and apple trees.

0.4 m., SW 198th. Turn L. *0.4 m.*, O 8. Turn R. *3.5 m.*, R turn for Beaverton. Straight. *8 m.*, Portland.

Historical Tour No. 3

From 6th Ave. exit on US 26, *2.7 m.* to turnoff for Oregon Museum of Science and Industry and Portland Zoo.

0.9 m., turn onto O 8.

3.6 m., Beaverton, Hall St. Turn L *1 block* to Farmington Rd. Turn R.

2.2 m., on R, R. R. Hardin home, 16775 Farmington Rd. In back stands old windmill and pumphouse built at turn of century. One of few of its kind left in state. *4.2 m.*, on L, pioneer house in early-day setting, with open, gently sloped fields behind the drowsy structure.

1.9 m., Farmington. Pool hall and tavern in shabby bldg. Barn across road is more photogenic. *2.1 m.*, jct., O 219. Turn L. *0.1 m.*, turn R onto Bald Peak Rd. At "Y" take R fork.

The road lifts in spasms of swells through throbs of wildflowers and freshets of greenery, with the world unfolding below it a last promise of pure delight. But affluent homes are rising, and one wonders about the vistas of the future.

5.5 m., **Bald Peak SP.** Cool grassy picnic ground under Douglas firs. View W: a vast bowl of shimmering green, billowed and plumed by groves of trees which enclose the meadows, each of the leas of a different size and shape, and the bowl tilted toward the serrated rims of the Coast Range. On a clear day, facing E, Mt. Adams, Mt. St. Helens and Mt. Hood seem to float above the far horizons of the Tualatin Valley.

Return to O 219. Turn L toward Hillsboro. *5.6 m.*, O 8 & S 1st St.

* Inside Hillsboro, **Pioneer Museum**, 641 E Main, contains many precious items, including miniature replica of early farm, whittled by descendant of founder, and high desk used by John McLoughlin.

Turn W onto O 8 at S 1st. *6.1 m.*, turn R onto Verboort Rd. *2.4 m.*, **Verboort.** Tiny community, on fecund plain, is scene of annual Sausage Festival, held first Sat. in Nov. Visitation Catholic Church, flanked by 140-ft. sequoias, is heart of settlement.

Return to Verboort Rd. *0.1 m.*, turn L onto Porter Rd. *0.8 m.*, on R, two rows of about 35 giant redwoods comprise handsomest private lane in Oregon. Trees were planted by John Porter, who came here with his parents in 1847. Porter purchased the land in 1854; his grandson, Edward, lives on S side of the redwood lane. Around 1870, says Edward Porter, his grandfather planted the seedling trees he raised in his nursery, from sequoia cones he had brought back from Calif.

1.4 m., O 8. (Old-fashioned bldgs. of Masonic and Eastern Star Home on L.) Turn R.

1 m., **Pacific University.** On campus stands oldest bldg. W of Rockies used continuously for educational purposes. It was built in 1850 of hand-hewn and rough-sawn Douglas fir from nearby forests to house Tualatin Academy, forerunner of PU. Contains chapel and museum.

0.3 m., downtown Forest Grove, rapidly parting with its hinterland charm for the prizes of "progress."

1.2 m., turn R onto Kansas City Rd. *4.8 m.*, **Kansas City.** All that remains of a settlement that was never really a town is creaky community hall. *0.2 m.*, turn R, toward Banks. *1.5 m.*, on R, old schoolhouse now used as barn. *0.2 m.*, turn L. (Note aged, remodeled house on NE corner plot; mixture of old and new.) *1.1 m.*, Jct., O 6. Turn R. Portland, 25 m.

Porter redwoods   Kansas City

Historical Tour No. 4

Int. 5 to jct., 99W, 7.5 m. 1.5 m., on 99W, Tigard.

14 m., **Newberg.** Here is located **Herbert Hoover Home**, also known as Minthorn house, at S River & E 2d. As a boy, Hoover lived here, in the mid-1880s, with his uncle Dr. H. J. Minthorn. A small room upstairs holds young Hoover's bed, dresser, chamber pot and washboard. Little of the furniture in the house was there when the Minthorns occupied it, but it is today representative of Willamette Valley home furnishings of the late 19th century. Less than 1 m. from Hoover Home is George Fox College, founded in 1885 by the Society of Friends as Pacific Academy. Hoover was member of first class. **Friends Church** (1892) at S College & E 3d, is impressive structure, with brick belfry tower. Almost all of Newberg's Quakers are staunchly conservative—not of the same persuasion as the American Friends Service Committee.

Turn R at O 240.

4.4 m., on R, **Ewing Young Marker.** Young, one of the great mountain men of the SW, came to Oregon in 1834. By 1835 he had crops growing on the rich soil of the Chehalem Valley, much of which he came to own. The marker is located almost in the center of his donation land claim. In 1837, Young led the first long cattle drive in the nation, from San Francisco Bay to the Willamette settlements. He died in early 1841, leaving no will and no known heirs. A meeting, held to appoint officers to administer his estate, also resolved to establish some sort of provisional self-government—the first concrete step toward political organization in Oregon. Five years after Young's death, an oak was planted in the soil of his grave. Today, the **Young Oak,** as it is known, is a mighty tree.

No road leads to the Young Oak from O 240. It can be seen, though, about 0.3 m. to the N, the L of two thick, round-topped oaks, with barns in the background.

　　* There is a way direct to the Young oak, providing you obtain permission to drive through a pasture. Continue W from marker 0.6 m. to sign pointing to "E. Young School." Turn R. 0.8 m., turn R. 0.5 m., on R, mailbox lettered "R. 1 Box 256." Owner lives in house back of box. The sheep along the meadow truck trail and the pungent barns behind the oaks are as delightful and charming as the Young Oak is historic.

Return E on O 240 to 99W. Turn R. 2.3 m., Dundee, a quiet, filbert town.

3.8 m., jct., O 18 bypass—to Coast. (See *Cross-Coast Range Roads.*)

1.9 m., on L, turnoff to Yamhill Locks County Park. 1 m., **Yamhill Locks Park.** As early as 1851 a steamer plied the Yamhill River. In the 1880–90s, steamboats made scheduled trips to Dayton, on the Willamette, a few m. below this site. Boats left Portland early in the morning, served free lunch to passengers, and arrived at Dayton about 4 p.m. Next morning they departed for Portland. Boat locks were built in 1900 in response to farmers who wanted competitive transportation rates. Ironically, for 25 years after locks were built, they were seldom used, other cheap transportation being available. Then locks were used by strong towboats to pull log rafts to Willamette sawmills. In 1959 Yamhill County paid the U.S. Govt. $1 for title to the locks and to the Yamhill River Dam, built in 1898. The dam was breached by the Oregon Fish and Game Commission to facilitate passage of anadromous (ascending from the sea) fish in the Yamhill and its tributaries. Grassy, shaded riverside park never seems to be crowded. Overnight camping. Park contains about a dozen old growth Douglas firs, among the last of those which a century ago were numerous in the valley.

Ewing Young Oak

Yamhill Locks   Marker in Yamhill-Carlton Pioneer Cemetery

Return to 99W. Turn L.

0.5 m., **Lafayette.** School on NW side of 3d & Monroe is typical of early auto-day schools being retired. House on SW side is typical of Yamhill County dwellings built in the 1860s. Across road, on E side, is a home equally old—and beautifully kept up. It was assertedly once the home of the remarkable Abigail Scott Duniway, distinguished suffragette and author. One of the most distinctive 19th-century houses in Willamette Valley. Adjacent walnut grove gives house a genteel, rustic atmosphere.

At Market St., turn R 3 *blocks* to 6th St.—**Yamhill County Museum.** Bldg. erected circa 1885 as "mission station"; was the United Brethren Church; still later, named Poling Memorial Church. Furniture includes 1849 pulpit chair from Methodist church at Yamhill and Joel Palmer bed from Dayton.

  * Turn W on Bridge St. 3 *m.*, **Trappist Abbey of Our Lady of Guadalupe.** Only one in Oregon; only 12 in country. Abbey, on low hill, overlooks productive farm and calm Yamhill Valley.

0.7 m.—S on 99W from Bridge St.—turnoff W on private road. *0.2 m.*, handsome house (1892). When it was built, the owner insisted that the carpenters drill ahead of every nail.

1.7 m., jct., O 47. Turn R.

The beauty of O 47 is chiefly in the imagery the land and its distant vistas will evoke in the poetic. To the E ruffle the whorled fields and family farm orchards that remind a man from Abraham Lincoln's country of the Illinois prairie. Westward, beyond pastoral scenes of sheer joy, the hirsute hills curl from the far edge of the saucered plain and arch misty green and haze blue into the foam-waves of the Coast Range. On a summer day the sun drips golden shadows on the feathered slopes and in evening the moon is a brassy gong hung on an invisible peak or a jack-o-lantern rolled into a saddle of the cordillera. Then shards of the wind, splintered by the foothill woods, come lancing into the meadows, gathering capes of dust around them, until they stub their jagged edges in a marshy ravine and fall flat, the last ripple of breeze bending the grass under a drowsy-eyed cow. From the jct. to Forest Grove at least a dozen roads venture W toward the foothills. None of them possesses staggering scenery, but all are tonic for sore nerves.

4.5 m.—from jct.—Carlton, a sleepy settlement with early 20th-century brick bldgs. and a municipal swimming pool right off the road.

Jct., Meadow Lake Rd.—to Coast. (See *Cross-Coast Range Roads.*)

2 m., turn R for **Yamhill-Carlton Pioneer Memorial Cemetery.** (*0.4 m.*, on L, cemetery.) From cemetery ridge, extraordinary view of Coast Range, which sweeps as a tidal wave across the W sky. Cemetery holds graves of men and women, and large number of children, dating back to 1860s.

Return to O 47. Turn R. *0.2 m.*, on R, **Zimmerman Century Farm.** (*0.1 m.* up gravel path, barn built in 1868, by the kind of craftsmen no longer around.) Owner George Zimmerman says: "The barn was built without a

Century-old handwork in Zimmerman Century Farm barn

single nail. Timbers are morticed in and dowel pins put in to hold the timbers together." Floor was used a century ago for threshing wheat by horses, he adds. Barn is still in use—to feed lambs in winter.

Return to O 47. Turn R. *1.3 m.*, Yamhill. About one block of businesses, with houses across the road from the stores. *3.2 m.*, Cove Orchard. Grocery-gas. Old school about 100 yds. back of store is now used as Grange hall. *5 m.*, Gaston. Just a break in the road. Beyond the onion fields the foothills seem to be breakers holding back the push of seaweed waves, and high in the E rises Bald Peak.

6 m., O 8. Forest Grove. (See *H-T No. 3.*)

22 m., Portland.

Historical Tour No. 5

Tigard, via Int. 5 and 99W—9 *m.*

See *H-T No. 4* for 99W to jct., O 47.

2.9 m. from jct., O 47—**McMinnville.** Home of Linfield College, established in 1857 as McMinnville College. McMinnville seems to have a plenitude of preautomobile-era houses. Just stroll or motor around town. Many of the houses have been greatly altered (and often not to the good); best example is 1883 structure at NE corner of W Ford & E 8th. House built with lumber from community's first school, when it was torn down. At one time house was city hospital, later remodeled into a duplex; currently used by a church which made additional changes.

Follow 3d (main street) E. Cross overpass onto Dayton-Salem Rd. *1.5 m.* from Ford St., Martin Lane. Turn R onto gravel. *0.2 m.*, on R, **Altimus House** (circa 1870). Muriel Altimus has lived in house since birth in 1897.

Return to paved rd., O 18. Turn R. *5 m.*, turn R onto O 221.

0.5 m., **Dayton.** One of Oregon's most historical small towns. It was the center of some famous donation land claims and a favorite "retirement home" for grizzled pioneers. Brookside Cemetery holds remains of several settlers who voted for American government at Champoeg. Everywhere one turns, the past is present; town is full of elderly houses.

City Park is site of two-story blockhouse, built in 1856 at Ft. Yamhill (see *Cross-Coast Range Roads*, O 22), and in 1911 moved by six wagons from Grande Ronde Indian Reservation. Across street—**First Baptist Church** (1886), wood-frame spire on red brick. **Pioneer Evangelical Brethren Church,** Church & 4th, built in 1850s as Dayton Methodist Church, has logs under its clapboards. **Joel Palmer House,** E side of 6th & Ferry, built in 1852. Much modernized, in very good taste. House directly S, on same side, is said by local antiquarians to be even older than Palmer House.

Backtrack on Ferry St. to NE edge of city park. Turn R onto O 221.

6.7 m., Grand Island Jct. Turn L. *0.5 m.*, **Grand Island,** in the Willamette River. Island is about 4 m. wide and 7 m. long; has about 40 families. A near-level, richly fertile land (a touch of Iowa), with fine houses and barns.

Ft. Yamhill, Dayton

Chief crops: beans, berries, hay, sweet corn, cherries. No stores, stations, schools. "It's a perfect place to live except when the river gets high, then it covers the ground," says a native. But floods are infrequent, and when they do occur, the river deposits a lot of silt, which adds to the island's fertility. "So," sums up the native, "it adds up to about even." Paved roads web the restful isle.

At Grand Island Jct., there is another charming side trip—this one in a different mood. Turn R on Amity Rd. *1.9 m.*, Webfoot Rd. Turn R. *1.2 m.*, on L, shrouded in a tangle of second growth woods, **Ebenezer Chapel**, 19th-century church long abandoned. Behind the one-room stone shell, all its windows broken, is an uncared-for cemetery, the grave markers dating nearly a century ago. The moss-encrusted tombstones, screened by the thick undergrowth and low branches, and the eerie silence of the darkling bog have a mystique which extends beyond the need for historical data.

Return to O 221. Turn R.

2.4 m., cool grove of Williamson SP and jct. to Wheatland Ferry.

Straight, *5.5 m.*, Lincoln, once an out-country shipping center; now down to a store.

Turn R onto Bethel Rd. *0.1 m.*, on L, **Brush College Grange Hall**, where for many years Brush College, a typical rural grade school, held classes. The pioneers could be as euphemistic as are the moderns.

Grand Island   Wheatland Ferry

1.9 m., to highway "Y"; follow L fork. *0.5 m.*, on L, **Spring Valley Presbyterian Church**, atop a rise shared by a small, shaded cemetery. Bell arrived 'round the Horn from England in 1859, same year church was erected.

From W end of church, view SW includes a white house unusual in appearance because of bell tower. Explanation: bldg., now a home, was once a school. Everything remodeled but tower.

Return to O 221. Retrace route to Wheatland Ferry Jct.

Turn R. *1 m.*, **Wheatland Ferry** across Willamette.

Approximately *0.5 m.* S, on E bank (private rd.), the Jason Lee Mission was established in 1834. Log mission school was first educational facility in Oregon. Great flood of 1861 wiped out all traces of "Mission Bottom," long after Lee had moved school to Chemeketa, now Salem.

0.5 m. from ferry landing, turn R, or S, onto Wheatland Ferry Rd. This pike is dotted with pioneer houses. Driving it is a journey through a corridor of mid-19th-century Oregon. Only a few places are listed here: *0.9 m.*, on R, 1860s house. *0.1 m.*, on R, barn built without nails, of 1850s vintage. *0.1 m.*, on R, house that may have been put up as early as 1840s. *0.2 m.*, on L, charming house much in dispute. Owner and friends insist it was built between 1837–39 by Elijah White, early co-worker and later sharp critic of Jason Lee, as Old Mission Hospital. If true, bldg. would be oldest in Oregon. Others insist it was not constructed until 1865.

2 m., jct. Turn E toward Brooks. *1 m.*, O 219. (N, *16 m.* to Champoeg SP. See *H-T No. 6.*)

Straight, *0.7 m.*, Int. 5. Portland, *37 m.*

Historical Tour No. 6

9 m.—via Int. 5 and 99W—Tigard.

Jct., O 217.

Turn L. *2 m.*, road "T." L, *0.3 m.*, **Durham School.** Oldest of two structures was put up in 1920. Has the homey touch of a Ford flivver.

Return *0.3 m.* to "T." Straight *1.5 m.* to jct., 99W. Turn L. *10.7 m.*, jct., O 219. Turn L.

3 m., on L, historical marker, **"Willamette Post."** On the closest knoll to the E stood the first trading post in the Willamette Valley. It was opened around 1811 by the Astor Company, which established Ft. Astoria, at the mouth of the Columbia. Later, British interests took over. The fact that this trading post existed was responsible in some measure for the early settlement of French Prairie. In 1861 the nearby Willamette River flooded heavily and carried away every vestige of the post.

0.3 m., jct., Champoeg.

* L *2.4 m.*—to Champoeg SP—through the chlorophyl-rich **French Prairie,** once a primitive sea of grass, and still luxuriantly carpeted with rich tints of flowers. The undulating land was named after French-Canadian fur trappers who settled here after retiring from Hudson's Bay Co.

3.9 m.—on O 219—on L, sign stating that buried here are Philippe Decre and Francois Rivet of the "Lewis and Clark 1805 Expedition." The data is technically correct, historically incorrect. Decre and Rivet may have been with Lewis and Clark at Ft. Mandan, in North Dakota, during the first three months of 1805, but they were not members of the expedition which reached Oregon.

A plaque on a stout, moss-beaded boulder a few inches away notes the names of others buried here. No cemetery is evident, though some small, very old wooden headstones, laid almost shoulder to shoulder, are hidden back of the rock. The names on the plaque include such pioneers as Joseph Gervais, Etienne Lucier, Louis La Bonte and Michel La Framboise.

A few yards ahead is a "country-style," red brick bldg. that was the St. Paul creamery and is now a community hall.

0.1 m., on R, **St. Paul Catholic Church,** oldest parish in the state. One of the fairest church scenes in all Oregon. It stands facing the small town, and behind it the meadows run free. Church built in 1846, of red brick made in ovens on the grounds, to replace log structure put up in 1836. Replica of log church to immediate R.

Though St. Paul has less than 300 population it is state-known for its three-day July 4th Rodeo.

Follow O 219 *0.3 m.* to St. Paul Cemetery. Many French Prairie settlers buried here.

1.7 m., turn L onto county road.

3.4 m., **Robert Newell House.** House was built in 1852 and restored in 1959 with mid-19th-century furnishings. Also on grounds: pioneer schoolhouse; old Butteville jail; replica of George Gay Home, first brick house W of Rockies. Built near Wheatland in 1841, house stood a century before it crumbled away.

Replica of George Gay home

    0.1 m., to S, **Champoeg SP.** Here is ground steeped in history. An Indian village, *Cham-poo-ick*, had long been flourishing by the time the first white men saw it in 1811. Hudson's Bay Co. had a post here for years, with their first warehouse S of Oregon City; and village was the shipping point of Willamette Valley wheat.

    These meadows, on the S bank of the Willamette, are most famous in Oregon annals, however, for the event of May 2, 1843. On that day the settlers of Willamette Valley posed the question of provisional government. The French-Canadians were bitterly opposed, owing their allegiance to their benefactor, Hudson's Bay Co. According to perhaps romantic legend, Joe Meek shouted, "Who's for a divide?" He traced a line with his boot toe and those who favored organization of a "civil community" followed him. Supposedly, he and his cohorts numbered 50. Also supposedly, 50 men betook themselves to the other side. Still supposedly, after a brief, troubled discussion between them, Etienne Lucier, the first white settler on French Prairie, and Francis Xavier Matthieu, who lived with him, placed themselves on the "American side" and the count was 52 to 50 for provisional government. Actually, the exact figure is not definitely known—some French-Canadians, according to some historians, angrily boycotted the "election"—and there has never been a really authentic account of what did take place that day.

    The last political meeting at Champoeg took place July 5, 1843. A written constitution was approved, and officers elected on May 2 were sworn in. Hudson's Bay Co. withdrew in 1852, but the settlement continued as a river landing, grain market and mercantile center. But doom struck in December 1861 when the Willamette, swollen by heavy rains, all but washed away the village. It was never rebuilt.

The park contains two historical museums, gleaming swales, and a fine CG.

Return to Robert Newell House jct. Turn L.

0.5 m., on R, 1875-built house, known locally as **Champoeg Farm;** rambling structure with unusual blockhouse-shaped "sentry tower" holding bell. On L, wooden warehouse, memento of riverboat days.

0.5 m., "Y."

  * R fork. *0.7 m.*, on R, Champoeg Cemetery. Narrow gravel lane leads to pastoral burying ground. Some of the graves occupied by German-born emigrants, who came to the new world in mid-19th century, seeking freedom. Their children and grandchildren lie near them.

2.4 m., jct. L, Butteville, much less of a town than 100 years ago. Hasn't had a PO since 1905. Store-gas.

  * Straight at jct. *0.6 m.*, turn L for **Butteville Cemetery.** *0.5 m.*, on gravel, cemetery. F. X. Matthieu, of Champoeg fame, and the sage of Butteville, lies here.

From Butteville, *4 m.*, Int. 5. *18 m.*, Portland.

Historical Tour No. 7

From SW 4th & Morrison, *4.2 m.*, on Macadam Rd., turn L onto Sellwood Bridge.

0.4 m., turn L onto 6th Ave. *1 block*, L onto Spokane St. *1 block*, **Oaks Pioneer Museum,** formerly St. Johns Episcopal Church of Milwaukie. Built in 1851 and moved to this site from Milwaukie in 1961. Plaque reads: "Oldest Oregon church in continuous use," a statement that can be interpreted several ways.

Just N of church is replica of first white residents' dwelling in present Portland—log cabin put up in 1842 by William Johnson. Original site was near SW Macadam & Ross Island Bridge.

Return to Macadam Ave. Turn L.

3.5 m., **Lake Oswego.** With its gorgeous lake, lakeside homes and decorative houses spilled upon the hills bowling the sparkling water, Lake Oswego is the inland Capri of Oregon. Follow any road that leads above and around the lake.

1.8 m. (on O 43), turnoff L to **Marylhurst College.** The placid greenswards lead to Shoens Library, an architectural gem.

Return to road. Turn L. *2.4 m.*, turn R up W "A" St. *0.7 m.*, on R (just beyond West Linn H.S.), **Camassia Natural Area.** A small wilderness set aside for public use by the Oregon Chapter of The Nature Conservancy. Walk *70 yds.* up asphalt; take footpath at wire fence of athletic field.

0.1 m., on W "A," O 212 (Sunset).

Turn L. *0.1 m.*, turnoff R for **West Linn Inn.** One of the oldest and best-known of Willamette Valley hostelries. Paved walk just E of Inn leads *0.3 m.* to **Willamette Falls Locks,** opened in 1873 and still much used.

Return to O 212. Turn L.

Replica of Johnson cabin

In its first few miles, this road provides some of the sharpest, broadest overlooks of the lower Willamette River.

2.7 m., 12th St. Turn L. *0.4 m.,* **Willamette Park.** Though close to metropolitan population, the park seems secluded, as though hidden by a bend in the river. Boating, swimming, fishing.

Return to O 212. Turn L. Old settlement of Willamette, now part of West Linn. The Willamette Meteorite, most massive meteorite ever discovered on the American continent N of the Mexican border and the world's sixth largest, was found near here in 1902. The 15½-ton iron is now on display in the Hayden Planetarium, American Museum of Natural History, New York City.

2.5 m., Tualatin Jct. Continue straight. *0.8 m.,* Lake Oswego Jct. Turn L. *0.7 m.,* turn L at Mountain Rd.-Canby Ferry sign. *0.5 m.,* at "Y," take R fork.

The road now opens to views of land that rolls in hayfields, barns, farmhouses, groves that lean with the wind, pools of sunshine and troughs of slatted shadows. And one says for the thousandth time on trips such as these: And so close to the crowded city! That's the beauty of Portland—to go from it in spirit and tone in so short a time.

2.7 m., Wilsonville Jct. (R to Wilsonville, 6 m.)

1.3 m., **Canby Ferry.** On a weekday, yours might be the only car on a crossing. The river whispers, as though not to disturb itself, and it seems to shudder when an impatient motorist, seeing the ferry empty at the far bank, honks loud and long.

1.9 m., Territorial Rd. Turn L. Back of first house in Ellis Gardens, floral showplace.

1.6 m., US 99E. Turn L. *6.8 m.,* **Oregon City.**

Oregon City has more historic firsts to its credit than any other community in the state, including being the first incorporated city W of the Missouri. Here were started the first Protestant church, Masonic Lodge and newspaper W of the Missouri. Oregon City saw the first use of water power in the state, was the first settlement in Oregon to hear a brass band, had the first mint in the state, was Oregon's first capital. One could go on in this vein for a page.

Built on three distinct terraces, or benches, on the sheer bluff along the E bank of the Willamette, Oregon City was initially called Willamette Falls, the settlement being located where the wide, strong-flowing Willamette drops 42 ft. from a basaltic ledge.

In 1829 a mill site was chosen at the boiling falls by Dr. John McLoughlin, the fabled "Whiteheaded Eagle" of Ft. Vancouver. Here McLoughlin located a 2-sq.-m. land claim, upon which a hamlet was born, starting with retired trappers and voyageurs of Hudson's Bay Co. In 1842, McLoughlin, who was responsible for platting the city, gave it its name. During these years he was Chief Factor of HBC's far-flung Western operations. But his relations with

Willamette Falls Locks

the British-owned firm grew increasingly difficult, and in 1845 he resigned and moved to Oregon City where he completed construction of a two-story colonial frame house on Upper Main St. Here he became an American citizen and in this house he lived until his death in 1857, passing away six weeks before his 73d birthday. Thereafter, the house was occupied for some time by members of his family; later, was used as a hotel. In 1909 the house was moved to a park which McLoughlin had presented to the city 59 years earlier.

Municipal Elevator, downtown, built to lift local pedestrians 90 ft. from business to lower residential level, has become tourist attraction. Each rider on the free elevator receives a "Life Time Pass." Before the first elevator was opened, in 1915, citizens had to climb flights of wooden stairs to the bluff, the first flight being constructed in 1874. Until then, there were only slippery paths.

At Main & 10th, uphill *0.2 m.* to the **McLoughlin House**, now a national historic site. McLoughlin and his wife buried on grounds, having been removed from wall at NE corner of 5th & Washington in summer of 1970. Due N of house is **Barclay House**, built in 1846 by Dr. Forbes Barclay, surgeon at Ft. Vancouver and intimate of McLoughlin. In 1937, Barclay House was moved from site of present Masonic Temple to McLoughlin Park.

Continue E on 7th St., where McLoughlin House stands. *1 block* to Washington St. Turn L. At 916 Washington is 1885 house whose Victorian style, gingerbread carvings, cupola and bay windows make it a classic period house of its era.

Return to 7th St. Turn L. *0.6 m.*, 7th angles R to become O 213-Molalla Ave. *0.7 m.*, on Hilda St., turn L. *0.3 m.*, **Mountain View Cemetery.**

Historically, one of the, if not *the*, most important of Oregon cemeteries. Scenically, one of the fairest, with enormous vistas beyond the well-tended grounds. Some famous names are found here, including Forbes Barclay and William Barlow. Best known is Peter Skene Ogden (see front cover for illustration), peerless trailblazer, Chief Factor of the Hudson's Bay Co. operations at Ft. Vancouver, and a giant figure in NW history.

Return to O 213-Molalla Ave. Turn L. *0.6 m.*, Beavercreek Rd. Turn L. *4.5 m.*, Beavercreek store. Straight, *0.1 m.*, on L, **Bryn Seion Welsh Congregational Church** (1884). On last Sun. each June, church holds *Gymanfa Ganu Blynddol*, Annual Song Festival, with music in Welsh and English. Singing starts after lunch at nearby Grange hall.

Return *0.1 m.* to Beavercreek Rd. Turn R. *0.6 m.*, on L, **Holly Knoll Museum**, an "old-fashioned village" patterned after the Salem Township, Neb., Mrs. Fern Fredrickson knew in her girlhood.

Return to O 213-Molalla Rd.

Turn R. *0.1 m.*, Warner Milne Rd. Turn L. *0.7 m.*, Linn Ave. Turn L. *0.5 m.*, turnoff R to **Ainsworth House** (1851). The white Mt. Vernonish, four-pillared, balconied house was a showplace in its day and is one of best preserved and best looking pioneer homes in Oregon.

Ainsworth house, Oregon City   Gravestone in Canemah Cemetery, Oregon City

Return to Warner Milne Rd. Straight, *1 block t*o Warner Parrot Rd. Turn L. *0.3 m.*, just beyond Canemah Ave., turn L onto dirt lane. *100 yds.*, the restored **McCarver House** (1850), sometimes called Locust Farm, because of adjacent locust grove. Legend has it house was prefabricated in Maine and was first prefab house on West Coast.

Return to Warner Parrot Rd. Turn L. *0.6 m.*, South End Rd. Turn R. *0.8 m.*, turn sharp L onto 5th Ave., which becomes Miller. *0.3 m.*, turn L on 4th St. to street marked Canemah Cemetery. *0.2 m.*, turn L onto Blanchard. *0.5 m.*, over bumpy gravel trace, **Canemah Cemetery,** on bluff curtained from river overlook by thick foliage. Markers date from 1850s.

Backtrack to Miller & 4th. Continue straight on 4th. *0.2 m.*, Miller St. Turn R. *0.1 m.*, 99E. Turn R. *2.2 m.*, Oregon City, at 9th & 99E. *5.4 m.*, turn R on Washington St. in Milwaukie. *0.4 m.*, on R (2746 Washington), **Hager Pond.**

Paul Hager and family live in 1875-built frame house in which Hager was born. He inherited from his father the pond, an ancient mill bldg., an old water wheel, a 19th-century pumphouse, a mellowed barn and the terraced land flanking the pond. On this acre and a half, the Hagers have developed for their own joy a lovely rustic cameo. The pond, fed by spring water, is populated by hundreds of rainbow trout. Ducks coast on the unruffled waters or lounge on the small rock islands. Chickens cakewalk around the barn as though they own the place. The pump house is a pigeon roost. The Hagers, who do not fish or kill their fowl, delight in their pets, which have included milk goats, rams, rabbits and raccoons. Best time to visit is weekend afternoons.

2 blocks N to Harrison. L to 21st St. **Milwaukie City Library.** Duck pond in rear is restful place, with a sort of rural Japanese touch to it.

From library, *1 block* W to Main St. Turn R. *0.5 m.*, Millport Rd. Turn L. *50 yds.*, 99E. Straight, *0.2 m.* to River Rd. and **Pioneer Cemetery.** An old burial ground stretching toward the river. The graves of many well-known local personages, (and a few of state importance) are here, close by the Waverly Golf Course.

Return to US 99E. Turn L. *4.7 m.*, Morrison St. bridge, Portland. L for downtown.

Historical Tour No. 8

13 m., on 99E, Oregon City, at 5th & Main. (For Oregon City, see *H-T No. 7*.)

0.4 m., **Willamette River Viewpoint.** Best local view of stream, falls, boat locks and industrial complex. Here, too, is historical marker giving brief history of Oregon City.

8.2 m., Canby, a hustling valley town.

* For Canby Ferry, turn R on Ivy. *1 block*, turn L onto 1st. *1 block*, Holly. Turn R. *0.3 m.*, at "Y," take R fork, Ferry Rd. *2.4 m.*, ferry, for Willamette River crossing to Wilsonville and Lake Oswego.

Church bldg., 3rd & Elm, was constructed by Methodist congregation in the 1870s, according to local historians, and has been home of various denominations here. Would make an excellent museum.

Marker at Willamette River Viewpoint, Oregon City

OREGON HISTORY

OREGON CITY - SUPPLY POINT FOR PIONEER EMIGRANTS WAS FIRST LOCATED AS A CLAIM BY DR. JOHN McLOUGHLIN IN 1829. THE FIRST PROVISIONAL LEGISLATURE OF THE OREGON COUNTRY WAS HELD HERE IN 1843 AND LAND AND TAX LAWS FORMULATED. OREGON CITY WAS THE CAPITAL OF THE OREGON TERRITORY FROM 1845-1852. THE FIRST PROTESTANT CHURCH (METHODIST) WEST OF THE ROCKY MOUNTAINS WAS DEDICATED IN 1844 AND THE FIRST NEWS PAPER (OREGON SPECTATOR) AND THE FIRST MASONIC LODGE WERE ESTABLISHED IN 1846.

Chestnut Apts., 525 SW 4th, built in 1890 as Knight homestead house, has dumbwaiter from hall into basement, to bring up firewood and put fruit down. Myrtlewood tree growing by porch only one in Canby area.

1.4 m., on L, **Barlow House.** There is debate as to whether it was built in 1854 or later; certainly, it is more than 100 years old. The two rows of black walnut trees are the growth of seeds brought 'round the Horn and planted circa 1860 by William Barlow, son of Samuel K. Barlow, chief builder of Barlow Toll Road, first wagon trail across the Cascades.

0.1 m., turn R toward Barlow. *0.4 m.*, **Barlow Pioneer Cemetery.** A patch of untended high grass and wild, thorny bushes which hold the remains of some of Barlow's early white settlers. One of smallest community burial grounds in state. There is so little to Barlow now, scarcely anyone gets buried here anymore.

Return to 99E. Turn R. *1.9 m.*, **Aurora.** Turn R at road marked Freeway-Donald. *0.2 m.*, Main St. Turn R. *0.2 m.*, turn R. *0.1 m.*, on L, **Keil House.**

Dr. William Keil was leader of Aurora Colony, a communal undertaking of old-country Germans and "Pennsylvania Dutch" founded here in March 1857. Keil named town Aurora Mills, after his daughter; name changed to Aurora in 1894. Shortly after colony was established, Keil built large, three-story home with two-deck porch across E front. One of the most impressive-looking mid-19th-century houses in NW.

Return to Donald-Freeway Rd. Turn R. *0.6 m.*, on Cemetery Rd. Turn L onto gravel for **Aurora Community Cemetery** (*0.3 m.*), where Keil and other Colony pioneers sleep.

Return to Main St. at 99E.

In and around Aurora are other Colony houses of the late 1850s and 1860s. For example: on 3d, between Main & Liberty (these houses are painted white) and the yellow house N of grocery store on Main. **Ox Barn** (1862) has been restored as a museum. Behind it is **Steinbach Pioneer Cabin,** relocated and somewhat remodeled. Shed near cabin holds steam-engine thresher

Barlow Pioneer Cemetery   Steinbach Cabin, Aurora

and wagons. To L of Ox Barn is **Kraus Family House,** donated by descendants of a pioneer colony family. Aurora has more antique shops than any town its size in Oregon. All these seem to be in "antique" bldgs., including what was a general store about 60 years ago.

4.4 *m.,* Hubbard. Turn R on G St. *2 blocks* to 2d. Turn L. *1 block* to H St. **Hubbard Community Church.** This elderly house of worship, with its tall, stern steeple and venerable belfry tower, is reminiscent of so many churches that dotted the valley at the turn of century. Most have been torn down.

Return to G St. at 99E. Turn R.

2.3 *m.,* jct., O 211. Turn L, or E, onto O 211. 3.7 *m.,* Meridian Rd. Turn R. 0.6 *m.,* **Elliott Prairie Church** (1893), a pretty picture on the serene grasslands.

Return to O 211. Turn R. *1.3 m.,* Barlow Rd. Turn L. *1.1 m.,* turn R onto Sconce Rd. *0.4 m.,* **Rock Creek Church** and cemetery. The simple, unadorned church was built in 1858 by people too busy for frills. Pews said to be the originals. Church now used solely for funeral services, about the only occasion some old-timers see each other.

Continue *1.6 m.* to end of road. Turn R toward Marquam-Molalla. *0.1 m.,* on R, **Smyrna Church,** established in 1891 as Congregational; now United Church of Christ. For several decades it was the center of rural life in this area.

Continue straight on Marquam-Molalla Rd. *0.4 m.,* turn R. *2.4 m.,* Monitor Rd. Turn L onto Clackamas Rd. No. 9. *4 m.,* Monitor, a tiny farm service hamlet typical of the hinterland.

Turn L toward Mt. Angel. *2.2 m.,* turn R toward Mt. Angel on County Rd. No. 640. *2.6 m.,* **Mt. Angel Cemetery.** *1 block,* turn L onto Main St., **Mt. Angel.**

Four days each year, in late Sept., Mt. Angel stages a "Bavarian" folk extravaganza, *"Oktoberfest."* Town is jammed with visitors. Businesses have taken on year-round German names and designations. For instance: sign on

One of many businesses in Mt. Angel displaying German signs
Harvey Mikkelson and steam engines

bldg. housing law office reads *"Advokat"*; Shell Oil station has pole-sign, *"Tankstelle"*; and tavern between attorney and gas pumps is known as *"Tiny's Gemutliche Bierstube."*

Turn L at Charles St. *0.1 m.,* turn L onto Church St. *0.7 m.,* turn R to Mt. Angel Abbey. *0.6 m.,* **Mt. Angel Abbey,** a Benedictine community established here in 1884. One of the finest views of Willamette Valley is from parking lot. Below the butte, which the Indians had called *Tap-a-Lam-a-Ho,* indicating a mountain used by them for communion with the Great Spirit, the valley is a gorgeous tapestry stretched to the Cascade foothills. Still—everytime one comes here, the valley seems more settled—more houses, even apartment houses now, and fewer trees.

Return to Mt. Angel at Charles & Main. Turn L. Straight on Main, toward Mt. Angel College. *0.5 m.,* **Mt. Angel College,** a former Catholic institution where the winds of humanitarian unorthodoxy are blowing.

3.6 m., at "T," turn L toward Silverton.

0.3 m., on L, gravel lane into **Mikkelson Farm.** Harvey Mikkelson has largest collection of steam engine threshers in NW and perhaps W of the Rockies.

1.5 m., **Silverton.** Despite the influx of many families, particularly Californians, into area, Silverton's business district retains a distinctive look of the late 1920s and early 1930s.

  * Silverton is sited in a topographically striking area, especially S toward Sublimity, *12 m.* on county road that dances over and between the Waldo Hills. The famed cartoonist, Homer Davenport, who was born in a pioneer house 5 m. S of Silverton, said, "From this old porch I see my favorite view of all the earth affords."

Continue through town on O 214. The road beyond Silverton rolls over airy billows of green. The summer heat diminishes as the road mounts and breezes filter in from the woods.

13.7 m., parking lot, North Falls of **Silver Falls SP.** Trail to overhang of falls. *0.5 m.,* turnout, for spectacular long-range view of North Falls. *1.5 m.,* turnoff to Silver Falls SP picnic area. *0.4 m.,* parking for South Falls.

Silver Falls SP supposedly has largest concentration of waterfalls in U.S.-14, five of them more than 100 ft. high, the highest, 178 ft.; 10 waterfalls within a 3-m. radius. With its many firs, hemlocks, cedars, and maples, and acres and acres of grass, and fine facilities, this scenic park is a true Oregon treasure.

0.3 m., through park, to O 214. Turn R toward Stayton-Salem.

This wavy countryside, with its hundred pastel nuances, is so pleasurable to behold that it becomes part of a fascinating trip, not just a link between interesting places.

9.9 m., turn L toward Stayton-Mill City.

2.6 m., **Sublimity,** said to have been so named by its founder "for the sublime scenery in the hills around town." Before Oregon achieved statehood, Sublimity College was established by the United Brethren in Christ, and

North Falls, Silver Falls State Park

Milton Wright, father of the airplane Wright brothers, was an early teacher. The college, which was really a high school, folded in the 1870s, but Sublimity survived the shock and managed to stay on the map.

2 m., **Stayton,** a cannery town rapidly becoming diversified. House at E Burnett & N 3d, circa 1900, is a sterling example of quasi-Victorian architecture, with the builder throwing in every idea that came to mind and apparently some that didn't. With its gingerbread and its witch's-hat cupola, it seems to have stepped out of Mother Goose. Modifications have toned down original design—which is a pity—but it's still a sight.

Continue on N 1st toward Scio. The country looks as prosperous as the land is fecund. One can easily understand why the pioneers, viewing for the first time meadows such as this, called Oregon their "Beulah Land."

8.2 m., Scio, a one-street flour mill town.

Cross bridge. 0.1 m., turn L toward Lyons-Mill City. 2.1 m., turn R on Fish Hatchery Rd. 3.3 m., CB. 2.3 m., **Providence Pioneer Church** and cemetery. (See back cover for illustration.)

The church, staring down upon the valley from a knoll, has an air of vigilant righteousness, as though built by Jeremiah and maintained by avenging angels. The analogy may not be too far-fetched. The church was built as Baptist in 1854 by a sturdy band of moralists headed by Elder Joab Powell, pioneer circuit rider and one of the most colorful figures in Oregon's ministerial lore. A powerfully built man, with broad shoulders, piercing blue eyes and graying hair, Powell was known throughout the region for his booming voice, fiery tongue and burning evangelism. No farm household short of being stone deaf could fail to tell Powell was coming by the off-tune rendition of "The Judgment Day, the Judgment Day is rolling on; Prepare; O prepare!" "Uncle Joab," as his parishioners called him, was anything but dull. Before he started his preaching, usually in shirt sleeves, he'd jam a chaw of tobacco into his mouth. Then he'd open with, "I am the Alpha and Omegay." Whenever his sermons didn't properly arouse his listeners, he lamented, as though consigning the unenthusiastic to perdition, "There is not much rejoicing in Heaven tonight." During his 23 years of preaching in Oregon, he was said to have baptized about 3000 souls, many of them in chill Crabtree Creek. The cemetery, back of the church, is laid neatly on the quiet hill, with seldom any sound but the wind to reach the graves. Both Powell and his wife lie here. The epitaph on Ann Powell's stone may be a commentary on the death of her restless, relentless, fire-and-brimstone spouse: "There remaineth therefore a rest to the people of God."

0.1 m., turn R toward Crabtree. 0.4 m., turn R at "T." 1 m., turn L. 2.6 m., turn R to Scio. 5.2 m., Scio. 0.2 m., turn L toward Jefferson. 8.9 m., **Jefferson.**

On N bank of Santiam, Jefferson was once a gusty riverboat town, outcompeting nearby Syracuse and Santiam City, both long faded from the scene. **Jacob Conser House** (1854) is city hall and library. Cafe at Main & Union was part of Jefferson Institute (1857). This section was moved here in 1899 and false front added. Methodist Church (1871), Church & 2d, is one of oldest in Santiam Valley.

At Main & 99E (where Foodtown Store is located), turn R onto 99E. 1.1 m., turn L. Cross RR track. 2.3 m., on R, **Silas Haight House** (1846).

The small, white-columned mansion was called "Little White House" by the pioneers because it was patterned, in more modest dimensions, after presidential White House. The grandfather and father of present occupant, Mrs. Cool, a Haight by birth, were born here.

Return to 99E. Turn L toward Albany. Stay on 99E (not freeway) toward Millersburg. 2.7 m., at Millersburg Market, turn R. 0.8 m., on L, pioneer house (circa 1860). Long veranda facing two doors and five windows. Square stone chimney.

Return to 99E. Turn L, or back toward Jefferson. 1.7 m., turn L onto freeway toward Salem.

5.1 m., turn off at Ankeny Hill exit. Turn L at end of exit. Cross viaduct. 0.2 m., road forks. Bear R. 100 yds. from fork, on L, **Anderson House** (1855). Very attractive frame mansion; symbol of prestatehood affluence. Anderson family has occupied house since it was built.

Return to freeway. Turn N. Portland, 58 m.

FOSTER'S PLACE
AND
THE BARLOW ROAD

THIS IS THE PLACE WHERE PHILIP FOSTER TOOK UP HIS
NATION LAND CLAIM IN 1843. STARTING AT THIS POINT
1846, FOSTER AND SAMUEL K. BARLOW BUILT A TOLL ROAD
KNOWN AS THE BARLOW ROAD), A CUT-OFF ON THE OLD OREGON
TRAIL. IT CROSSED THE CASCADE RANGE TO AVOID THE
DANGERS AND HARDSHIPS OF THE COLUMBIA RIVER GORGE.
152 WAGONS REACHED THE WILLAMETTE VALLEY OVER THIS
CUT-OFF IN THE FALL OF 1846, THE FIRST OF THOUSANDS
TO FOLLOW.
FOSTER'S PLACE BECAME A WELL-KNOWN LOCALITY ON THE
OLD OREGON TRAIL. HERE, HUNGRY, TRAVEL-WORN EMIGRANTS
OBTAINED FRESH VEGETABLES AND FRUIT. HERE THEY FOUND
RICH PASTURE FOR THEIR TRAIL-WEARY LIVESTOCK.
"FOSTER'S PLACE" AND "BARLOW ROAD" PLAYED IMPORTANT
ROLES IN THE HISTORY AND DEVELOPMENT OF THE OLD
OREGON COUNTRY."
THEY WERE BOTH PIONEER PROJECTS.

ERECTED OCT. 1946
BY OREGON COUNCIL, AMERICAN PIONEER TRAILS ASSN.

Plaque at Eagle Creek

Historical Tour No. 9

Follow US 26 to Sandy, 24 m. Turn R, or S, onto O 211. This road follows the path of the Oregon Trailers who took the Barlow Cutoff.

2.2 m., on R, Sandy Ridge School, an old schoolhouse. Through the windows, students can see Mt. Hood, horses and meadows.

3.5 m., on R, old Eagle Creek School—directly S of modern brick school. Note bell tower above entrance.

0.1 m., jct., O 224.

At jct., on L, a plaque on large boulder legends the site of Philip Foster's farm and business enterprise and the end of the extended Barlow Road. Foster's large, well-furnished log cabin was located about 50 yds. back of marker. Thousands of emigrants ate at the Foster house—the first white dwelling the early pioneers saw in Oregon. They paid 50 cents for a dinner consisting of fresh beefsteak, boiled potatoes, cole slaw and hot biscuits, served with tea or coffee. The comers turned their stock into the Foster pasture, buying a "cut of hay" for their animals. The caravans also could purchase fruit grown in Foster's orchard, grain ground at his grist mill, and, starting in 1848, two years after he opened to Oregon Trail trade, medicines, hardware and other supplies at his general store. From Eagle Creek the wagons forded the Clackamas River, to the W, and continued on toward Oregon City and other parts of the Willamette Valley.

Across the road leading to Estacada, and partially hidden by two trees, stand three rough-grained, weathered, stone steps, the remains of the general store Foster owned, and possibly the oldest remains of any store in Oregon.

First house on R beyond stop sign on road leading to Oregon City is Burnett House, built in 1860. Much of the house has been unaltered. Across the road, and in front of a house built in 1887 by one of Foster's sons, stands oldest lilac bush in state. It was planted in 1844 from a stalk of purple lilac Mrs. Philip Foster brought around the Horn. The lilacs have never failed to bloom. Bush is now more than 35 ft. high, has a width greater than 40 ft., and in circumference measures more than 100 ft.

Philip Foster and members of his family are buried in a private cemetery on a hill above the jct.

Continue on O 211.

5.4 m., **Estacada,** hub of a vast recreation area. (See, this section, *Clackamas River-Mt. Hood National Forest Tour.*)

Continue on O 211. *12.6 m.*, Colton, rural hamlet dominated by tall church, on L. *8.3 m.*—through open farm country that reminds one of Ernest Haycox' novel of pioneer settlement in this area, *The Earthbreakers*—**Molalla.** Office Cafe has collection of early-day logging tools and equipment above inside of front door.

Turn L, or S, on Molalla Ave. *0.4 m.*, on R (second house past nursing home), **Dibble House,** built in mid-1850s by 1852 emigrant Horace Dibble. Two-story house has six rooms, two downstairs fireplaces, parlor, buttery and cellar. Timbers and lumber were all hand prepared.

Continue W. *1.1 m.*, turn R at "Y" onto County Road No. 25. *5.3 m.*, Wilhoit, just a pleasant spot in the road. Continue straight ahead. *1.3 m.*, what was once Wilhoit Springs, an abandoned mineral spa. (Private property;

Grave of Philip Foster above Eagle Creek   Old pavilion, Wilhoit Springs

Scotts Mills County Park

visitors not sought.) At turn of century the place was booming, with hotel, cottages, store, etc. Dances were held in pavilion, seen from road.

0.6 m., on dirt road, **Mandrones Mine,** possibly only operating coal mine in Oregon. (No mine visitations.) Coal not used for fuel; crushed for soil conditioner, for organic farming.

Return to Wilhoit. Turn L. 5.2 m., over roller-coaster road that at times seems to fly off into space; lane, on L leading to **Scotts Mills County Park.** 0.1 m., one of loveliest small parks in Oregon. Butte Creek cascades over craggy cliff into rock wall basin, making a very pretty picture.

Return to highway. 0.1 m., **Scotts Mills,** rustic settlement that in recent years has become haven for big city refugees, who want to do their own thing in an idyllic setting. **Friends Church** (1894), 5th & Grand View, is architecturally impressive.

At highway, turn R, or N, onto O 213. 2 m., Marquam. Turn L, or W, onto Mt. Angel Rd. 0.1 m., on R, **Marquam Methodist Church** (1890).

Return to O 213. 9.9 m., Liberal. First PO called Molalla was here, established in 1850. Today the area, once completely rural in character, is giving way to affluent homes, industry and stores.

0.5 m., on R, **Wagon Wheel Park,** inviting rest and picnic stop on Molalla River. 1.4 m., Mulino. Old schoolhouse, church and flour mill bldg.

10.9 m., Oregon City. 13 m., Portland.

Shunpiking

Before Int. 5, the high-speed N-S freeway was built, the key routes through the Willamette Valley were US 99W and the older US 99E, both flanking the Willamette River. At Junction City the roads combined, as they still do, and US 99 was the main artery clear to the Calif. border. You'll see much more of Oregon by Shunpiking, taking 99W & 99E, as well as roads branching off them, then you'll observe from the freeway.

West Side Shunpiking

9 m.—via Int. 5 and 99W—Tigard. (See H-T No. 6.)

14 m., Newberg. 2.3 m., Dundee. (For both, see H-T No. 4.)

3.8 m., O 18 bypass—to Coast. (See *Cross-Coast Range Roads.*)

* 1 m., jct., O 221—Dayton and Wheatland Ferry. (See H-T No. 5.)

1.9 m., turnoff to Yamhill Locks. 0.5 m., Lafayette. 0.7 m., turnoff to beautiful old house. 1.7 m., jct., O 47. (For all, see H-T No. 4.)

2.9 m., McMinnville. Jct., O 18—for Dayton. (For both, see H-T No. 5.)

1.2 m., jct., O 18—to Coast. (See *Cross-Coast Range Roads.*)

5.6 m., Amity. **Amity Church of Christ,** "Oldest Christian Church West of the Rockies." Founded here 1846; present bldg., 1912.

13.1 m., Rickreall, stop-signal crossroads. Jct., O 22—to E. (10.5 m., Salem.) Jct., O 22—to Coast. (See *Cross-Coast Range Roads.*)

For a delightful back-country excursion, try the following:

* At Rickreall, turn R onto O 22. 0.2 m., turn L onto O 223. 0.1 m., on R, house is said to have been built in early 1870s. 0.7 m., on L, red barn is pioneer structure in this area. 4 m., Dallas. Some of downtown wouldn't look out of place if horse and buggy days came back. **Polk County Courthouse,** built in 1889–1900 of local sandstone and covered with ivy—or Virginia creeper—is work of art compared to antiseptic addition.

5.6 m., Falls City Jct.

(4 m., jct. Falls City here, named for the Little Luckiamute River falls at W end of town, is earthy logging settlement, with its nose pressed against the pocketbook. But it's a lot bigger and more up-to-date than what's around Black Rock, 4 gravel m. W. At jct., L fork runs out in 16.5 m. at Valsetz, a company lumber town. It derived its name from the Valley & Siletz RR, built to haul out logs. Before the auto became the only way to travel, Valsetz folks would sometimes ride the V&S to the big city or Dallas, mostly in the caboose. There was no charge.)

8.5 m., Pedee. A sign on the door of the lone store reads: "Please Call Again"; but the store has been closed for good.

Polk County Courthouse

3.5 m., Ritner Creek CB. 1.7 m., Kings Valley. A sawmill supplies the industry, and store-tavern is the business section. First postmaster was Rowland Chambers (1855). His descendants still farm land around the settlement. 0.6 m., under black walnut tree (planted in 1846), marker commemorating founding of Kings Valley in same year. Behind tree is house a Chambers built in 1889. 0.2 m., on L, unoccupied country church, which locals claim was put up about 1870. House back of it, hammered together with square nails, is probably five years younger.

1.4 m., Hoskins Jct.

(R on Hoskins Rd. 0.7 m. to Earl Price mailbox. **Watson House**— built in 1852—on L, 100 yds. up private lane, is oldest in Kings Valley and asserted to have been first plastered house in state. 1.1 m., Hoskins. The place had quite a history. First there was Ft. Hoskins (1856–65). Then came a RR yard, with a big roundhouse. A community arose and a CB was erected above the Luckiamute. Well, the CB isn't there now; all that remains of the RR yard is a shop bldg., probably put up about 1914; and the total mercantile community consists of a tavern called "The Fort." It's the only suggestion of Ft. Hoskins existant.)

0.2 m.—S from Hoskins Jct. on O 223, on L, mailbox of Norman Chambers. (0.3 m., up rocky lane, unused, dilapidating King house, built in mid-1850s. Owner says: "I'd like to snap my fingers and have it disappear.")

6.2 m., jct., US 20.

5.6 m.—from Rickreall, on 99W—Monmouth Jct.

　　* 0.3 m., Monmouth, a farm market center being rapidly changed by the growth of Oregon College of Education.

　　* Jct., O 51. (12.5 m., mostly paralleling Willamette River—Salem.)

A meandering journey touching a quiet corner of the past begins at Monmouth Jct.

　　* 2.3 m., on O 51, **Independence**, for some the "End of the Oregon Trail." **J. S. Cooper Block** (1897), with castle-like turret and flagpole, is example of elegant small-town valley architecture 70 years ago. Turn R. 1.4 m., turn L toward Wigrich. 2.6 m., turn R at Wigrich. 3.1 m., **Buena Vista**, settled in 1847. A few old bldgs. still standing, but active business is only a store. (0.4 m., **Buena Vista Ferry**, crossing Willamette. E landing leads to Int. 5.) 4.4 m., turn L toward Albany. 6.9 m., US 20. Turn L. 0.3 m., across bridge, Albany.

4.5 m.—from Monmouth Jct.—turnoff R for Helmick SP.

　　* 1.2 m., Helmick SP. Picnicking and swimming on banks of Luckiamute.

3.8 m., turnoff L to Wilson Game Management Area.

　　* 0.5 m., Wilson GMA, primarily devoted to rearing game birds, mainly pheasants. Visitors shown through operations on request. Best time is May, during hatching season.

12.3 m., **Corvallis**, seat of **Oregon State University**. Of interest at OSU: Natural History Museum, Horner Museum (devoted to Oregon history), Herbarium and Entomological Collection, and Geological and Paleontological Collection. **Benton County Courthouse** (1889), downtown, has distinguished-looking clock tower.

Jct., US 20 and O 34—to Coast. (See *Cross-Coast Range Roads*.)

Jct., US 20—to Albany, 12 m.

Jct., O 34—E to Int. 5, 9 m.

A longer but more interesting way to Junction City, US 99, is known locally as Peoria Rd.

　　* In Corvallis, turn E at NW Van Buren. Follow O 34. 1.2 m., turn R at Peoria Jct. 0.9 m., house on R built circa 1880. 3.4 m., turn L onto Oakville Rd. 1.4 m., **Willamette United Presbyterian Church**, organized in 1850, the oldest of its denomination W of the Missouri, supposedly first psalm-singing congregation in Oregon, and best-known pioneer church in mid-Willamette Valley. Wide-spreading oaks frame the structure, one of the most attractive religious edifices in the state. Turn R onto Peoria Rd. 0.2 m., on L, old Oakville School. 1.7 m., main Peoria Rd. Turn L. 3.3 m., Peoria Park; boat landing on the Willamette. 0.3 m., Peoria store. (First st. N of store—10 yds.—leads W 0.1 m. to 1892-built warehouse. A century ago there were four grain warehouses on the Willamette here, with a capacity of 60,000 bushels of wheat, and Peoria was a thriving steamboat loading town. But coming of RR to E—Shedd and

Oakville Church   McFarland Free Methodist Community Church

Halsey—doomed Peoria.) *3.3 m.* Halsey Jct. (*5.3 m.*, Halsey.) *10 m.*, Harrisburg. *4 m.*, Junction City.

13.1 m.—from Corvallis—on L, **McFarland Community Free Methodist Church.** Early village house of worship, no longer in use.

1 m., Bellfountain Jct.

* *3.4 m.*, Bellfountain, a wide curve on a rural road that never had more than 50 persons, but in 1937 its high school, now a grade school, won the state basketball championship, defeating Lincoln of Portland for the title, thus writing the most remarkable chapter in Oregon athletics.

3.4 m., Monroe. **McAllum Museum of Western Americana** boasts one of largest collections of Winchester rifles and shotguns in U.S.

8.5 m., Junction City, US 99. (See US 99.)

East Side Shunpiking

5.2 m.—from E exit of Morrison St. bridge, on 99E—Milwaukie. *6.8 m.*, Oregon City. (For both, see *H-T No. 7.*)

(For Oregon City via Lake Oswego and West Linn, see *H-T No. 7.*)

Jct., O 213. (For Silverton, see *H-T No. 8.* For Molalla, see *H-T No. 9.*)

8.6 m., Canby. *1.4 m.*, Barlow house. *0.1 m.*, turnoff to Barlow. *1.9 m.*, Aurora. *4.4 m.*, Hubbard. *2.3 m.*, jct., O 211. (For all, see *H-T No. 8.*)

1 m., Woodburn, home of radio station KWRC, famed for its "talk show" programs.

3.1 m., on L, **Samuel Brown House** (1858). White-painted, second story porch, latticed front, two chimneys. Barns and out buildings are out of an 1860-ish album.

0.3 m., Gervais Jct.

* Turn R. *0.5 m.*, **Gervais,** whose business section seems 60 years back in time. Sizeable numbers of "White Russians" and Spanish-speaking people have moved into area, giving Gervais trilingual acoustics.

3 m., continuing W, **St. Louis Catholic Church,** center of tiny hamlet. According to life-long elderly parishioners, Marie Dorion, the remarkable Iowa Indian, who was first woman to cross plains (with Astor Overland

Expedition in 1811) and settle in Oregon, lies buried under present church. If so, her body had been removed from Catholic Cemetery here, where she had been laid to rest in 1850. Present church was put up in 1890; first church, log structure, was erectd in 1840s. Climer residence, 1½ blocks NW of church, served as rectory for early priests; is one of oldest bldgs. in state, and is distinguished by log beams, wooden pegs and hand-planed, grooved boards. Parts of inside have never been changed. About 100 yds. N of lane leading to Climer house is old St. Louis school, a real antique piece.

1 m. W, O 219. N, *8.6 m.* to St. Paul, *10.3 m.* to Champoeg SP. (See *H-T No. 6.*)

5 m., Brooks. *1 m.,* Quinaby Rd.

* Take Quinaby Rd. *1.2 m.* W to Schreiner's Gardens. Open to public only in May, when iris bloom.

1.2 m., on R, white colonial-style house with water tower in rear.

6.5 m., **Salem,** state capital and site of late summer State Fair. Historic murals in **Capitol** provide graphic education on Oregon's background. Stirring view of Willamette Valley from dome. **Bush Pasture,** 600 Mission St., SE, is 80-acre city park containing rare trees and shrubs. **Bush House Museum,** Victorian mansion (1878) has some of the original furnishings and household articles of pioneer tycoon Asahel Bush. **Bush Barn Art Center** (Salem Art Museum), adjacent to Bush House, sponsors exhibits of NW artists. **Willamette University,** 900 State St., founded in 1842 as Oregon Institute, with the assistance of famed—and disputatious—missionary Jason Lee, is oldest institution of higher learning in NW. On the grounds of the old **Thomas Kay Woolen Mills**—12th & Ferry—stand what could be the two oldest bldgs. in Oregon, the **Jason Lee House** and **Parsonage,** both reputedly built in 1841.

Jct., O 22—to Coast. (See *Cross-Coast Range Roads.*)

Jct., O 22—to E. (See *Trans-Cascade Roads.*)

Leave Salem on 99E, which later turns into Int. 5.

12 m.—from downtown Salem—turn off Int. 5 at Ankeny Hill exit for Anderson house (*0.3 m.*) Return to freeway. *0.7 m.,* turnoff at Jefferson exit. *5 m.,* Jefferson, which is on a piece of fragmented old 99E. *1.1 m.,* turn L for Silas Haight House (*2.3 m.*) Return to 99E. *2.7 m.,* Millersburg. Turn R for 1860 house (*0.8 m.*) Return to 99E. (For all, see *H-T No. 8.*)

4.8 m.—from Millersburg on 99E—**Albany,** famous for its rare metals industry, infamous for its stinking fumes. World championship timber carnival, in early July, draws competing loggers from as far away as Australia.

Jct., US 20—to Coast. (See *Cross-Coast Range Roads.*)

Jct., US 20—to E. (See *Trans-Cascade Roads.*)

6.5 m., Tangent. Across RR tracks, abandoned church dating back to 1870s.

5.7 m., Shedd.

* E on Plainview Rd. *1.5 m.* to **Thompson Mill,** Oregon's oldest plant, and forming the prettiest picture.

Methodist Church on NW corner of Plainview Rd. & 99E was established in 1853; present structure built in 1873. Church bldg. on SE corner 1 block S of Plainview Rd. has iron-grill fence landing and stained glass windows. Despite rundown condition, it has a patrician haughtiness. Ought to be restored; inside even more appealing than exterior.

5.3 m., Halsey, a small feedmill town in the vast seed-growing area of the Willamette Valley. Air pollution from burning of fields has triggered much bitter controversy. **Halsey Christian Church,** on SW corner of road to Peoria, is oldest in town, which was born in 1871.

Jct., O 228—to Brownsville and Sweet Home. (See *Trans-Cascade Roads.*)

0.5 m.—from Halsey Greyhound depot—turn R for visit to an unusual Nature Conservancy forest.

    * 0.9 m., turn L onto Power Line Rd. 3.1 m., on L, gate that is entry to a 90-acre tract of virgin oak on the Big Muddy. The land was homesteaded by the grandfather of Mrs. Lee Foster in 1872 and the grove has never been plowed or logged. It is a sterling example of the natural oak and ash forest and valley meadow land that existed before homesteaders entered the Willamette Valley. There is not even a trail through the grove. A 10-acre virgin grove, on the Little Muddy, is behind the pre-20th-century Foster home, 0.3 m., on R, farther up the road.

8.3 m., **Harrisburg,** a river town with many touches of the Willamette steamboat days. Lumberland, 1st & Smith, was built over pioneer May & Senders general store. Riverboats moored across the street. Other landmarks of the past: old leather shop, Smith near 2d; Odd Fellows Hall, 2nd & Smith; Christian Church, 6th & Smith.

Jct., Coburg Rd.

    * 0.8 m.—on Coburg Rd.—on R, **Davis House,** built in 1850s, as was adjacent barn. 8 m., Power Line Rd. (0.5 m., the handsome **Ward House** —1877.) 3.5 m., rural schoolhouse (1910). 0.5 m., **Macy House,** probably built in mid-1850s. 0.5 m., **Coburg.** Century-plus dwellings at 163 S Willamette and, on N Willamette, 145, 152 and 209. 6.8 m., Eugene.

County road at S end of Harrisburg leads N to Peoria and Corvallis. (See *West Side Shunpiking.*)

The bridge across the Willamette S of Harrisburg wasn't always there. There wasn't a span prior to 1925; before then, a scow was used to ferry vehicles and teams. The scow was a vast improvement over the first ferry, started in 1848, which was made up of two boats lashed together with a platform for transporting a wagon. The horses and oxen had to swim behind.

4 m.—from Harrisburg—Junction City.

Shunpiking—US 99

Junction City, where 99W & 99E merge into 99. But the town received its name from the anticipation—unfulfilled—of a junction of two RR lines in 1871. Scandinavian Festival, four days in early August, is one of the great folk celebrations of NW.

1.8 m., jct., O 36—to Coast. (See *Cross-Coast Range Roads.*)

12.7 m., **Eugene**, seat of **University of Oregon. U of O Museum of Arts** is noted for its Oriental Collection. University Library contains extensive Oregon historical collection.

A panorama of Eugene, the upper Willamette Valley and the surrounding hills can be seen from Skinner's Butte, reached from N High St.

Hidden in the growth of the burgeoning Eugene are some very interesting old places. They include bldgs. at 433 E Broadway (1868), now a restaurant; SW corner, 13th & University (1886), now U of O Faculty Club; 1268 Jackson (1878), for years the home of world-famous geologist, Dr. Thomas Condon; 1611 Lincoln (1868), locally renowned for its "Rural Gothic" architecture; County Clerk's Office (1853), in Lane County Fairgrounds, 13th & Monroe; 1006 Taylor (1876); 414 Lawrence (1889); 260 W 6th (1868); 340 W 7th (1882); 170 E 12th (1855); and McMurphey House (1888), better known as "Castle on the Hill," on S slope of Skinner's Butte, at 303 Willamette. **Lane County Pioneer Museum,** at NE corner of fairgrounds, has wealth of homesteader artifacts. Maude I. Kerns Art Center, in early church bldg. at 1910 E 15th, has full schedule of arts and crafts exhibits.

A breezy, back-country rd., twirling from Eugene to Lorane, 22 *m.*, catches glimpses of deer crossing or moving in the brush. But houses are closing in on the home of the deer.

* W on Chambers St. to rd. Lorane is a peaceful little village with pastoral church and homey Grange hall. *2.5 m.* S of Lorane, **Mountain House Hotel,** or Cartwright House (1853). Was PO, stagecoach inn and telegraph station. One of the first wire messages received was of President Lincoln's assassination. Lorane is 13 m. from Cottage Grove and 15.8 m. from Drain, both on 99.

Jct., O 126—to Coast. (See *Cross-Coast Range Roads.*)

Jct., O 126—to E. (See *Trans-Cascade Roads.*)

6.8 m., Goshen. The Eugene spilloff has inflated the hamlet to the point where it has its own spit-and-polish fire dept.

Jct., off adjacent Int. 5, O 58. (See *Trans-Cascade Roads.*)

5.5 m., Creswell. From a rural crossroad it has bloomed into a bedroom of Eugene.

9.2 m., **Cottage Grove,** one of Oregon's most ambitious and sparkling little cities, with a downtown that glitters in neon. Most interesting part of town is S on River Rd. from Main St. Here are some intriguing vintage houses. Examples: 553, 625, 653 S River Rd. But most interesting is first house from Main, on L, **Dr. Snapp House,** with witch's-hat front. It is used as a museum during Bohemia Days celebration in mid-July. From Main St., on River Rd., *0.2 m.*, Dr. Snapp house. *0.1 m.*, footbridge across Coast Fork of Willamette. *0.3 m.*, CB—which locals claim to be the only RR CB in U.S. Pioneer Museum, in 19th-century Catholic church, is at H & Birch.

One of the most adventuresome off-the-beaten-path trips W of the Cascades starts at Cottage Grove. It leads to the ghostly, sprawling mining camp of **Bohemia,** center of the 225-sq.-m. Bohemia Mining District. This heavily

Footbridge at Cottage Grove   Covered railroad bridge at Cottage Grove

timbered region of gorges, wooded scarps and jagged peaks is home to turbulent mtn. streams and to wildlife which have been pushed into the dark re-
cesses of the diminishing forest primeval by the relentless incursion of man.

On a spring day in 1863 a man named "Bohemia" Johnson, supposedly
hiding in the Calapooya Mtns., accidentally discovered gold. There followed
the usual swarm of prospectors; within two years, 100 claims were staked. No
great finds have been made, but there is the wake of the usual lore, with
legend holding that the Bohemia district has several "lost" mines—Lost
Frenchman, Lost Dutchman, Lost Lode of Trestle Creek, Lost Mine of
Fiddlers Green.

Eventually, the major metals taken were silver, lead, zinc and copper.
Though the feverish mining days are now history, old-timers insist there is
more ore in the hills than was taken out—the common talk of old-time mining
men everywhere in Oregon.

* E on Main off US 99. (Street sign directs to Dorena Dam.) *1.7 m.*,
turn L. *1.9 m.*, turn R and cross Row River CB, which leads into Lang
Rd. *0.9 m.*, from turnoff to CB, Mosby mailbox. Turn L. *0.1 m.*, **Mosby
House** (1862), built on an 1853 Donation Land claim. Return to Dorena
Rd., just beyond the same CB. Turn R. *1.3 m.*, jct. (R fork: *3 m.*, turn-
off to Baker Bay Park, Lane County park on Dorena Reservoir; *3.8 m.*,
Dorena CB; *2.1 m.*, Dorena.) (L fork: *7.3 m.*, passing **Dorena Dam,
Dorena Reservoir** and Harms Park, Dorena CB; *2.1 m.*, Dorena.)

Dorena: store-cafe-gas. *2 m.*, Culp Creek. Jct. here. Both roads go to
Bohemia but one to the R, Sharps Creek, is steeper and more trouble-
some. Road ahead is slightly longer but is the more gentle and safer
route. *4 m.*, Disston. *18 m.*, passing two FS CGs, top of ridge. (Last 2 m.
are steep but safe.)

Turn R and you travel the ridge road for 6 m., with magnificent views
to N and S. The road looks down on abandoned mine bldgs. and numerous mine tailings. Having come to Bohemia, climb Fairview Mtn., if you
feel in shape. (Not hazardous, but no ascent for cardiacs). From this
zenith the views catapult across great gobs of space. On a clear day, you

may see from the Pacific to the Cascade peaks and S to Mt. Shasta in Calif.

Retrace route or return to Disston Rd. by way of Champion Mine Rd. near E of ridge (rougher and more trying), or the steeply descending, twisting Sharps Creek Rd., at W end of ridge.

* For another satisfying—but far less absorbing and challenging—side trip out of Cottage Grove, turn L on 6th St. toward **Cottage Grove Dam,** 6 *m.,* and another 6 *m.,* past **Cottage Grove Reservoir** to London, a backwoods scratch on the Coast Fork of the Willamette.. Rod and Reel Trout Farm, 2.2 *m.* S of London, requires no license and is open year-round for rainbow trout fishing.

17.6 *m.*—from Cottage Grove—Drain. Town was site of one of Oregon's first normal schools, long gone. Still remaining is CB, on 1st St., 0.1 m. S of A St.

Jct., O 38—to Coast. (See *Cross-Coast Range Roads.*)

3 *m.,* on R, Jesse Applegate marker. Home of one of Oregon's foremost sons stood 0.5 m. W of here. It was used as the first court of the Provisional government.

Applegate marker near Yoncalla

Applegate House

2.1 m., Halo Trail.

* Turn L, or E. 0.6 m., turn L toward Applegate Sec. 0.4 m., to house built by Charles Applegate, one of the three illustrious Applegate brothers, in 1856. Perhaps the least-known of Oregon's historic pioneer homes.

0.4 m., Yoncalla, small shopping point in a tangled vale of choppy hills. House directly S of station is kind that was prominent around here in horse-vehicle days.

14.2 m., **Oakland,** a town of 800 that looks like a tintype of the late 19th century, with its many weatherworn brick bldgs. Stearns Hardware has been in business since 1887. City Library in 1890 bldg. that was a drug store. "Oakland Museum" seems a redundancy; the whole town has a museum air.

2.6 m., **Sutherlin.** Mercantilist D. W. Banker Bldg. (1916) seems to set the tone for the architecture and spirit of town. Old steam locomotive and ancient caboose, which served lumber camps, in City Park.

5.4 m., Wilbur. 0.5 m., turn L, or E. 0.2 m., on R, United Methodist Church congregation dates back to 1853. Present structure, of much more recent vintage, retains flavor of early style.

2.5 m., from turn to church, "water falls" on the N Umpqua River. They form such a classic picture of shimmering delicacy as to bring to mind the image of weeping willows.

0.2 m., across bridge, Winchester.

5.1 m., **Roseburg**, gateway to the Umpqua recreation area, one of fairest sections of Oregon. **Lane House**, now a museum operated by the Douglas County Historical Society, at 544 SE Douglas, honors Gen. Joseph Lane, Oregon's first territorial governor, one of Oregon's first two U.S. senators and—a fact local historians would overlook—a staunch defender of slavery and a bitter foe of Abraham Lincoln. Actually, Lane did not live in this house; but he resided on the same block and sometimes took his meals here with his daughters. The Joseph Lane house was sited where the Douglas County Farm Bureau Cooperative now stands. Hamilton house (1895), SE Lane & Kane, was built by a circuit court judge. Another house bearing the marks of turn-of-the-century affluence, 1 block N on Kane (at Cass), was put up by merchant Napoleon Rice. **Douglas County Museum**, across street from fairgrounds (exit off Int. 5) is most architecturally unique museum structure in state and has the most imaginative and professionally arranged displays of any Oregon historical museum.

At Harvard, near downtown Roseburg, turn R for Lookingglass (*6.5 m.*), a country store which gained national publicity by installing a parking meter. People drive in from miles around to feed the meter. (See *Cross-Coast Range Roads, O 42, Winston.*)

Jct., O 138—to Diamond Lake and US 97. (See *Trans-Cascade Roads.*)

7.5 m., Winston. Jct., O 42—to Coast. (See *Cross-Coast Range Roads.*)

0.4 m., Winston-Dillard Community Park, on the banks of the S Umpqua.

1.2 m., Dillard, a mill town with lumber stacked along the road, even next to a restaurant.

Douglas County Museum

11.6 m., Myrtle Creek, a hardy logging and farming center that is more modern than the giant prehistoric animals who roamed these parts a few million years back. In 1927 a fossil tusk 10 inches in diameter and 6 ft. long was discovered around here.

10.4 m., Canyonville, at the N end of the canyon that was the most harrowing stretch of the Applegate Trail. One of the heroes of the ill-fated party which made the first attempt through the canyon, in 1846, was **Tabitha Moffat Brown,** who later played a role in the founding of Pacific University. Jct., O 227.

    * A pleasant, rustic backroad drive to Medford, *73 m.*, and the shortest route from Canyonville to Crater Lake. O 227 is sparingly dotted with small hamlets till it reaches O 62, the road to Crater Lake; the longest distance between hamlets (Drew to Trail) being 21 m.

10.8 m.—via Int. 5—Azalea. The store bldg. (all that is Azalea) was stagecoach inn.

11.9 m., Glendale. The road winds through second-growth timber, small farms humped over washboard acres, weary houses and sagging outbuildings. Glendale is a mill town whose "flivver" main street leans against RR tracks. The fanciest establishment in this town could be the tavern. The green hills make the prosaic town look even duller than it may be.

Back track *4.7 m.* to Int. 5. *4.8 m.*, Wolf Creek. **Wolf Creek Inn,** also known as Wolf Creek Tavern, dates back to 1857 and would be oldest hotel in state if it were still receiving guests, but only tavern is operating; a quiet place for local blue collars.

For visit to one of least known ghost towns in state, try following:

    * At S end of Wolf Creek, turn onto Coyote Creek Rd. The road nudges open woods, where slants of sunlight are bent into honey-colored pools and patches; rail fences, stretched lean and gawky; and musky glens latticed by drifting shadows. *3.5 m.*, on R, large log house, finished on the outside with Port Orford cedar bark. House, completed in 1932, belongs

Davis house, Golden   **Old house at Golden**

Old Catholic church at Golden

Log structure on road from Grave Creek bridge to Wolf Creek

to son of miner who came here in 1884. Owner has his own narrow-gauge track from woodshed to house, with small ore cart for hauling. Just W of house is miner's cabin built in 1891. Behind it, up a dirt path at the split-rail edge of homesite, is first and only Golden school, long deserted. *0.5 m.*, the ghost town of **Golden,** less than 100 yds. in length. It flourished from about mid-1890s to mid-1910s. All that has survived is a vacant sugar-pine house, picturesque church structure, general store bldg. and a carriage shed. The scraggly pear and apple trees close by add symbolic poignancy to the haunted scene. Across the creek are mementos of the mining days: heaps of rocks and gravel still naked and raw, livid wounds in the thicket that time has not healed, and a crude miner's shack half-hidden in the foliage.

There is a longer, more rugged and even more scenic trip leading out of Wolf Creek.

* Take Wolf Creek Rd. W for Grave Creek, Almeda and Galice. *10.1 m.*, on R, an unidentified log structure that looks like an early-day trading post and is one of the more interesting and puzzling sights along this lightly traveled road. *4.9 m.*, confluence of Grave Creek and Rogue River, at bridge, which doesn't seem to belong, it being modern and concrete in the raw hinterland. Jct. here, with R fork heading NW, to branch into lanes that dead end in the Rogue wilderness, lead to coastal Gold Beach, or eventually reach Coos Bay, *79 m.* N of Gold Beach, *3.8 m.* beyond Grave Creek bridge, viewpoint of the rotting remains of the old Almeda gold mine, across the Rogue. *0.2 m.*, Almeda Bar Rec. Area, a county park on the river. *3.3 m.*, a sign on the store reads: "This is Galice." And so it is. (Store also has cafe, gas pumps.) *0.3 m.*, jct. (Agness, *41 m.*; Gold Beach, *66 m.*) *4.4 m.*, **Indian Mary Park**, a grassy, leafy Josephine County CG and picnic area on the Rogue. *1.6 m.*, on R, **Hellgate Viewpoint.** The most famous canyon scene on the Rogue. Here the river fights its way

Ruins of Almeda Mine

Galice

between rocky cliffs that stick out big toes into the stream. One of the most dangerous sections of the swift, turbulent, tricky Rogue. 5.8 *m.*, Merlin, a quiet mill town. 3.8 *m.*, Int. 5. 4.8 *m.*, Grants Pass.

5.2 *m.*—from Wolf Creek exit at Int. 5—Sunny Valley exit.

  * 0.4 *m.*, Grave Creek CB, with six windows on each side.

16.2 *m.*, **Grants Pass,** in the heart of the many-splendored Rogue River country. Wilson house, NE Jackson & 6th, is kind of rambling baronial mansion Grants Pass had more of 60–70 years ago.

Jct., US 199—to Coast. (See *Cross-Coast Range Roads.*)

Jct., Applegate Valley Rd.—to Jacksonville and Medford. (See *Cross-Coast Range Roads, US 199.*)

9.9 *m.*, Rogue River Jct.

  * 0.2 *m.*, **Rogue River,** in an idyllic location in the shimmering Rogue River Valley. Little wonder it has attracted so much attention from so many Californians. Big annual event is National Rooster Crow on last Sat. in June. Town is gateway to Valley of the Rogue SP—fine CG, boat ramp to Rogue, complete picnic facilities.

(For a short side trip replete with varied interests, take Pine St. N. It becomes E Evans Rd., which rambles carefree through melodious Evans Valley to Evans Creek CB at Wimer—9 m. from town. Retrace route 2 m. to Minthorn Lane, cross creek, and return by W Evans Rd. to Palmerton Park, a local arboretum. At corner S of park, turn L, cross the creek and drive through town on Main St. E Main curves around Harper Hill, skirting the Georgia Pacific plant, passes a side entrance to Valley of the Rogue SP, and continues on to the Rock Point Stage Station

[1863] and the Rock Point bridge, named for rock formation in river below.)

2 m., **Birdseye House**, large log structure constructed in 1856, with many of the logs taken from the original stockade of the short-lived Ft. Birdseye (1855), which stood less than 0.1 m. back of house. The oldest home in S Oregon still in use. Please do not trespass on grounds.

4.8 m., turn L onto Sardine Creek Rd.

  * 2.2 m., Old Oregon Historical Museum. Rich collection of S Oregon artifacts. Covered wagon on grounds was rolling about 1885. 2 m., Oregon Vortex, a commercial "House of Mystery" which supposedly has been scientifically debunked, but continues to puzzle optically-illusioned tourists. Bldg. was originally assay office for gold mining co.

Hellgate view, Rogue River

Birdseye house

Return down Sardine Creek Rd. to highway. Turn L. *1.6 m.*, Gold Hill-jct., O 234.

Gold Hill was scene of an early S Oregon gold discovery, but the first settlement in these parts was long-gone Dardanelles, on the S side of the Rogue. It was given the name by W. G. T'Vault, who received the first Donation Land grant in the area, and in his cabin established the first PO in Jackson County, in 1852. Before he arrived, he had already made a name for himself in the territory, having been, among other things, editor of the first newspaper in the NW, *The Oregon Spectator* (Oregon City). Remains of old gold

Covered wagon at Old Oregon Historical Museum

mines can be seen on Nugget Butte, due N of town. First two houses E of 4th St. on 1st Ave. were put up around 1890. Library started as a schoolhouse around 1900 and was city hall for some years. House at 535 4th Ave. was saddlery when original town stood on N side of RR tracks. IOOF bldg. was put up in 1891; front has been remodeled. Grange hall, 275 4th Ave., dates back to 1890. Tavern at 4th Ave. & 4th St. was hotel in "old town."

* Follow O 234 *5 m. to* Sam's Valley Jct. Turn L. *2 m.,* Sam's Valley. Abandoned general store, on L, is last reminder of hamlet's mercantile community. *1.6 m.,* road rejoins O 234. Turn L. *7.4 m.,* end of O 234, at jct., O 62. (For O 62, see *Trans-Cascade Roads.*)

5.3 m.—from Gold Hill—on L, view of Table Rock, standing nearly 1000 ft. above the Rogue. A treaty concluding the 1853 "Indian War" was signed on a slope of the mesa. As usual, it didn't do the Indians much good.

2.7 m., museum turnoff.

* *0.4 m.,* **Crater Rock Museum,** housing one of the finest geologic collections in state—as well as many other items of interest.

2 m., Central Point.

* Short cut to Jacksonville—*5.5 m.*

4 m., **Medford,** largest city in S Oregon and processing center for a prosperous orchard area.

Display at Crater Rock Museum

Jct., O 62—to Crater Lake and Klamath Falls. (See *Trans-Cascade Roads*.)

Jct. (7 m. N on O 62), O 140—to Klamath Falls. (See *Trans-Cascade Roads*.)

Jct., O 238—to Applegate Valley and US 199.

* *4.5 m.*, **Pioneer Village**, a stockaded representation of early S Oregon, embellished by period entertainment, including "old-fashioned melodramas" and silent Westerns.

0.5 m., **Jacksonville**, a living museum of the second half of the 19th century. Intelligent restoration has preserved the charm of Jacksonville, born as a bruising gold camp and almost finished when the gold ran out and the county seat was moved to Medford. There are so many interesting places, most of them on the main stem, California St., that discussing them all would take several pages. Jacksonville is one of the few towns where you can be your own guide. Just stroll about town; there seems to be a plaque on every bldg. Among the more colorful sights: **Jackson County Museum**, built in 1884 as county courthouse; **Dowell House** (1859); **Catholic Church** (1858); **McCully House** (1860), now a doll museum; **Methodist Church** (1854), probably the oldest church in Oregon consistently used as house of worship; **Table Rock Saloon** (1859); **U. S. Hotel** (1880); **IOOF Bldg.** (1855), whose upstairs was used by Jewish pioneers as a synagogue; **Beekman Bank** (1862); **Brunner Bldg.** (1855), now town library; **Beekman House** (1880). Probably the oddest structure is the **Nunan House** (1890), 635 N Oregon. The three-story, 18-room house was constructed of local brick, sandstone, sugar pine, hardwood, cement, and iron grill ornamentation. It has nine gables,

Stagecoach used for tourists on Jacksonville street   Dowell House, Jacksonville

Samuel Colver House, Phoenix

stained glass windows and porch gazebo. **Jacksonville Cemetery**, a short walk from downtown, includes graves of W. G. T'Vault, one of the most spectacular and disputatious of all Oregon history-makers; C. C. Beekman, the legenary banker; and Peter Britt, pioneer photographer and artist. Concerts of the annual **Peter Britt Music and Arts Festival**, staged in Aug., are held in the air-conditioned ballroom of the U.S. Hotel and on the greensward of the Peter Britt Estate.

For remainder of O 238, see *Cross-Coast Range Roads, US 199*.

4.5 m.—S on US 99 from Medford—Phoenix. **Samuel Colver House** (1855), on R, built of logs sheathed with sawed lumber, has been a stagecoach stop, inn, distillery, etc., and is now antique shop.

7.1 m., **Ashland**, home of Southern Oregon College and site of world-famous, summer annual **Shakespearian Festival.** Exquisitely landscaped **Lithia Park** is background for Globe Theater. House at 1639 Jackson Rd. (circa 1863) was constructed as warehouse. A few years later it was remodeled into a dwelling and stood on the old Oregon and California Stage Rd. Abandoned for decades, it has recently been restored as nearly as possible to its original design.

Jct., Dead Indian Rd. (what a horrible name!)—to Lake of the Woods. (See *Trans-Cascade Roads*.)

Jct., O 66—to Klamath Falls. (See *Trans-Cascade Roads*.)

16 m.—up and over the summit of the Siskiyou Mtns.—Calif. line.

Trans-Cascade Roads

Int. 80N—Portland to The Dalles

The road has its trans-Cascade conclusion at Hood River but the terminal point here is The Dalles—so designated as to make 80N compatible with the listing of other trans-Cascade roads.

From Portland to Hood River, see *The Great Heartland, Mt. Hood Loop*.

Hood River, a quiet county seat, is the gateway to thousands of acres of apple and pear trees. The county claims to be the world's largest producer of d'Anjou pears and the home of pear vodka. Blossom time, in the spring, lures thousands of visitors to the white-tinted orchards, whose buds unfold beneath the great cone of Mt. Hood, ablaze with virgin snow.

(For Lost Lake and other interesting places near Hood River, see *Mt. Hood Loop*.)

0.5 m.—on 80N, from Hood River city center exit—jct., O 35 (see *Mt. Hood Loop*) and White Salmon Bridge, across Columbia.

5.3 m., Mosier Exit. (Scenic Loop).

* 0.5 m. Mosier—a TV scriptwriter's dream of a downright neighborly crackerbarrel burg. First Christian Church (1910) is town landmark. Mosier Trading Post started as such at turn of century and was lodge hall and other things before it became trading post again.

2 m., on L, mansion built about 1914. One of the princeliest houses in rural Oregon.

The "Scenic Loop" winds up to and along a plateau that affords such moving views of the Columbia River and its basaltic cliffs and rock canyons as cannot be seen from the freeway. This was once the main road— US 30—and squirming around it at 30 m. per hour, you can understand why a water-level route was desperately needed. There is still a pioneer character to the tawny plateau, which breaks into ridges and drops into deep defiles.

4.3 m., turnoff for Rowena Crest Viewpoint (see back cover for illustration). Seen from Rowena Crest: the graceful geometry of the road at three levels; the imperial march of the Columbia; and, on the Wash. side, groaning cliffs, the wind-bleached town of Lyle, and the Klickitat River pushing into the Columbia. It's very breezy on the Crest, so hang on to your hat, or wig.

2.1 m., turnoff for Mayer SP, on Columbia shore. Picnicking, boating, swimming. The turnoff marks the end of the "Scenic Loop" but let's continue on the old road. 1 m., Rowena—a store and little else. 8 m., The Dalles.

Mosier Trading Post

6.8 m.—on 80N, from Mosier Exit—turnoff to Rowena and Mayer SP.

7.6 m., turnoff to city center, The Dalles. (See *Central Oregon, Int. 80N.*)

US 26—Portland to Madras

US 26 is the most direct road from Portland to the heart of Central Oregon and is thus widely traveled. It reaches its grandest majesty at an early stage, when it sweeps up Laurel Hill, below the beacon of Mt. Hood whose slopes in spring are aswarm with rhododendrons.

13 m., Gresham, only a few years ago a placid market town and site of Multnomah County Fair. Fair was moved to indoor Portland and Gresham is burgeoning as another "progressive" suburb.

11.3 m., Sandy. The folksy touches of yesteryear's agrarianism are being effaced by the swift pace of modernization.

Jct., O 211. (See *The Great Heartland, H-T No. 9.*)

(From here to jct., O 35, see *The Great Heartland, Mt. Hood Loop.*)

From jct., O 35, 4.5 m., Frog Lake Jct. 2.6 m., Clear Lake Jct. 1.6 m., Timothy Lake-Olallie Lake Jct. (For details on these, see *The Great Heartland, Clackamas River-Mt. Hood National Forest Tour.*)

2 m., Bear Paw FS CG, on a cool stream.

3.3 m., jct., O 216.

* From forest coolness, the road—O 216—slips into a semi-naked landscape, clothed only by small trees and shrubs. 19 m., Wapinitia, which

dwindled from a homesteader stronghold to a store. (R, *13 m.* to Sim-nasho, through a drab part of the Warm Springs Reservation.) *7 m.*—on O 216—jct., US 197. *2 m.,* Maupin. (See *Central Oregon—US 197.*) *13.4 m.*—from jct., O 216, on US 26—Simnasho Jct.

    * *6.5 m.,* **Simnasho,** once an important settlement of the Warm Springs Indian Reservation. Little remains of what was here half-a-century ago—except a shack that was a school, the old missionary church, and the wooden sidewalk between the church and what was the minister's home. Turn R at Wapinitia-Kah-nee-ta Jct. The road first rides a high, naked plateau exposed to long and graphic panoramas of the Central Cascades. The range is seen as a continuum, arising from valley floors and stretch-ing as a barrier far as can be seen. Then the road enters a sea of yellowish, reddish, purplish, salmonish, brown-green rock-cropped hills—the painted waves achurn above the raw-sculptured gorge of the Warm Springs Can-yon. *13.4 m.*—from Simnasho—Kah-nee-ta Jct. Turn L. *1.2 m.,* **Kah-nee-ta,** a beautiful spa operated by the Confederated Tribes of the Warm Springs Reservation. This warm-water oasis in a saucer of juniper hills has become the foremost resort of Central Oregon. Day visitors can also swim, mineral bathe, picnic, hike, ride horses. Return *1.2 m.* to jct. Angle L. The road climbs out of the canyon to charge across an arid plateau.

Simnasho Church

9.3 m., on R, rimrock wall of kind seen often on Oregon desert. Top looks like a fortress parapet. *1.1 m.*, Warm Springs Agency, administrative center for the reservation, on US 26.

18.3 m.—from Simnasho Jct., on US 26—Warm Springs Agency. (Observe interesting design of wooden chapel of Catholic Church at approach to Agency.) The most popular road to Kah-nee-ta is from Warm Springs.

5 m., jct., Pelton and Round Butte Dams.

* *2.6 m.*, turnoff to Pelton Dam. *9.3 m.*, turnoff to Round Butte Dam.

10.5 m., Madras. (See *Central Oregon, US 97.*)

O 22—Salem to US 20

2 m.—from Market St. exit, Salem, on Int. 5—O 22 exit. *7.7 m.*, Aumsville Jct. *4.5 m.*, Sublimity-Silverton Jct. *2.2 m.*, Stayton Jct. *6.7 m.*, Mehama —jct. O 226.

From Mehama on, O 22 is one of the fairest, most exciting stretches of highway in the state, given that special quality of scenic joy by the dazzling N Santiam River.

0.8 m.—from Mehama—Elkhorn Rd.

* Turn L at Forest Guard Station for Henline Falls. The 16.8-m.-long road, which follows the Little N Santiam, is rather squiggly, but the green world is sheer pleasure and there are several CGs along the way. Drive through the tiny hamlet of Elkhorn, cross Henline Creek, and continue *1.5 m.* Small parking area across shallow ditch on L, or N, side of road. There is no sign pointing the way but an easily seen trail angles NW and in 100 yds. reaches **Henline Falls.** Henline Creek hurls itself almost 60 ft. into a steep gorge, though in summer the flow is greatly reduced. An old waterwheel stamp mill is at the falls, a remnant of a long-abandoned mine. The shaft of the mine comes out here; it goes back about 0.3 m. Other old mines are in vicinity. Inquire about them at Pearl Creek Guard Station, in area.

3.2 m., North Santiam SP. Picnic and/or fish.

2 m., Fishermen's Bend Park (BLM). Camping. Unique feature here is a picnic table more than 80 ft. long, whose top is one board, cut from a giant Douglas fir.

1.6 m., turnoff for Mill City. A spread-out town divided by the river. It may be the only Oregon town in two Oregon counties (Marion and Linn).

3 m., Gates. **Santiam Trading Post Museum,** a complex of structures dating back to 1875, consists of former stagecoach hostelry, PO and feed store.

3 m., Packsaddle County Park, start of annual Whitewater Challenge— boating the high, roaring Santiam—held late in May.

1.5 m., **Niagara Park** entrance.

* Niagara Dam, seen from parking area, was hand built in last century, but nothing much came of it, or of town, which at one time was gusty little burg. No trace of it remains. Maybe it was all a joke, starting with the naming of the town after a small falls in the river. . . . The N San-

Santiam Trading Post   Niagara Dam

tiam, chanting noisily, riffles and chutes and giggles in a green-steel blue current, frothed by a foamy crackling of whitecaps, through a fern-rock gorge. Few rivers in Oregon look more refreshing or clear or pioneer rivery than the Santiam here. A path through the forest is a foot-journey into solace. The trail follows an overhang, but is perfectly safe. Deer also use the path. See if you can discern their tracks.

5.4 m., Detroit Dam. Behind it the N Santiam is backed up 8.5 m., creating Detroit Reservoir—for all appearances a winding, dreamy, deep blue lake.

4 m., Mongold SP; considered part of Detroit Lake SP.

1.8 m., **Detroit Lake SP**, one of the finest and most popular of all Oregon SPs. CG, boating, fishing, swimming, water skiing. Advisable to make reservations as far in advance as possible.

1.5 m., Detroit, a fresh-face tourist juncture on the shores of the reservoir. Jct., Breitenbush Springs and Olallie Lake.

  * *10.5 m.,* following the gurgly Breitenbush River, **Breitenbush Springs,** two natural hot-water spas within 1 m. *19 m.,* FS Guard Station and resort at **Olallie Lake,** largest in a region of more than 100 lakes and tarns. Nearby 7210-ft. Olallie Butte reached by 4-m. trail, affords breathtaking pan-a-vistas of this magnificent terrain. At least 50 water formations are visible without field glasses. Some seem harsh and cold; others appear as liquid sapphire under a lambent sun. Olallie and other lakes sometimes seem as crowded as an overflow convention—so don't expect to be alone in the wilderness. (For roads and recreation lands N of Olallie Lake, see *The Great Heartland, Clackamas River—Mt. Hood National Forest Tour.*)

4 m., Idanha. The hamlet, once the E terminus of the Corvallis and Eastern RR, has become a tourist stop. The first clear glimpses of Mt. Jefferson are from here. More abundant views are ahead, as O 22 climbs the Cascade slope.

10.5 m., on R, Riverside FS CG. A modest-size overnight area in a grove lulled by the Santiam.

2 m., Marion Forks.

* Follow Marion Lake Rd., on L, *4.3 m.* to parking area. Foot trails lead to Lake Ann and Marion Lake, at edge of Mt. Jefferson Wilderness. *0.2 m.*, Marion Forks Salmon Hatchery. FS CG adjacent.

13.5 m., lava flow— from Nash Crater—estimated to be 3800 years old.

1.4 m., jct., US 20. (See this section, *US 20.*)

O 226—US 20 Turnoff to Mehama, O 22

O 226 begins 5.5 m. from Int. 5 Albany overpass on US 20.

2 m., Riverview Rd.

* Turn L for rural tintypes. *1.8 m.*, on R, house built circa 1870 with square nails. Barn in rear was put together about same time, with wooden pegs to hold rafters together—which they are still doing. Original shake roof was casualty of Columbus Day 1962 storm. *1.1 m.*, road forks. Take L fork. *1.6 m.*, CB built in the 1930s. Still in use. Return to forks. Continue straight toward Scio. *1.3 m.*, CB—also in use. Return to forks. Take L fork back to O 226. Turn L.

0.9 m., **Crabtree.** Turn L on Hungry Hill Rd. *1.6 m.*, CB—in use. Return to Crabtree. Store was opened about turn of century and some of it looks it. Stained glass windows in Crabtree Christian Church (1909) were taken from an earlier church. Tavern has board sidewalk around two sides of it.

7 m., Scio, Oregon's center of Czech-American activities. (For Scio area, see *The Great Heartland, H-T No. 8.*)

Covered bridge near Crabtree   **Shimanek Covered Bridge**

2.2 m., Richardson Rd.

* Turn L. *0.7 m.*, **Shimanek CB**, across Thomas Creek. Put up in 1927, remodeled in 1966. One of the last CBs with portal style architecture. To some, Shimanek has the misty delicateness of a Japanese print; to others it smacks of New England CBs in-country from salty fishing villages.

4.5 m., on R, Hannah CB, across Thomas Creek.

1.6 m., on R, Jordan CB, spanning Thomas Creek. Below bridge there has been churned up a weird rock formation, with Thomas Creek bursting into a powerful jet stream through the gap of an abandoned dam.

6.3 m., Lyons, a logging town on the N Santiam. *1.3 m.*, Mehama, a smaller logging town. O 226 joins O 22 at Mehama.

US 20—*Albany to Bend*

1.5 m., Albany to Int. 5 overpass.

5.5 m., jct., O 226. (See O 226, preceding.)

7 m., **Lebanon**, famed for its annual June Strawberry Festival, topped by the "world's largest strawberry shortcake." Town also boasts "largest plywood mill in the U.S.A." Pioneer homes, in diminishing number, dot residential streets, mostly near business section.

3.1 m., on R, Sodaville Jct.

* *1.6 m.*, **Sodaville.** The 1-acre Sodaville Springs SP, established on land donated in 1871, was quite famous for its soda water springs. But just about everything has been torn down or dried up. Straight ahead from SP. *0.2 m.*, turn R. Follow curve to R. *0.1 m.*, turn L. *0.1 m.*, at 2301 Maple, house reputedly built in 1872. A bizarre structure that compels attention. Gables face in all directions; two-storied veranda. In its

Rock formation in Thomas Creek near Jordan River covered bridge

Sodaville   Old, unoccupied house at Sodaville

day the largest and most expensive dwelling in the area. Sodaville Evangelical Church, nearby, was there when town was an important market place, long ago. Many historical traces in and around Sodaville: houses, barns, fences, hand pumps, etc. (see front cover for illustration).

2.2 m., Waterloo Jct.

* 1 m., Waterloo. A lovely county park, with mineral springs and river falls, on the S Santiam, in an area that once held flour and woolen mills.

8.4 m., Crawfordsville Jct. (See O 228 below.)

0.4 m., Sweet Home city center. In prehistoric times a mighty forest was spread over this area. All that's left of it now is silicified fossil wood—some of it gorgeously colored with clear marked grain and rings structure. Other reasons which bring rockhounds to the Sweet Home area are banded agate, carnelian agate, crystal-lined geodes, and fire-engine red jasper.

3 m., Foster, a casual roadside settlement gateway to Foster Dam and the aquatic-sports Foster Reservoir.

2.6 m., jct., Green Peter Dam and Quartzville. (A popular off-the-highway drive because of water sports facilities and historic interest.)

* 5 m., Green Peter Dam. The reservoir, holding the tributaries of the Middle Santiam, has become a water sports bowl. 4.3 m., Thistle Creek Access. Boat landing. 1.6 m., Whitcomb Creek Park. CG, picnicking, boating. 7.4 m., Dogwood PG. 5.8 m., Yellowstone Rec. Site. CG. 1.1 m., Quartzville Guard Station (FS). 0.4 m., jct., FS Rds. 1158 and 1177. Follow FS 1158, on L. 2.3 m., site of Quartzville, which in the mid-1860s was a feverish gold town, with 500 claims filed and 1000 inhabitants. Within a decade, Quartzville had become a ghost town. A second gold rush, in the 1890s, brought it back to life, but by 1902 the ghost had returned. People still flock to the area to pan for gold in the legendary creeks of yore but what was once Quartzville, with cabins, store and

saloon, is now a delightful park in the folds of the forest. FS rds. lead 30 m. to O 22, 3 m. E of Detroit. To reach O 22 by this route, follow FS 1158 for *11 m.*; then take FS 1105.

8.5 m.—from Green Peter-Quartzville Jct.—**Cascadia SP.** Giant firs rising back from the giggly, dimple-faced S Santiam. There is more spiritual satisfaction in an hour here than in a month of TV viewing.

15.5 m., **Iron Mtn. Trail.** From the parking area a 1.6-m. FS trail winds very gently into sloped woods, and alpine flowers seem always at your side. A fine way to break a long drive.

1.7 m., **Tombstone Prairie.** Long before the whites arrived, this ruffle of green was where the Indians gathered to powwow. Then the whites built a wagon road and the prairie became a CG for freighters.

6.3 m., **Pioneer Wagon Rd. Historical Marker.** At this point the old rd. crossing the Santiam Highway was part of the Willamette Valley and Cascade

South Santiam River at Cascadia State Park

Mountain Wagon Road, completed in 1869. There are still a few folks around who remember paying toll on it; it became a free rd. in 1915.

3.5 m., jct., O 126. (See this section, O 126.)

3.2 m., jct., O 22. (See earlier this section, O 22.)

5 m., turnoff for Hoodoo Bowl, one of the NW's finest ski areas.

1 m., Santiam Pass. Unobstructed views of 7841-ft. Three Fingered Jack and 7802-ft. Mt. Washington.

5 m., turnoff for **Suttle Lake,** a deep-blue basin set in a forest of tall evergreens. It and its companion, **Blue Lake,** an aquamarine crater reflecting the corniculate peak of Mt. Washington, are popular recreation areas.

0.9 m., turnoff for Camp Sherman (4 m.).

4.8 m., primary turnoff for Camp Sherman and nearby **Springs of the Metolius River** (4.5 m.).

    * The 46-m. Metolius, probably the swiftest and coldest small stream in Oregon, is the frigid, saltant child of icy springs spouting from the blind, mysterious base of 6415-ft. Black Butte. For 20 m. the coursing river points N, aiming at 10,495-ft. Mt. Jefferson. It zings through open woods of ponderosa pine and western larch, dotted with incense cedar, Douglas and lowland fir, and Engelmann spruce. Almost halfway through its length the stream bends E, forming the S boundary of the Warm Springs Indian Reservation. Then, in a dramatic climax, it rushes through a rocky gorge more than 1500 ft. deep at points, to pour into Lake Billy Chinook, the creation of Round Butte Dam, where the Metolius is merged with the Deschutes and Crooked rivers. The Metolius is regarded as one of the best rainbow trout streams in the West. The Metolius Rec. Area—famed for its warm days and crisp nights—includes guest ranch, resort and cabin facilities. Square dancing at Camp Sherman Community Hall brings together the dudes and wranglers. Camp Sherman is make-up point for pack trips to Mt. Jefferson and Three Sisters Wilderness. Wizard Falls fish hatchery at Camp Sherman.

4 m., another turnoff to Camp Sherman.

5 m., **Sisters,** a complete small town which knots together the strands of US 20, O 126 and O 242. For scenery, one of Central Oregon's most attractive towns, because of proximity to Three Sisters.

From Sisters to Bend, US 20 seems to lilt through upland meadows, so green and fertile, even into late summer, and under the cooling vigil of snow-capped peaks, so close and unblemished.

0.4 m., Sisters SP. A wayside picnic area in a stand of old-growth pine along Squaw Creek.

14 m., **Tumalo Emporium.** Restaurant immersed in 1890 decor and music. Has feel of country inn and rural store. The Pioneer Museum holds furnishings that might have been seen in old Tumalo house, and bldg. is relic of Tumalo town, started early in the century.

0.1 m., on R, Tumalo SP turnoff.

    * *1.1 m.* Camping on the Deschutes. Nights can be very windy and chill but fishing is normally fine.

0.3 m., Cline Falls Jct.

   * 10 m., county rd. through pungent backcountry to Cline Falls SP.

2 m., Tumalo SP Jct. Another rd. to the park.

2.8 m., on R, Sawyer SP turnoff. A juniper and pine haven on the Deschutes.

1.7 m., **Bend.** (See *Central Oregon, US 97.*)

O 228—Halsey (US 99E) to Sweet Home (US 20)

2 m., Int. 5 (18 m. S of Albany via freeway).

3.7 m., Brownsville turnoff.

   * 0.5 m., **Brownsville,** an early woolen mill town seeking to revive the glory days of its "mauve decade" of the 1890s. Stores and bldgs. in business district are false-fronted. Balconies of Masonic Hall were put up in early 1960s to give old structure an older and more elegant look. First Baptist Church, Main & Walnut, is kind of church structure Brownsville knew many years ago. Historical Museum is loaded with Linn County relics. S end of city park, along Calapooya River, was Kirk's Ferry, town's original name, and on the supply trail from Oregon Territory to the California gold fields. **Moyer House** (1881), built in the Italian villa style popular at the time; one of the most magnificent 19th-century homes anywhere in Oregon, and is alone worth a trip to Brownsville. Informal tours through house.

1 m., on R, **Atavista Farm.** House, which owners say was built in 1875, is as resplendent on the Moyer House and, from a landscaping perspective,

Atavista Farm near Brownsville

Gazebo behind Atavista Farm   Calapooya River covered bridge at Crawfordsville

much handsomer. Gazebo pavilion was put up in 1957 of parts from a 19th-century porch.

5.9 m., Calapooya River CB. It isn't used, except by kids who want to rest their horses and by old-timers who want a quiet spot to palaver.

0.1 m., Crawfordsville. Single-story cafe bldg. was built as two-story general store in 1890.

0.3 m., jct., Mabel and Marcola.

* The 30-m. road to Springfield, following in part the Mohawk River, is a good drive for a look at ex-hamlets (Mabel and Wendling) and villages (Mohawk and Marcola) which are destined to become middle-class suburbs of Eugene and Springfield. Two CBs on this trip—Wendling and Earnest, E of Marcola. (Wendling—4 m. E of Marcola.)

3.7 m., on R, Holley Christian Church, established in 1871. Sign reads: "Come as you are." Prized Holley purple or Calapooya blue agates are found SW of town.

4.3 m., Sweet Home (US 20.)

O 126—Eugene to Redmond

This is the McKenzie River Road, far better known as a recreation pike than as a trans-Cascade highway. The McKenzie River is so attractive—it has been called "the most beautiful clear green river in America"—and the fishing is so good, and camping places so plentiful, that thousands feast upon it every summer day. It has a rustic atmosphere with only a few pretentious touches—but garish commercialism is building up.

4 m., **Springfield.** It is hard to believe that this mill town of almost 30,000 had less than 1000 people 35 years ago and practically rolled up the sidewalks of its business block when the sun went down. Today Springfield is spread so far and fancy that even the locals sometimes get lost. Since 1957 the town has held an annual mid-July Oregon Broiler Festival. Thousands of chickens are barbecued, to the accompaniment of much hoopla.

5.7 m., Hendricks Bridge SP, a tree-shaded wayside picnic area and boat landing on the McKenzie. *8.3 m.*, Leaburg, a small hamlet scattered along the road. *2.2 m.*, on R, **McKenzie River Salmon Hatchery.** *1.9 m.*, on R, **Leaburg Dam.** Cross bridge to park and **Leaburg Trout Hatchery.**

1.6 m., **Goodpasture CB**, a 165-ft. span across the McKenzie built in 1938. A lot of people park on the S side of the bridge to fish.

Beyond the bridge, the McKenzie ripples so sweet and dimplish in summer—a different stream from the snow-bloated, mad demon of early spring.

0.9 m., Vida, just a place for river folks to pick up their mail. *0.5 m.*, on R, **House of Horses Museum.** Martha Shelley, self-taught painter and wood carver, has filled her galleries with artistic presentations which express her love and knowledge of "horses, horses, horses."

2.3 m., Ben and Kay Dorris SP. A small PG on the McKenzie, with boat landing area. Good fishing sites. *0.5 m.*, on R, trail (0.1 m.) leads down to a large overhanging rock, known to early travelers as Rock House or **Stagecoach Rock.** Stagecoach drivers would stop here on cold days and, in a cave under the rock, build a fire to thaw out their passengers.

8.1 m., Morton Memorial SP. Picnic in the woods on the bank of the McKenzie. *0.3 m.*, Finn Rock. The store and rest area derive the name, in part, from the big rock on the McKenzie. Some people say the peculiar formation resembles a shark's fin—but the place was named after pioneer settler Ben Finn. Anyway, it's a great place to fish.

3 m., Blue River, a village that seems to share the moods of the McKenzie. Blue River Reservoir Jct., L.

  * *1.5 m.*, Blue River Dam (270 ft. high) and **Reservoir.**

4.3 m., on R, Cougar Reservoir Jct.

  * *3.7 m.*, **Cougar Reservoir,** a 6-m.-long lake created by a 452-ft.-high dam backing up the S fork of the McKenzie. Three FS CGs. *1 m.*, on R, Rainbow Jct.

Martha Shelley in her House of Horses Museum, Vida

0.4 m., on L, **Holiday Farm,** a 19th-century stagecoach stop that has been converted into a restaurant, with much of the original atmosphere retained. Herbert Hoover, who was an avid McKenzie angler, stayed here often.

3.5 m., McKenzie Bridge FS CG. Delightfully rustic. *0.5 m.*, McKenzie Bridge, the last settlement on the road before reaching the E side of the Cascades. From here to Sisters, via O 242 (see below), there is not a single gas station or store.

Jct., Foley Springs.

4.5 m., a popular 19th-century hot springs resort, stagecoach station, and Foleysprings PO—now closed to public. The road goes on 5.2 m. to edge of Three Sisters wilderness.

0.3 m.—on O 126—Jennie Harris Wayside. A patch of forest canopying the McKenzie. *3.4 m.*, Paradise FS CG. A large camping area 1 m. into the woods.

0.7 m., jct., O 242. (For O 242, see below O 126.)

6.8 m., Olallie FS CG, small tent and trailer retreat providing a feeling of seclusion.

7.4 m., on L, turnoff for Ice Cap FS CG and Koosah Falls.

0.2 m., on L, Ice Cap FS CG, modest-size retreat in the woods. *0.1 m.* R from CG entrance, **Koosah Falls.** Koosah (Chinook for sky) was once called Middle Falls, being the second of three falls created when the ancient bed of the McKenzie was blocked by a number of lava flows from Belknap Crater, more than 10 m. off. It was all very recent—no more than 1500 years ago. Tamolitch Falls, to S of Ice Cap, was once called Lower Falls, and is reachable only by trail.

0.4 m., on L, **Sahalie Falls,** once called Upper Falls. The falls thunder out of pine hill clefts to cascade about 70 ft. into ponds backed by glistening, spongy moss. Trail leads to pool and to point above falls.

1.5 m., Clear Lake turnoff.

0.5 m., **Clear Lake.** FS CG. Resort. The transparent lake, in a 2000-ft. depression formed many centuries ago by the vast McKenzie lava flow, which piled up a dam across the old Santiam Valley, is fed by giant springs gushing from the NE shore—the same springs that created the McKenzie River. The lake is not only the coldest in the Cascades—almost a constant 41 degrees—but the clearest. Well-preserved tree trunks that bordered the original stream can be seen at a depth of 40 ft.

2.2 m., on L, Fish Lake FS CG. If you're expecting a lake, you'll be disappointed. Just a CG by a meadow.

From Fish Lake to US 20, both sides of the road are at the edges of deep fields of lava.

1.5 m., jct., US 20.

29 m.—O 126 and US 20 are one—Sisters.

16 m.—from Sisters, on O 126—on R, Cline Falls SP turnoff.

0.3 m., Cline Falls SP. A pleasant picnic and fishing pause on the banks of the trotting Deschutes. Follow stream to falls N of park.

Clear Lake off O 126

1.8 m., on L, **Reindeer Ranch.** Largest herd of reindeers in W, and perhaps in coterminous USA, are here. The animals are rented for commercial purposes, primarily during Christmas season.

2.3 m., Redmond. (See *Central Oregon, US 97.*)

7 m., Powell Butte, a lively rustic crossroad.

12 m., Prineville. (See *Central Oregon, US 26.*)

O 242—Jct., O 126 (Near McKenzie Bridge) to Sisters, US 20-O 126

This is, without doubt, the slowest, narrowest, crookedest, loneliest, most vulnerable and spectacular road across the Cascades. It used to be an important mtn. pike, but you seldom see a truck on the road now, and it is kept open only for recreation purposes. Snow generally closes the rd. about Thanksgiving, and it isn't plowed open until summer. So it's free for travel only about five months of the year. On all this route there isn't a single tourist accommodation. On the W slope, the road passes through woods dominated by fir; on the E slope, it's pine tree land, quiet and fragrant and cool, with the shoulders covered by pine needles, beer bottles and soda cans.

8.9 m., on R, gravel parking strip for Proxy Falls.

  * 0.5 m. trail into Three Sisters Wilderness to **Proxy Falls** and same distance—the trail splits—to **Lower Proxy Falls.** Upper Falls forks around island of firs and splashes in twin columns down terraces that are so evenly spread they seem hand-made. Then, united, Upper Falls spills lustily over thickly green-mossed stumps to a pool which has no visible outlet. Geologists say the water drains into porous lava and reappears elsewhere—no one knows where—as a lake, stream or spring. Lower Falls is an even more impressive cataract. Like the Upper Falls, it descends in two branches. But its drop is steeper and the flow fuller. It emerges from a

thicket to race down a bulging rock wall, leaving an "island" of trees in the middle. Once on the canyon floor, it reforms as a stream and heads for the Pacific. Both falls plunge about 200 ft. and were formed by a lava dam that can be traced to a volcanic flow originating from Collier Cone on the flank of N Sister.

1.4 m., Lower Alder Springs FS CG. Just space enough for a few tent sites—with the forest all around. *0.1 m.,* Alder Springs FS CG. An even smaller place—with some historic interest. During the wagon-road days, it was a corral for stock being driven across the range. (1-m. trail to glorious Linton Lake.) *0.2 m.,* snow gate. From the end of Nov. through the end of June, the gate is generally closed. Beyond this point the road puffs up Deadhorse Grade, so named because a draw horse keeled over dead on this spiraling ascent. In less than 5 m. the rd. climbs almost 1200 ft. If you don't get dizzy from the winding, the scenery may make you heady.

4.9 m., on R, Frog Camp FS CG turnoff.

* 0.3 m., Frog Camp FS CG. Only a few tent sites, but camp is popular take-off point for trips into Three Sisters Wilderness.

0.4 m., **Sisters Viewpoint.** One of the grandest panoramas of the Three Sisters. The early Methodist missionaries, who settled Salem, called these

Proxy Falls (upper)   **Proxy Falls (lower)**

alpine beauties Faith, Hope and Charity—but others decided that mountains didn't have the virtues of man.

0.3 m., on L, Scott Lake turnoff.

* 1 m., Scott Lake FS CG. Scott Lake is a lovely mirror for the Three Sisters.

2.7 m., **Belknap Crater View.** The cinder cone on the L is Big Belknap Crater; the lava cone on the R is Little Belknap Crater, which was responsible for the vast dumps of lava in the foreground.

0.6 m., on L, turnoff to West Lava FS CG. A small CG that is an island in a lake of lava. 0.7 m., on R, Huckleberry Lake turnoff.

* 1 m., tiny lake on border of lava fields.

2 m., **Dee Wright Observatory,** above 5324-ft. McKenzie Pass. In the center of the most extensive lava flows in Oregon. Astronauts destined for the moon came here to practice.

"Nowhere in the continental United States," says the FS, "is there a more impressive view of recent volcanic activity or a greater variety of volcanic forms than at McKenzie Pass. On a clear day one can see the crest of the Oregon volcanic Cascades from Mt. Hood to Three Sisters. Broken, rugged lava flows cover seventy-five square miles, and cinder cones, land islands and glaciers dot the landscape."

View from Dee Wright Observatory at McKenzie Pass; Mt. Washington in background

Mt. Hood is 78.5 m. from the observatory; Mt. Jefferson is 28.5 m. off. North Sister, Middle Sister and Mt. Washington are all less than 10 m. away. Some of the clearly observable landmarks have fascinating names: Bald Peter, Horsepasture Mtn., Little Brother, and The Husband.

The 0.5-m. Lava River Trail, starting and ending near the observatory, is, at least in places, part of the McKenzie Salt Springs and Deschutes Wagon Road, constructed between 1866–72. The rd. was built across the lava fields, despite the torturous terrain, because it was 1000 ft. lower in elevation than the older Scott Trail (1862), which crossed the summit near N Sister. Upon completion, toll was charged. It became a free county rd. in 1898—12 years before the first automobile wheezed over the summit in 1910—and a state highway in 1917. Some folks say it hasn't improved much since then; but neither has the scenery deteriorated.

A marker on the Lava River Trail reads: "You are standing near the western edge of a lava flow from Yapoah Crater. The flow is eight miles long and about a half mile wide. . . . Geologists believe this flow is about 2700 years old, one of the most recent in the area. . . . Do not leave the trail. The blocks of lava are unstable and extremely sharp."

Oh yes, one more thing: There are rest stations at the pass. A lot of people find them convenient at this location.

The road uncoils down the E slope of the Cascades, and, when the lava runs out, gushes of ponderosa pine fill the space.

11 m., on L, Cold Spring FS CG. A fine time to visit here is in autumn, when the quaking aspen turn into sheets of burnt gold.

4 m., Sisters. Here O 242 is swallowed by US 20 and O 126.

O 58—Eugene to US 97

Prior to construction of Int. 5, O 58 was the most feasible route from the Willamette Valley to San Francisco. It is still the best way to Klamath Falls.

6 m.—from Eugene, on Int. 5—start of O 58.

9 m., **Pleasant Hill**, founded by Elijah Bristow, veteran of the War of 1812, in 1846. Only three mementos of old settlement remain: replica of a fireplace built with the original stones of the 1846 cabin; the cemetery, one of Oregon's oldest burial grounds (with second Pleasant Hill schoolhouse on ridge); and Pleasant Hill Church, oldest of the First Christian denomination in state.

5 m., Lowell Jct.

* *1 m.*, Lowell, gateway to nearby Dexter, Fall Creek and Lookout Point Reservoirs. Primary recreation is boating.

21 m., Oakridge, largest community on O 58, with less than 4000 persons.

2.5 m., turnoff for Hills Creek Reservoir. (Packard FS CG 5.5 m. S of turnoff.)

7.2 m., McCredie Springs, site of an early spa.

11.3 m., turnoff for Salt Creek Falls.

* Narrow FS rd. to top of falls, *0.2 m.* PG and turnaround. Foot trail from O 58 to bottom of falls. FS CG. **Salt Creek Falls**, on the head-

Colliding Rivers

waters of the Willamette, leaps 286 ft. from an overhanging cliff into an emerald gorge. Falls are second highest in Oregon.

4.2 m., turnoff L for **Waldo Lake,** Oregon's second largest natural lake.

* Five FS CGs within 10 m., including one that can be reached only by boat.

1.5 m., W turnoff to **Odell Lake.** Gouged out by an ancient glacier, it is 6 m. long, 3 m. wide and has sounded depths to 2000 ft. Flanked by 8744-ft. Diamond Peak and the reflected 7811-ft. Maiden Peak. One of the state's best known fishing lakes.

5 m., E turnoff to Odell Lake.

2 m., turnoff to **Crescent Lake,** a vividly blue alpine pool, also popular with fishermen and campers.

* 2 m. to lake. 5 m., end of paved rd. around W side of lake. 9 m., edge of **Diamond Peak Wilderness.** No vehicles in this wonderworld of nature.

17 m., jct., US 97. N, *57 m.*, Bend. S, *80 m.*, Klamath Falls. (See *Central Oregon, US 97.*)

O 138—Roseburg to Diamond Lake and US 97

No matter how highly this road has been recommended, you will affirm that it has not been overpraised. Easy to drive, never boring, free of commercialization, and with excellent side trips available, it is unquestionably one of the finest river drives in the state.

16.4 m., on L, **Colliding Rivers Viewpoint.** Here the N Umpqua, swift and deep, funnels into a white water chute and smashes head-on into the rapids of Little River, racing in from the S, in a dramatic rocky canyon scene. Picnic area at Viewpoint.

* Turn S, or to the R going E—across road from Viewpoint— for unusual Forest Tour along Little River. *1.8 m.*, log pond. *5.2 m.*, Cavitt Creek CB. (Across bridge, turn R up Cavitt Creek Rd. *1 m.*, picnic in the woods. *3.3 m.*, Cavitt Creek Falls. CG.) *4 m.*—beyond CB—parking for Wolf Creek Falls Trail. (*1 m.*—across footbridge and uphill past weird rock formations of volcanic tuff, to a falls that cascades 75 ft. to a pool and then plummets 50 ft. in a second drop. Picnic near falls.) *1 m.*, on R, parking for Wolf Creek Nature Trail. (*0.3 m.*, across small dam, trail through flowery woods.) *0.2 m.*, Wolf Creek FS CG. *0.2 m.*, logging camp built about 1942 and used by church for summer camp program. *2.9 m.*, Emile (pronounced *E'-mile*) BLM CG. *1.1 m.*, Coolwater FS CG. *10.4 m.*, Lake in the Woods FS CG. Old trail cabin, pretty lake behind dam, and two delightful waterfalls—each *0.7 m.* down either Hemlock Falls Trail or Yakso Falls Trail. Forest Tour follows Little River all the way—except for side trips in parentheses.

1.1 m.—from Colliding Rivers Viewpoint—Glide. Tourist facilities.

5 m., cataracts and riffling white water of the N Umpqua combine for striking river scenery. (Beyond this point, fly angling only.)

6.3 m., Susan Creek SP, in a jumbled canyon on the river.

The Umpqua is a temperamental stream and from bend to bend you cannot predict its behavior. It will be smooth as glass, a pool without a ripple in it, and suddenly it will clash against rocks, break into white-topped, blue-

Angling on the North Umpqua

Fishing on the North Umpqua near Rock Creek

North Umpqua River scene   Steamboat Falls

bellied riffles, swirl, froth and snarl. And then it will be peaceful again, the face of innocence. The road almost hugs the river for 32 m., and *always* there is the thick, real forest.

3.9 m., Fall Creek FS CG, near a narrow cleft of the stream. *2.5 m.,* Bogus Creek FS CG. *3.4 m.,* Steamboat. Cafe-gas-groceries. *0.6 m.,* Steamboat Falls Jct.

  * *0.6 m.,* road forks. (L, Cottage Grove, *49 m.,* over a rough, narrow rd., with no town or station between.) Straight *5 m.,* turnoff for **Steamboat Falls.** (Straight at turnoff—*26 m.* to Bohemia Saddle; *44 m.* to Oakridge. Neither road is bad in fair weather and both are very sparsely settled.) *0.8 m.,* Steamboat Falls FS CG. Steamboat Creek finds an opening in the wide rock bed, executes a 90-degree turn, slides in sheer tide into a small pen, and roars down a wall that looks like the exterior of a SW pueblo. The drop isn't very high, but the sound and the fury and the odd geology make up an impressive happening.

7.7 m.—from Steamboat Falls Jct.—Horseshoe Bend FS CG. *0.8 m.,* Dry Creek Store.

  * Follow Bradley Trail back of store for *3 m.*—an arduous climb—to **Dog Creek Indian Cave.** Trail passes grave of pioneer Bill Bradley, whose favorite gun is bolted to the headstone. He was killed, according to the inscription, "while attempting to subdue a wild horse." The inside walls of the cave are covered with pictographs, some suggesting hunting scenes.

In its higher stages the trail winds through virgin timber, salal, and fern, and Oregon grape and fir needles carpet the red soil. Rock chimneys and natural arches are within short hiking distances. And, in spring, the purple blooms of the rare Kalmiopsis are found. When the wind is still and there are no voices on the ridge, the chant of the Umpqua is heard as a call coming from the far end of a tunnel. Early curiosity seekers carted away all easily removable artifacts from the cave. It is hoped the FS will give the cave the protection it deserves.

12 m.—past views of Eagle Rock, Brobdingnag formation which towers imperiously above the surrounding forest, and the much-photographed walls of columnar basalt of Soda Springs—turnoff to Toketee Lake. FS CG. *8 m.*— with the grand view along the way being the needle-like spire of 9182-ft. Mt. Thielsen—turnoff to Clearwater Falls FS CG.

North Umpqua east of Steamboat

12 m., **Diamond Lake,** as diversified in recreation as any lake in the state and in so scenically bounteous a setting that its admirers call it "Gem of the Cascades." Village, lodge, FS CG—the works.

7 m.—from Diamond Lake village—turnoff to Crater Lake National Park.

* *16.9 m.,* via west rim lake road, Crater Lake Lodge.

15 m., jct., US 97. *63 m.,* Klamath Falls. (See *Central Oregon, US 97.*)

O 62—Medford to Crater Lake and Klamath Falls

7 m., jct., O 140. (See *O 140* below.)

3 m., turnoff for Eagle Point.

* *0.6 m.,* **Putman Brothers,** last stone-ground flour mill in Oregon, in 1872 bldg.

3.2 m., jct., O 234. (See *The Great Heartland, Shunpiking—US 99.*)

0.7 m., Butte Falls Jct.

* *16 m.,* Butte Falls. This amiable settlement of about 400 is "fenced in" by cattle guards. (A rd. SE tugs 20 m. to O 140. Bountiful views of Mt. McLoughlin, which early settlers called "Snowy Butte.")

5.6 m., Shady Cove, nestled against the frothy Rogue River. Deer are sometimes seen at edge of trees beyond E side of rd. in N part of town.

2.3 m., jct. O 227—to Canyonville. (See *The Great Heartland, Shunpiking—US 99.*)

The drive up this Rogue River highway is exhilarating in every sense. Farmsteads give way to ranches and ranches to woods as the country thins of year-round residents. It is a very busy road—too busy for most people to enjoy, and those who close their eyes until they reach Crater Lake miss much beauty.

8 m., Casey SP, in gentle woodlands along the Rogue. Boat ramp. *1.5 m.,* McLeod SP, a Rogue wayside leaning against a heavily hirsute hillside. Boat ramp. *7.8 m.,* Laurelhurst SP. Camp on the shoulder of the Rogue. Good fishing. *5 m.,* Prospect. Store, station. *11 m.,* Union Creek Camp, near the Rogue River Gorge, through which the white water stream plunges in youthful exuberance. *1.4 m.,* jct., O 230.

* *24 m.*—chasing the leapfrog Rogue through the shifting tones of the Umpqua National Forest—O 138, at SE corner of Diamond Lake. South Shore Picnic Area good place to pause.

16 m., Crater Lake Lodge Jct.

* *4.8 m.,* Crater Lake Lodge, at rim of **Crater Lake,** and starting point of Ranger-guided and bus tours around lake.

From 1853, when the lake was first seen by a white man, until 1869, when two daring travelers reached Wizard Island and bestowed the present name upon the waters, this faerie ultramarine bowl was known as Deep Blue Lake, Mysterious Lake and Lake Majesty, all appropriate.

The lake, chaliced in the caldera of an extinct volcano, Mt. Mazama, which may have reached a height of 15,000 ft. before its suicidal eruption eons ago, is walled by cliffs whose majestic proportions and configurations would anywhere else be an object of wonderment. Combined with the lake, one of

Crater Lake

the deepest, bluest and most beautiful in the world, the total is so devastating upon the senses as to render silence more credible than words.

It is believed that until 1888 the lake had no fish. In that year, William Gladstone Steel gently slipped 37 fingerlings into the lake, survivors of the 600 he scooped from the Rogue River and hauled in a bucket the long and tormenting miles, pausing at every stream to freshen the water. Over the roughest terrain he carried the bucket in his hand. He regarded it as something of a miracle that the few survivors had sufficient life to swim away, even feebly. Crater Lake now has a fish population of thousands.

The National Park is more than the lake: it comprises baroque volcanic formations, the richly tinted "Pinnacles," velvety meadows and dreamy marshes, more than 500 species of flowering plants and ferns, more than 70 species of birds and many animals. Look for the red, yellow and black flair of the western tanager; listen for the silvery tones of the hermit thrush. John Muir wrote: "A thousand wonders are calling. Look up and down and round about you."

18 m.—from Crater Lake Lodge Jct.—jct., O 232.

* *3 m.*, Kimball SP, at the headwaters of the deep blue, transparent Wood River. CG in pine and fir. *24 m.*, jct., US 97—for N.

7 m., site of Old Ft. Klamath, established in 1863 and active until 1889. Reconstructed guardhouse has pictorial museum. The Modoc leaders hanged for their part in the "Modoc War" are buried here, their graves fenced to protect them from vandals. In death, they receive more care than they did in life.

7 m., jct., US 97. 23 m., Klamath Falls. (See *Central Oregon, US 97*.)

O 140, Jct., O 62, 7 m. N of Medford—to Klamath Falls

This is the newest, safest, swiftest and most scenic route to Klamath Falls.

34 m., turnoff R for Fish Lake FS CG. Fish Lake is one of the best mtn. lakes for rainbow trout in this part of the Cascades.

6.5 m., turnoff for **Lake of the Woods**, a soul-stirring beauty. Above the Shasta fir and white fir forests which engulf the lake rises the white symmetrical cone of 9495-ft. Mt. McLoughlin. A trail leads to its summit, from where the eye roves into Calif. CG, PG, lodge, cabins, store.

* Adjacent to the lake is the roadless 23,071-acre **Mountain Lakes Wilderness**, a wildlife sanctuary. Pack trains make up at Lake of the Woods for climbs to the 6000- and 7000-ft.-elevation lakes.

6.8 m., turnoff N to **Upper Klamath National Wildlife Refuge**, where majestic lake and hill scenery, the whooshing of waters and the thousand tongues of bird and mammal life-forms make puny the voice of man. Here, happily, the hunter, the shotgun and the bird-call invitation to slaughter are not welcome.

* 24 m., skirting the Refuge, Fort Klamath, on O 62.

24 m.—from Refuge Jct.—along W shore of Upper Klamath Lake, whose clear and marshy waters are home or waystops to nearly every kind of North American waterfowl, Klamath Falls. (See *Central Oregon, US 97*.)

Dead Indian Road—Ashland to O 140

Until the completion of O 140, this foolishly named rd. (can you imagine a "Dead White Man Road"?) was the swiftest route from Medford and Ashland to Klamath Falls. It is still a fine rd., but has been superseded by O 140, at least from Medford. 38 m., at Lake of the Woods, O 140.

O 66—Ashland to Klamath Falls

At one time O 66—or the Green Springs Road, as it is sometimes called—was the main route between the Rogue River settlements and the Klamath Basin. It followed, though imprecisely in some instances, the paths of explorers and the Applegate Trail and was traveled by freight and stage lines. But, because it is so up-and-down, and twisty and narrow, and because better roads were built, O 66 has been relegated to a secondary position. 18 m., Tubb Spring SP, a forested wayside with a "different" roadside fountain. 33 m., Keno. Store-cafe-station. 12 m., Klamath Falls. (For Klamath Falls, see *Central Oregon, US 97*.)

Central Oregon

Oregon's "Old West" lies E of the Cascades. It is an immense land, with much of its charm hidden—especially from those who race through it.

Int. 80N—The Dalles to Jct., O 74

The Dalles. Cut into a boulder in City Park are the words: **END OF THE OLD OREGON TRAIL 1843–1906.** Even while the covered wagons were still arriving en masse, The Dalles had become a prominent port for steamboats. When Wasco County was created in 1854, it embraced all of Oregon E of the Cascades and parts of what are now Idaho, Montana and Wyoming. Only physical reminders of that era are the Surgeons Quarters, sole remaining bldg. of Old Fort Dalles (1850) and now **Fort Dalles Museum,** 15th & Garrison; the first county courthouse (1859) which stood at present city hall site, 3d & Court, but has been relegated to weedpatch W of natatorium, at W end of city; and **Pulpit Rock** (see front cover for illustration), a natural lectern of upthrust conglomerate from which early Methodist ministers preached to emigrants and Indians (12th & Court). The Dalles, in addition to the fort, has three other museums: **Carpenter's,** a collection of early American hand tools, especially those used by a carpenter of the 19th century (4th near Union); **Nichols,** in the rear of the no-longer used St. Paul's Episcopal Church (1875), geological and paleontological objects, but most impressive is the beautiful, unblemished church chapel (Union near 5th); and **Winquatt,** artifacts of mid-Columbian Indians (1 m. E of town—take R turn from US 197 just before approaching bridge across river). Other points of interest in this very historic city include: **St. Peter's Church** (1897), 3d & Lincoln; **Smith Callaway Chapel,** second courthouse of Wasco County, 3d & Union; **Government Mint** (1862), which never produced a coin, now rear section of storage warehouse at 710 E 2d; The Dalles Mural, a dramatic 92-ft.-long, 9-ft.-high mural depicting chronology of The Dalles region, in U.S. National Bank, 401 Washington; house at 112 W 4th, which has the stained glass windows, gingerbread and ornate iron grill fence that was prominent in the architecture of the late 19th century; and **Sorosis Park,** the highest point on Scenic Drive—classic views from the observation point of the city, Mt. Hood and Mt. Adams.

2.8 m.—from city center exit, The Dalles—Jct., US 197—to S, and The Dalles bridge, to N. (See US 197 below.)

1.8 m., turnoff for **The Dalles Dam.**

8.1 m., on R, view of **Long House,** Celilo Village.

0.2 m., jct., O 206.

Nichols Museum, formerly St. Paul's Episcopal Church, The Dalles

* L, *0.2 m.*, Celilo Park, greensward on the river, where Indians fished for centuries before the white man's dam erased their cherished Celilo Falls. R from jct., *0.3 m.*, Celilo Village, Indian hamlet.

* O 206—Celilo Jct. to Condon. A high and open rd., racing across wheatlands where distance seems fixed and time rooted. Few people pause to fill themselves with the immense panoramas, probably because few outsiders travel this Fulton Canyon Rd. Here, as nowhere else, the march of power towers reaches its apex of symbolism: with a bit of imagination they appear as "men from Mars."

3 m., Deschutes River SP. Camp, picnic or fish on historic grounds. Here the wagon trains on the Oregon Trail forded the Deschutes. Women and children were sometimes ferried across in canoes by Indians, who wanted clothing as toll. Some of the emigrants resented the Indians acting as whites—charging for service.

Long House, Celilo Village

7.9 *m.*, on R, pioneer church bldg. in a locust grove, so known to people hereabouts as "Locust Grove Church." Once the lily of the valley to its parishioners, church bldg. has been used as pig, sheep and hay barn.

4.5 *m.*, Wasco, looking larger than its 400 or so population. A grain town that also thrives from being at the jct. of O 206 and US 97. (For side trip: take Airport Rd. *4 m.* to Klondike. Store, started during homesteader days, and early school, both abandoned. The gold that comes to Klondike farmers is off the wheat. From Klondike a 3.5-m county rd. will bring you back to O 206, E of Wasco.)

"Men from Mars," scene along O 206

Old Locust Grove Church now used as a barn

15.2 m.—from Wasco, on O 206—Burres SP, wayside on the John Day River. *25.5 m.*, Condon. (See this section, O 19.)

(*41 m.*, continuing on O 206, spiraling through and over and around seas of grain, Heppner, O 74. For more on O 206 between Condon & Heppner, see O 19, Condon.)

7.2 m. on 80N, from jct., O 206—Biggs Jct., US 97. (See this section, US 97.)

* *0.2 m.*, L for bridge to Yakima; *0.1 m.* more, to R, Biggs, freeway facility. Tourist accommodations.

5.5 m., Rufus, a dry jumble of a roadside stop. Turnoff for **John Day Dam,** largest on the Columbia touching Oregon.

2.3 m., turnoff for John Day Dam Viewpoint. *2 m.*, turnoff for John Day River Rec. Area.

(John Day was a young Virginian who came W in 1811 with the Astoria-bound Wilson Price Hunt party. Becoming sick near the Snake River in Dec., Day was forced to fall behind. His journey to Ft. Astoria, which he reached with rescuers the following May, was a nightmare. He suffered severe hunger and illness and was robbed and beaten by Indians, who left him naked near the mouth of the river bearing his name. Late in June 1812, he set out with Robert Stuart for St. Louis, but in a few days became paranoid and wild and was returned to Ft. Astoria. Places named after him are probably the only ones in Oregon honoring a man acknowledged to have been violently insane, but there are doubts about the mental status of some other men whose names dot the state.)

23.6 m., jct., O 19. (See this section, O 19.)

* 0.4 m., **Arlington.** This may be Oregon's most modern small town. It was built anew because construction of the John Day Dam caused Columbia water to inundate the old town. City park, a token of grass and saplings, faces river pond. Out here, in the naked aridness, the park is an oasis, especially when the wind breezes through the water.

9.3 m., jct., O 74. (See this section, O 74.)

US 197—80N to US 97

11.9 m., Dufur Jct.

* 0.8 m., **Dufur**, a sleepy market town with an aged business section. The old-timers say they can recall when the hills were covered with apple

Cowpoke comes flying off a brahma bull at All-Indian Rodeo

Action at All-Indian Rodeo, Tygh Valley

trees; some of the largest orchards in the state were here. Nobody seems to know why the land was turned to grain—probably more profitable. In spring the hills, as all along the way to Maupin, are so moist-green you think you can squeeze the color out of them. Later they turn golden, rust, black and, in winter, white.

10.6 m., summit, Tygh Ridge. The high ridge to the L was trod by the ill-fated Meek Cutoff Party of 1845.

5.7 m., on L, home of colorful All-Indian Rodeo, held in mid-May.

1.2 m., jct., O 216.

* *6 m.*, on L, at site of old schoolhouse, rough rd. leads N *2.5 m.* to Conroy Homestead, early 20th-century plains house. *0.3 m.*, beyond, reachable only by foot, two small rock piles mark location of at least two graves of the Meek Cutoff party. *3 m.* beyond Conroy Homestead, on dirt trace, ruts of old Military Wagon Road. Along the way there are barns, houses and fences built by the pioneers and no longer occupied or maintained. *1.7 m.*, on O 216, **Sherar's Bridge**, once an important waypoint on The Dalles-Canyon City toll road. Nothing remains of the inn, stagecoach station, livery stable and houses owned by Joseph Sherar, who collected exorbitant tolls from stockmen and travelers to cross his bridge, also gone. The present span is not of that vintage.

The Deschutes River, a frothy, greenish stream, swirls and ripples through a low, rocky canyon. Cinder-colored ledges extend from the cliff to form a trough, so that the stream has to fight its way through the narrow pen, creating riffles and cauldrons as it battles its encagement. Under permit by federal treaty, members of the Confederated Tribes of the Warm Springs Reservation fish on both sides of the stream from rocks or home-made platforms. All other Indians prohibited.

Vestige of early homesteader days on Smock Prairie; Mt. Hood in background

Smock Prairie School

20.3 *m.*—through bleak, windswept land—US 97. (See this section, US 97.)

Turnoff W to Tygh Valley for historical side trip to Barlow Rd. country.

* 0.3 m., Tygh Valley, site of the late-summer Wasco County Fair. *5.8 m.*, Wamic, where stood the E gate of the Barlow Toll Rd. From Wamic Store, *0.5 m.*, Three Corners. Turn L. *0.9 m.*, Four Corners. Turn R. *0.3 m.*, Lone Pine Cemetery. *0.2 m.*, Harvey-Nelson Corner. Turn L. *1.4 m.*, Rock Creek. *0.4 m.*, on R, early log cabin, or shed. *0.7 m.*, Gate Creek, which was for a while site of a toll station. *1.2 m.*, on R, pioneer **Smock Prairie School.** *0.2 m.*, Barlow Rd. (Straight, *16.2 m.*, down rough White River Rd., which many emigrants used, O 216.) At Barlow Rd., turn R, going W on dirt rd. *1.2 m.*, cattle guard on Smock Prairie

Wheelchair fishing at handicapped fishing ramp, Deschutes Canyon Access Road

meadow. (24 m., O 35.) Beyond the turnoff—from the cattle guard to Rock Creek Dam and Reservoir, 5 m.—the FS rd. is narrow and at places impassable for low-centered vehicles.

6.8 m.—from Tygh Valley Jct.—jct., O 216, to W. (See *Trans-Cascade Roads, US 26.*)

2.8 m., **Maupin**, atop a plateau commanding awesome views of the Deschutes canyonlands. The town is the starting and the return point for one of the most unusual and gratifying rail trips in the West. The Burlington Northern mixed freight leaves Maupin each day, except Sunday, at (supposedly) 2:53 a.m. standard time, for Bend. Passengers are carried in an old passenger car hitched on as a caboose. The train winds through the Deschutes River Canyon, pausing at several points. A favorite getting-off spot is South Jct., 31 m. S of Maupin. The train crew, which keeps abreast of such things, advises passengers where the "most fabulous" trout fishing is. But for those who want to see a wild gorge, a rocky cavern hidden in a crease of silence, a rage of Nature, and camp beside a clear, talking-to-itself river, fishing is not all-important. The return schedule from South Jct. daily except Sat. and Sun. is 1:48 a.m. and arrival in Maupin is 3:01 a.m. On Sat., the train leaves South Jct. at 9:13 a.m. and reaches Maupin at 10:20 a.m. But, to be safe, check schedules.

0.8 m., jct., **Deschutes River Access Rd.**

    * Opened several years ago, this BLM stream pike penetrates deep into relatively unsullied canyon country, with high, multicolored bluffs and some strange rock formations. The sight of deer is not rare and birdlife is plenteous, particularly chukars, pheasants, blue herons, turkey vultures, geese, ducks and mountain jays. 3 m., Handicapped Fishing Ramp, supposedly the only such facility in the nation. Wheelchair anglers love it. 5 m., view of Sherar's Falls. 10 m., Beavertail Rec. Site, with BLM CG. 7 m., Macks Canyon. BLM CG. Indians camped here several thousand

years ago. The BLM asks you to help preserve the evidence of their existence for archeological study. Nearby Cedar Island is blue heron rookery.

Beyond the jct. the rd. (US 197) climbs to a plateau and runs through savage landscape, as frightening to the city eye as any terrain in the state. Note the rock piles used as corner posts.

21.2 m., US 97. (See US 97 below.)

Shaniko Jct. (12 m., Shaniko. See US 97 below.)

US 97—80N to California Line

This is the great artery of central Oregon, the most important N-S road E of the Cascades. But the best viewing is off it.

0.3 m., Biggs, heavy-duty freeway stop.

9.3 m., **Wasco** (pop. about 400), which will seem larger in retrospect, after you have driven about 75 m. You won't find another drug store until you reach Madras. Jct., O 206. (See this section, 80N.)

Now the road is a black band cut through the enormous wheatlands of Sherman County, one of the great grain baskets of Oregon. Grain elevators in this area are part of the landscape. In most towns they are just off the highway.

8.8 m., **Moro**, smallest county seat in Oregon, with about 300 people. But, being a market place, it looks bigger; and, being modern, it has up-to-

Deschutes River Canyon from access road

Indians fishing at Sherar's Falls; view from Deschutes River access road

date motels. **Sherman County Court House** (1899) looks even older on inside than it does on outside. *9.6 m.,* Grass Valley, another grain elevator village. Unlike Wasco and Moro, it shows signs of fatigue. *0.5 m.,* jct., O 216. (See preceding, *US 197*). *12.2 m.,* Kent. That potato-shed-looking structure across the road from the Kent store housed the only generator in town before electricity was brought in from the outside.

O 218–Shaniko to Fossil

15.8 m., **Shaniko.** In recent years there has been an effort to turn Shaniko into a touristy "ghost town," an Oregon Knott's Berry Farm—without the berries. The "church" was a schoolhouse carted in from Bakeoven, to the NW. The town never had a church. "Boot Hill" is a fake; the town never had a cemetery. The caboose never rolled into Shaniko.

Still, though land values have soared, the population increased (up from 39 to 75 in a decade), and modernization introduced (TV and a two-unit motel in a stationary trailer), Shaniko remains Oregon's most interesting natural town, still more rooted in the past than caught up with today's thing-umajigs. Unlike Jacksonville, it hasn't been invaded by artists and artisans; most of Shaniko's citizens are elderly males who are native to the high plains.

Sherman County Courthouse

Founded in 1876 by August Scherneckau (the Indians pronounced it Shaniko) as Cross Hollow, the settlement was lifted from obscurity in 1900 when it was made a RR terminus. The boom which followed gave it the title of "Wool Shipping Center of the World." The usual frontier town took shape—with gaudy hotels, saloons, scarlet houses, livery stables, a department store, etc. Dull moments were few. Millions of sheep grazed on the plateau; eight-horse (or mule) freight wagons tinkled into town, piled high with wool; cowhands and sheepherders swaggered from saloon to saloon, whooping and scrapping. Then came battles between cattlemen and sheepmen; the last such skirmishes in the state were fought here.

For a brief decade Shaniko lived high. Then another RR was built, to the W, and Shaniko dwindled as a shipping and trading center. In 1950 the last tracks into town were torn up. And few sheep are now found in this area.

Shaniko today has several outdoor and indoor museums, all charmingly amateurish and bucolic, and probably the largest collection of buggies and buckboards in the state; a narrow two-story city hall that was boarded up for 25 years before being "restored"; a blockhouse-shaped structure which was for years the town's waterworks; a rambling schoolhouse that lost its last pupils decades ago; board sidewalks; homesteaders' cabins, some long empty; and the **Shaniko Hotel**—built in 1900 as the Columbia "Southern Queen of the Highland Hostelries." A horse trough in front is always filled with water.

The dining room, containing the beautifully carved back-bar of an early saloon, is a miniature museum of central Oregana. Food is served family style at old-fashioned, oilcloth-covered tables.

Beyond the town and across the wavy highlands, far on the W lip of the plain, Mt. Jefferson and Mt. Hood mushroom white above the ocher-purple plateau, like coned clouds frozen in the blue-burnished sky.

Jct., O 218. The direct rd. to the wonderful world of Wheeler County.

Buggy and wagon museum, Shaniko   **Antelope Loop**

*7.7 m.—with many switchbacks in the lower part—Antelope. The switchbacks are gentle and, at points, the pastel Antelope Valley appears as a set of cameos framed by tawny hills. Antelope a decade ago was a sleepy portrait of stagecoach days. But almost all the colorful bldgs. have burned or been torn down. It's just a trickle of houses under a lane of poplars now. Antelope Community Church (1896) has been restored to as near as possible original condition by citizens. Back altar, once part of Willowdale Church, was shipped from the East as gift from pioneer Episcopal bishop. Store-cafe-gas-PO—all in the same family.

0.3 m., jct. (W, 13.4 m., US 97. The small farms of homesteader days have given way to a few large ranches.)

Turn L with O 218. 1.1 m., on R, Brown's Agate Beds. Commercial digging in sagebrush rangeland. 2.7 m., Ashwod Jct.

(19.5 m., **Ashwood.** At one time it boasted the liveliest saloon and the biggest dance hall in the county. It's very quiet now. Store, grade school, grange hall, a few houses—and Ash Butte, with its "witness tree," as its constant companion. Double rainbows over nearby Greater Butte, which photographs pink, never fail to awe. Fine rockhounding around Ashwood —particularly the green moss beds of Darrel Friend and the petrified wood of the Tom McDonald Ranch.

(For the adventurous, there is a 41.5-m. gravel rd. from Ashwood SE to US 26, 2.8 m. W of Mitchell; a far-off rd. threading through vast, still range country where the complaint of a crow may be heard for miles and where a newcomer is an object of curiosity. This distant, half-hidden land, kneaded by the incessant elements, is veined by creeks and mounded by the grotesquely attractive hills of the "Mitchell Sea," vaults of tree leaves and plant fossils millions of years old. The rd. passes **Painted Hills SP,** in whose Eocene Clarno formation the fossils are abundant.)

From Ashwood Jct. to Fossil, O 218 is hauntingly strange and aloof and inconstant. From Antelope to Fossil there is not a store or station, few houses, and little traffic. The terrain is ever shifting—in formation, color, elevation and mood. For miles & miles the road winds downhill, often deceptively, so that one has the impression of a camera moving in gradually from long-range panning to detailed closeups.

11.1 m., Clarno, on the John Day River. During the homesteader days, Clarno had a PO, its site being wherever the postmaster lived. Clarno is still on the map, though only one family lives here. (There is also a small Grange hall.) Beyond the river, the rimrock hills have been fluted, spired, pinnacled and turreted by wind sculpturing. The natives discourage climbing these hills—infested with rattlers, they say.

3.4 m., Clarno SP. Remarkable salmon-colored rock battlements here, overlooking road. From a distance they appear as the ruins of a Roman fortress.

16.3 m., jct., O 19. 0.3 m., **Fossil.** (See this section, O 19.)

19.6 m.—on US 97 from Shaniko—Antelope Jct. (*13.7 m.*, Antelope.)

Suddenly the bleak, acrid, rocky landscape turns lush with grass—the miracle of water. The transformation is short-lived, but while there is sight of cattle and meadows the world seems different.

0.7 m., Willowdale. Store-cafe-station.

2 m., turnoff to Priday Ranch (6 m. E), popular commercial agate beds.

14.4 m., jct., US 26. *0.5 m.*, **Madras**, which was a crude homesteader trading center until the drought and the depression. The construction of dams and reservoirs—meaning the impounding and transportation of stream water—have brought "green gold" to the valley and made Madras not only an agricultural pivot point but the hub of a vast recreation area.

For a close-up of some of the rec. area around Madras, follow below:

* Turn W at D St. *0.8 m.*, turn R at Belmont Lane for Round Butte Dam. *6.8 m.*, turn L for Round Butte Dam Viewpoint. *1.7 m.*, turn R. *0.7 m.*, **Round Butte Dam.**

View from Round Butte Dam

The drive to the dam is one of the most soul gripping in central Oregon. Mt. Jefferson seems to be erupted from the plain and Mt. Hood, Three-Fingered Jack and the Three Sisters are apparitions which float in the bluish-amber sky. On one side of the road, at places, are greening fields, lavishly sprinkled and aided by an intricate system of irrigation ditches. On the other side of the road there are deep, unfolding vistas of desert rimrock, mesa, sage and gutted wasteland. The road rides high above the valley which feeds into Madras, and the views from the ridge pike extend clear to the Ochoco Range.

These are the views from the Round Butte Dam Observatory: slightly to the L is Mt. Jefferson; ahead is Mt. Hood. Below to the L, beyond the juniper, is the Metolius River. Directly below is Lake Billy Chinook, which holds the waters of the Metolius, the Deschutes and the Crooked rivers. Beyond Billy Chinook Lake gleams Lake Simtustus, which is the amalgamation of the rivers under the name of the Deschutes. (Lake Simtustus CG is 5.5 m. above the lake.)

Lake Billy Chinook, the reservoir behind Round Butte Dam, was given the name by the Confederated Tribes of the Warm Springs Reservation in commemoration of a tribesman who served John C. Fremont as guide and scout on his exploration of Central Oregon in 1843.

Return to rd. from dam lookout. Turn R toward Cove Palisades SP. *4.4 m.*, turn R for viewpoint of the water-carved, wind-eroded, sunbrowned canyon. *0.2 m.*, Viewpoint. The Deschutes and the Crooked are seen, together with a patch of the Metolius, forming Billy Chinook Lake. In summer the waters are specked with power boats, each with its own

Divide of Lake Billy Chinook into Crooked River (lower left) and Deschutes River (lower center) right of point of land; Mt. Jefferson in background

Petroglyph Rock, Cove Palisades State Park

shimmering peacock tail. Return to rd. Turn R. *0.7 m.*, Viewpoint. From here not only the confluence of the Deschutes and Crooked rivers are seen, but seven million years of Central Oregon geology are visible. The formation, with its yellow, brown, gray and black bed, contains volcanic and sedimentary characteristics. *0.5 m.*, Viewpoint. A centerfront look at a high tongue of land, now called "The Island" and known to the early homesteaders as "The Plains of Abraham." Nothing grows on it but sage and juniper; someday it may hold a resort and airstrip. *1 m.*, view of Cove Palisades SP from the rim of the gorge. *0.7 m.*, jct. Turn R to **Cove Palisades SP.** *1.8 m.*, marina. *2.2 m.*, bridge across Lake Chinook, Crooked River arm. *1.3 m.*, on L, a giant boulder covered with bafflling small-ringed craters, sunbursts, insect-designs and curlicues—a petroglyph perhaps several thousand years old, but its age remains as much of a mystery as its meaning. The boulder was found about 1 m. N, near the former rapids of the Crooked River. *0.2 m.*, camping area for Cove Palisades SP. Turn R for boat ramp on Deschutes. *0.4 m.*, parking area for boat ramp.

Return to Round Butte Dam Jct. Continue straight toward Culver. *0.3 m.*, turn R. *1 m.*, turn R. *0.9 m.*, turn L. Now the desert has been left behind and this road is warm in the bosom of the fertile valley. *0.8 m.*, Culver, a rural shopping and marketing place with a homebody flavor. *0.2 m.*, turn L toward Metolius. *4.6 m.*, Metolius, a potato storage hamlet that seems drowsy between spuds. *2 m.*, turn R onto Colfax Lane. *0.3 m.*, on R, up private lane, one of the oldest (circa 1900) homesteader houses in the Madras area; a representation of the homes the more well-to-do nesters put up in the early days. *0.2 m.*, US 97. Turn L. *1.8 m.*, Madras.

Site of old Culver; barn was formerly livery stable

1.8 m.—from Madras, on US 97—jct., US 26. (See *US 26* below.)

7.9 m., on L, Haystack Res. Jct.

　* *1.2 m.*, turn R onto Reservoir Rd. *0.7 m.*, Haystack Resort. The calm liquid basin, encircled by low juniper hills, has a relaxed, authentic Western character. *0.5 m.*, original site of Culver. Only three structures remain of old settlement: home (1898) that was hotel; barn that was livery stable; and behind barn, wooden water tank, to which early farmers traveled many miles to fill up. For years the tank was the only water supply in the area. *1.3 m.*, Haystack Res. FS CG.

3.7 m.—on US 97—on L, old country schoolhouse that has stood vacant for ages and ages—or so it seems.

3.9 m., **Crooked River Gorge.** The river steals through a deep, dark, fearsome rock canyon that echoes with horror. Viewpoint on S side of bridge. Peter Skene Ogden SP here is rest area. Park named after an explorer who was first white man in various parts of central Oregon.

3 m., Terrebonne. Turnoff L for **Smith Rock SP.**

　* Follow signs *3.3 m.* to canyon and take trail for views. The awesome canyon walls towering above the Crooked River appear as thunderous pillars of the seat of Jehovah. One almost expects proclamations to be roared from the heights, looking like so many imperious temples, with watchful mosques on the ridge beyond.

5.4 m., Redmond, a growing market center.

Jct., O 126—to E. (*19 m.*, Prineville. See *US 26* below.)

0.3 m., jct., O 126—to W. (See *Trans-Cascade Roads, O 126.*)

　* *2.3 m.*, on O 126, **Reindeer Ranch.** A most unusual spectacle, enjoyed by people of all ages.

4.8 m., turn R on SW Quarry Rd. for Petersen's Rock Garden.

　* *1.1 m.*, L on SW 61st St. *1.4 m.*, turn R. *0.5 m.*, **Petersen's Rock**

Garden. A fanciful construction of lagoons, castles, Statue of Liberty, bridges, fairyland tales, etc.—all in native rock; outgrowth of the hobby of a Danish immigrant farmer.

(From the garden, Bend can be reached by driving S on old US 97 to Tumalo, 6 m., turn L, and continue 5.4 m.)

11 m., **Bend,** fairest city of the plains, gateway to a vast and varied recreational area, and lavish in its number of motels. (The less expensive are off the main highway). The 25-m. Scenic Drive (a good starting point is the Chamber of Commerce, 1037 Brooks St.), visits three of the city's four parks, including forested Shevlin Park, along Tumalo Creek and three SPs,, including **Pilot Butte.** The butte received its name from early emigrants, who from the top of the cinder cone, 511 ft. above the plateau, charted their wagon train course. Almost the entire range of Oregon's Cascade peaks are visible, blazing white above the hazy, blue-green forests and ocher plain. Facing E, the earth tilts and changes from a geometry of irrigated farms to burnt up slope buttes and cones. Pioneer Park, which has fishing for children, is not on the Scenic Drive but is very close to downtown.

The most noteworthy of off-97 excursions out of Bend is **Century Drive,** also known as the Cascade Lakes highway. From jackpine on the sagebrush floor to stately Douglas firs providing green hems to ponderous white mountains, the road changes pace so quickly as to startle, bewilder and delight. There is an amazing variety of scenery and an abundance of recreational opportunities.

* Turn W on Franklin Ave. for Century Drive. Follow signs *21.3 m.* to Bachelor Butte Jct. (Turnoff for one of the state's best known ski areas.) *2.1 m.*, Todd Lake Jct. (*2 m.*, a bewitching lake looking up 3000 ft. to 9152-ft. Broken Top, the most rugged formation in the Central

Crooked River Gorge   Smith Rock State Park

Cascades. FS CG.) The road passes through a lava flow on L, and pumice field—*2.3 m.*, Sparks Lake Jct. The lake, extending S, is the jump-off point for the high primitive regions to the N and W. A 5-m. trail reaches the three Green Lakes, mounted in the saddle between S Sister and Broken Top. Two FS CGs near Sparks Lake. *1.4 m.*, Devil's Garden, a mtn. meadow near Satan Creek. FS CG. *0.5 m.*, Devil's Lake, a lovely alpine mirror so close to the dead forest of Hells Creek and the purgatorial remnants of past volcanic action. FS CG. *4.7 m.*, Elk Lake Jct. (Turnoff for Elk Lake Lodge.) **Elk Lake**, with more than 100 Rainbow and Eastern brook trout lakes within a 10-m. radius, is regarded as the recreational center of the Cascade lakes loop. (Mud Lake, 1 m. off, is stocked with Atlantic salmon and reserved for fly fishermen only.) The lofty peak of S Sister, a portrait of grandeur, is mirrored in the waters of Elk Lake; beyond the E shore, Bachelor Butte appears as a phoenix arisen from the ashes of its extinct crater. Pack trips for explorations in the Three Sister Wilderness make up at Elk Lake Lodge. Point FS CG at W end of lake; Beach FS CG at S end. *5.1 m.*, Lava Lake. Together with nearby Little Lava Lake, the source of the Deschutes River. *8.1 m.*, Cultus Lake Jct. (2 *m.*, lake resort. The small, shimmery lake, cooled by breezes sifting through stands of ponderosa, lodgepole and white pine, has become a prominent recreational area in recent years. Two FS CGs on E side; one—tent only—on W side, accessible only by boat or trailer.) *1.7 m.*, **Crane Prairie Reservoir Osprey Management Area**, first of its

Elk Lake

Osprey at Crane Prairie Reservoir   *Courtesy U.S. Forest Service by Milton J. Griffith*

kind in nation. About 50–70 nests of the fish hawk—often mistaken for the bald eagle—are scattered through the 10,600-acre area. The tall, reedy, gray, naked snags of trees killed when the reservoir was flooded in the early 1920s make excellent nests for the osprey, one of 47 rare species threatened with extinction. Other birds which find shelter in the management area include bald eagles, cormorants, blue herons and kingfishers. *6.3 m.,* Twin Lakes. (Between here and Wickiup Reservoir, 2.8 m. S, several FS CGs are sited.) *8.7 m.,* Pringle Falls, a swiftening of the Deschutes. FS CG. *7.2 m.,* US 97. Turn L. *25.3 m.,* Bend.

A shorter trip of scenic interest and arboreal fragrance is the drive to Tumalo Falls.

  * Turn W on Franklin. Follow Century Drive signs *2.6 m.* to Jct. Continue W on Galveston. *14 m.,* **Tumalo Falls,** a 97-ft. cataract deep in a pine forest. Tumalo Creek pours over a rockledge through a craggy cleft with power and abandon. Tumalo Falls FS CG has only a few tent and picnic sites—just the right size for those who seek seclusion in the companionable woods. Resume S on US 97 from Bend.

3.9 m., turnoff L for Arnold Ice Cave.

  * *11.7 m.,* on red-cindered FS Rd. 1821 to **Arnold Ice Cave,** whose floor is ice covered the year round. Before refrigerators, many Bend people came here for their ice. Along the way to Arnold Ice Cave, there are turnoffs to Skeleton Cave (FS Rd. 1854)—FS PG—and Wind Cave. FS PG.

Lava Butte

6.7 m., turnoff R for **Lava Butte Visitor Center.**

   * 1.1 m., parking area. The 5016-ft.-high butte, formed by an eruption in a fissure extending from Newberry volcano a millennium or two ago, is the center of the 8983-acre Lava Butte Geological Area, encompassing central Oregon's lava domain. The prominent cone, with observatory on top and vent and channel at base, through which roared fiery streams of lava, is the most popular site of Oregon's "Moon Country." From the observatory, the entire Oregon Cascades is a roll of peaks. Pine forests dress up the foreground, in all directions; and cropping up in the arid E are buttes and hummocks and low ranges and volcanic mtns. A trail from the observatory around the butte's crater to the parking lot takes 15 minutes to stroll and is very educational, being marked with explanatory signs about the flora and fauna of the butte and its environs.

0.5 m., turnoff R for Benham Falls.

   * 4.5 m., FS CG near Deschutes leap.

1.3 m., turn L to **Lava River Caves SP.**

   * Eons ago a flow of molten lava, pouring out from under the cooled and hardened surface, cored a tunnel nearly 1 m. long, 50 ft. wide and 35 ft. high. Some people regard this cavern as the most interesting and unique volcanic phenomenon in central Oregon. Lantern rental.

2.3 m., turnoff L for **Lava Cast Forest.**

* *10 m.,* on NW slope of Newberry Crater, a strewn mass of lava casts, shaped, as though of plaster, in the form of trees. These trees were engulfed by a lava flow and, before the wood burned out, the lava cooled sufficiently to mold. Perhaps the largest forest of lava-cast trees known. Wear heavy shoes and watch your step.

Turn R from US 97 for Sun River, grandiose resort complex.

* *1.8 m.,* country store. *0.5 m.,* resort.

8.7 m., on L, Paulina Lake Jct.

* *10 m.,* **Newberry Crater,** a caldera of a "burned out" mtn. that may once have been 12,000 ft. high. The fractured, jagged ramparts of the vanquished volcano are topped by the pinnacle of 7985-ft. Paulina Peak. Alpine trees and crags look down about 1600 ft. to the surface of Paulina and East lakes, divided in Newberry's massive crater. (Both lakes are renowned for trout fishing.) Other geological attractions are the crater's trackless obsidian flow, the scores of deep cones scattered around the slopes, the obsidian cliffs and 65-ft. Paulina Creek Falls. Tourist accommodations and other facilities on pine-bordered shores of lakes. FS CGs at both lakes. A steep 3-m. trail ascends from FS CG at W end of Paulina Lake to Paulina Peak. Much of central Oregon, from the burnished fringes of the plains to the Cascade snow coifs, is clearly visible.

5.8 m., Lapine, a highway community that will probably prosper, owing to its fine scenic location and climate. *1.8 m.,* jct., O 31. (See O 31 below.)

14 m., Gilchrist, an historic mill town with some fanciful architectural touches. *1 m.,* Crescent, a rural shopping and tourist-facility burg. *10 m.,* jct., O 58. (See *Trans-Cascade Roads.*)

8.1 m., Chemult, an old-time RR town with tourist facilities. *9.2 m.,* jct., O 138—to Crater and Diamond lakes. (See *Trans-Cascade Roads.*)

3 m., jct., O 232.

* *27 m.,* over mile-high Sun Pass, drenched in yellow pines, to O 62.

17 m., Thunderbeast Park, commercial exhibition of figures of prehistoric animals.

9.3 m., **Collier Memorial SP,** an open-air logging museum of early timber days. Much of the equipment provides fascinating configurations for imaginative photographers. Fishing in contiguous Spring Creek and Williamson River, both portraits of timeless wisdom and new-born innocence. CG and PG.

2.7 m., Chiloquin Jct.

* *1.3 m.,* Chiloquin, once a key settlement of the Klamath Reservation. **Klamath Indian Memorial Museum** in City Hall.

5 m., jct., O 62. (See *Trans-Cascade Roads.*)

6 m., Modoc Point. It was from here that the oppressed Modocs, consigned to land alien to them, began their return to Lost River, SE of Klamath Falls. This "insurrectionary" action brought on the "Modoc War" of 1872–73, fought in what is now Lava Beds National Monument of N Calif. The

Collier Memorial State Park

leaders of the small band were hanged at Old Ft. Klamath. (See *Trans-Cascade Roads, O 62.*)

Just below Modoc Point, US 97 swings around the E shore of Upper Klamath Lake, remnant of an ancient inland sea and second largest body of fresh water W of the Rockies. Great flocks of geese and ducks make the lake home each autumn before continuing S on their annual migration. Among the many other species of waterfowl which frequent these waters are the huge-beaked, snow-white pelicans, protected by law.

17 m., **Klamath Falls,** largest city E of the Cascades. Much of the colorful history of the area is dramatized in the excellently arranged collection of **Klamath County Museum,** in old National Guard bldg. at 1451 Main. **Baldwin Hotel,** 31 Main, built shortly after turn of century, is an official historic site. According to legend, "the once boisterous hotel holds such tales as the hiding of secret money in the hollow brass bed frames." Hotel has 32 hollow Western brass beds, 36 wood-burning stoves, early-day commodes, Quaker spinning wheel, 150-year-old mahogany sleigh bed, 17th-century cast-iron bed, Alladin lamp more than 100 years old, and cheval dressers. Lobby is from another age. Across street, in Veterans Park, is old Southern Pacific engine.

Within 0.3 m. is lovely Lake Ewana, graced by crowds of pelicans, and brief Link River. **Klamath Art Assn. Gallery** at Main & Riverside. Across street is **Favell's Museum of Western Art and Artifacts.**

Jct. ,O 66. (See *Trans-Cascade Roads.*) Jct., O 140— toW. (See *Trans Cascade Roads.*) Jct., O 140—to E. (See *O 140* below.)

* E on O 140, *5 m.,* O 39. *14 m.* S on O 39, Merrill, thriving potato and livestock center in rich Klamath Basin. *5 m.,* Calif. line.

16.4 m.—from Klamath Falls, on US 97—Calif. line.

US 26—Madras to John Day
Crooked River Road—Prineville to US 395

29 m. through zestful ranch country—**Prineville,** a well-laid-out plains town. It is also "agate capital of the U.S." and is strategically located in a prime thunder egg locality. Thousands of rockhounds flock here to try their luck at the hundreds of acres of public domain. (Inquire at Chamber of Commerce.) **Log Cabin Museum** (1880) recalls days of early nesters and stockmen. Old Crook County Courthouse is stamped with the brand of the range. **Ochoco Wayside,** 1 m. W, a juniper-covered butte, looks out over the city and Crooked River Valley and provides splendid view of Ochoco Mtns. Community-operated City of Prineville Railway is responsible for much of the town's revenue. Free rides in old passenger coach during summer.

1 m., turnoff for Post, Paulina, and points E; a stirring off-the-beaten-path motor trip.

1 m., turnoff S for Prineville Res. SP. (*15.5 m.,* SP CG on recreational reservoir.)

12 m.—on Post Rd.—Eagle Creek area, which produces highly valued red and black plume agates.

* The rd. from here on, to its conclusion, winds through a few striking rock formations, some low canyons, grasslands and wastelands, and passes, generally well off the pavement, deserted one- and two-room

Indian culture exhibit in Klamath County Museum   Room in Baldwin Hotel, Klamath Falls
Courtesy Klamath County Museum   *Courtesy Klamath County Museum*

schoolhouses, tumbling cabins and barns, and occasionally a working ranch. The rd. follows the Crooked River to its S fork. Down the river, all the way to the present site of Prineville, bumped and staggered the battered wagons and the confused, lost, sickly and bitter emigrants of the 1845 Meek Cutoff party.

11 m., **Post,** in the approximate geographical center of Oregon. Entire town consists of store, which is also the PO, tavern and gas stop.

1 m., turnoff on gravel rd. to Maury Mtns. (S *10 m.,* Homesteaders came to these rumpled hills to cut down trees for wood to build their shanties. The area is deposited with green, red, brown and golden moss agate and white plume agate.)

24 m., S Fork of Crooked River. Meek's Cutoff party came up from the S and turned W.

5.5 m., **Paulina,** so "Western" a setting you think it was created by TV. Pioneer ranchstead; general store (also PO, tavern and gas pump); dance hall, with sign requesting patrons to check guns, knives and clubs at door; a community church that had been the schoolhouse at Beaver Creek; and W of town, but belonging to it in character, a rodeo arena that must be the crudest and earthiest in the state. It's hard for modern travelers to believe that Paulina in the mid-1920s had three stores, a two-story hotel, restaurant, barber shop and blacksmith shop.

18.5 m., Suplee. A few ranch bldgs. in the vicinity but nothing remains at the old townsite. *17.6 m.,* Izee, after the IZ brand of an early rancher. Grange hall, school, teacherage—and that's all. *3 m.,* Bonham Jct. A few ranch bldgs. and a mailbox. Large herds of deer roam in open country along the S fork of the John Day River. *23.7 m.,* through meadow-rich Bear Valley, US 395. (See *Eastern Oregon, US 395.*) (*17 m.* N, John Day.)

Resume US 26.

Paulina Rodeo arena   **Paulina Community Church**

Pau-Mau Club, Paulina   Pioneer ranch, Paulina

5.5 m.—from Post Jct.—Ochoco Lake SP, a juniper tongue on the N shore of Ochoco Reservation. Boat ramp. CG.

2.4 m., on L, Mill Creek Rd.

* *7.6 m.*, **Steins Pillar,** a fist in the forest. Mounted on a natural rock pedestal, the solid rock column is 350 ft. high, 120 ft. in diameter.

6.9 m., jct., Ochoco Creek Rd.

* Formerly part of the main pike to John Day, this section is now a FS rd. Within 18 aromatic m. it passes the old Howard School, Ochoco FS CG (near ranger station), disintegrating log houses, and the Ochoco Mine (gold), where the town of Howard stood, near mouth of Scissors Creek. A 5-m rd. returns along Crystal Creek to US 26.

14.2 m., turnoff to Ochoco Divide FS CG, in the high, cool pines.

The rd. now descends the rolling Ochoco Mtns., in the wavy green Ochoco National Forest, and emerges in a stringy amber valley.

15 m., turnoff for **Painted Hills SP.**

* *6.2 m.*, the fossil-vaulted domes and ridges, banded with yellows, reds, ochers and greens, dominate the silent sea of an eerie nether world.

2.8 m., **Mitchell,** whose population of 175 or so makes it the largest town in an area of more than 3000 sq. m. Odd as it may seem to some, in this semi-arid land, Mitchell has suffered heavily from downpours and floods, the last serious deluge coming in 1965. When it rains heavily, be on the lookout for rocks washed down from the banks. Mitchell Baptist Church has all the architectural flavor of the region.

15.2 m., on R, Antone Rd.—turnoff for Camp Watson, one of the military outposts set up the 1860s to protect white settlers from the "rebellious" Indians.

* *0.7 m.*, stop at house on L to receive permission to use private rd.—and key, if gate is locked. *1 m.*, on R, ranch rd. gate. Close gate after entering. Follow rough rd. *1.5 m.* Take foot trail to R. *1 m.*—through woods polluted by junked cars and a host of other garbage—knoll enclosed by barbed wire. On knoll are seven grave markers of the men of the Oregon Cavalry. To their flanks are other grave markers, going back to 1876. All traces of the post, below the knoll, have been obliterated.

16.8 m.—on US 26—jct., O 19. (See O 19 below.)

The highway now enters **Picture Gorge**, a 500-ft. defile cut by the saw-blade current of the John Day River through 25 layers of basaltic lava flow. The narrow canyon was named for the ancient Indian writings on the brooding walls. Much of the art has been ruined by vandals.

2.7 m., on R, turnoff on Day Creek Rd., part of The Dalles-Canyon City Military Rd.

    * *0.5 m.*, turn at fork onto narrow rocky trace. *0.4 m.*, turn around at barbed wire fence. Walk through fence opening to end of shelf, **Mascall Overlook.** From here four distinct geological ages are visible: Columbia, Rattlesnake, John Day, Clarno. Many geologists hold that this is the finest view of Oregon's fossil beds.

4.8 m., Dayville, a pretty little cow town. Dayville Hotel, no longer in business, still makes a good photo subject.

0.7 m., on L, Stewart Ranch, one of pioneer spreads of Grant County. *2.4 m.*, on L, farmhouse and barn date back to first wave of homesteaders. *10.8 m.*, on R, turnoff on Fields Creek Rd.

    * *0.2 m.*, fossil beds on cut of slope at L of gravel rd.

10.9 m., Mt. Vernon, on the western rim of the cattle-rich John Day Valley.

Jct., US 395. (See *Eastern Oregon*.)

From Mt. Vernon to John Day the land is green and softly stretched, with affluent-looking ranches and houses on both sides.

8.6 m., **John Day**, the legendary cattle town of Oregon, now a modern market place. Glistening pastures reach out to the hem of the snow-ridged Strawberry Range of the Blue Mtns., giving the John Day Valley a rugged

View from Mascall Overlook   **Kam Wah Chung & Co. building, John Day**

charm. (For up-to-date information on trails leading into Strawberry Mtn. Wilderness, see Malheur National Forest Service HQ in John Day.) **Kam Wah Chung & Co.**, in City Park, is last vestige of Chinese settlement. Main part of structure was put up in 1867. Bldg.—which was herb doctor's office, assay office, store and social club—was closed in 1940. Seventh-Day Adventist Church, near Bridge & W Main, has "wedding cake frosting" on bell tower. Weatherford Collection of fossils in City Hall.

(Canyon City, 2 *m.* S of John Day, on US 395, is muted but graphic page of gold rush era. See *Eastern Oregon, US 395.*)

US 20—Bend to Burns

No major road in Oregon rides the desert so completely and for so long as does US 20 E of Bend. It is the loneliest, bleakest, ghost-ridden, poignant and most mysteriously awesome ranking pike in the state. Its domain is the "high desert," that vast plateau that was a continent of sorrow for thousands of homesteaders, duped into settlement by the RRs, land speculators and other fast-buck entrepreneurs. If the tears of the hapless homesteaders could have washed into the ground, at least a few acres might have been irrigated. The unwise settlers plowed up soil that was not fit for growing crops, turning the land against them until they had to flee for their lives. Today, the desert is used for little but grazing. The occasional remaining shanty, moaning its soul away in the obsequies of the wasteland winds, is grim testimony to the swindle and the land.

The rd. leaves Bend almost sadly, as though reluctant to say farewell to the green fields and high rectangles of baled hay close to the city. Then it pushes through a splurge of junipers, which wave good-by and then seem to turn their backs upon the traveler.

16 m., **Horse Ridge Summit,** commanding a far, broad view of the indigo-hued Cascades and the peaks of Three Sisters, Broken Top, Mt. Jefferson and Mt. Hood. **Western Juniper Natural Area**—600-acre tract—on Horse Ridge.

8 m., Millican, which old-timers still recall as a "one-man town," Billy Rahn being both the citizenry, and the mayor, as well as the storekeeper and the postmaster. A story—probably not true, but too good not to repeat—is that Billy once called a special election, absent-mindedly cast two ballots in a shoe box, immediately held another election, and this time triumphed properly. Store, station.

17 m., Brothers. Store-cafe-PO-station. And a pretty schoolhouse.

8 m., on R, Frederick Butte Rd.

* 31 m., Lost Forest, an ecological phenomenon. This rd.—for jeeps only when wet—connects to rds. leading to Christmas Valley, Fort Rock and Silver Lake. (See O 31 below.)

14 m., Hampton, largest settlement between Bend and Hines, near Burns. Store-cafe-PO-station. Clearly visible in the NW is Hampton Butte, another landmark in the grim trek of the Meek Cutoff party.

Gap Ranch

11 m., on R, **Glass Buttes.** Rising 2000 ft. above the desert, these buttes comprise one of the world's foremost obsidian outcroppings. Obsidian is the product of molten lava which rapidly cooled into flinty, glossy glass. The iridescence of the obsidian here reaches in thickness to a quarter of an inch and is characterized by kaleidoscopic coloring. Held to light, you have a glassy rainbow in your hand. Indians fashioned from the obsidian a wide variety of artifacts, from arrowheads and spear points to axes and chisels.

13.7 m., on L, the old, deserted, dolorous **Gap Ranch,** sole physical vestige of the livestock empire and legend of Bill Brown. Exschoolteacher Bill Brown came to the drylands from W Oregon in 1880 with a band of sheep. In time he built up the largest flocks of sheep and herds of horses in the state. He had everything, so it seemed, except the affection of the woman he adored, Mickey Hutton. To prove his honest intent he ordered a diamond brooch made in the shape of his brand, tied it around her neck, and announced, "Anything that wears that horseshoe brand belongs to me." Then, in the doggerel of a folk poem penned to describe the occasion: "She took it and she shook it and she stomped it on the floor/ And Bill was mortally certain she didn't love him anymore."

16.3 m., Riley. Store-cafe-station.

Jct., US 395—to S. (See this section, *US 395.*)

25 m., Hines, mill town.

2 m., **Burns.** (See *Eastern Oregon, US 20.*)

(*3.1 m.*, jct., US 395—to N. See *Eastern Oregon, US 395.*)

O 31—US 97 to US 395

20.4 m., on R, turnoff to **Big Hole.**

* 0.7 m., a sunken, roughly circular spot—perhaps volcanic-created—with an approximate 0.3-sq.-m. area and about 300 ft. below the rimrock flat. NE is Big Hole Butte.

1.6 m.—on O 31, from Big Hole turnoff—turnoff L for Hole in the Ground and Fremont.

* *0.5 m.*, rd. forks. L fork goes *1 m.* to **Hole in the Ground,** a round cavity about 1 m. in diameter and about 300 ft. deep. More likely it is the product of volcanic action rather than of meteor impact. R fork goes *2.3 m.* to site of **Fremont,** one of the many homesteader towns founded in the land rush of the early 1900s. Before Fremont folded, it had a creamery, cheese factory, hotel, general store, livery, blacksmith shop, dance hall and PO, and was an important stagecoach stop. When the homesteaders went broke, they quit the desert in droves. The towns they left behind soon fell prey to the elements, wood gatherers and vandals. The locations of most of these towns—there were dozens of them—have been obliteratd. Fremont is lucky. It still shows the splinters of the dance hall and a mounting block, made of steps sawed into a juniper stump. Block was used by long-skirted women who wanted to step into buggies without giving male onlookers a glimpse of their ankles. The windmill was put up about 1955 by Reub Long, rancher and well-known author. *3.5 m.,* Fort Rock Jct.

* Jutting out of the desert floor is a massive, sheer-cliffed basalt column, almost crescent-shaped, and more than 0.3 m. long. From a distance of 4 m., the rock appears as a great medieval fortress, with tremendous walls and stout parapets, and built on a mound, so that an assault would be even more difficult, since the invaders would first have to climb the exposed slopes. The dull brown shadows below the bastion can easily be imagined as a wide moat. *6.8 m.* from jct., the town of Fort Rock, which has dwindled from a lively burg to a thin cluster of weather-beaten frame bldgs. It looks now like the setting of a John Ford Western. At any moment you expect to see a lean-faced cowpoke ride laconically into town, to head for the saloon, that isn't there.

Fort Rock, *1.5 m.* N of town, is now a picnic-facility SP, as well as a National Historic Landmark. *1.3 m.* W of rock, on graded rd., **Fort Rock Cave,** known to the older settlers as Cow Cave. Here in 1938, Dr. Luther Cressman found about 75 woven sagebrush sandals. They were treated with preservative so could not later be tested for age by the Carbon-14 dating process, which did not start until 1949. A partly worn-out sandal, found after the C-14 method was discovered, proved to be about 9000 years old. Some of the sandals found earlier could have been older—or younger.

One of the wildest, most inhospitable sections of the desert is **Devils Garden,** a 4200-acre area "walled in" by a rim of lava. Here, among the juniper and sagebrush and shattered lava, the only sound is that of the shrilling wind, a phantom sweeping back and forth in its invisible cloak. Only one rd. enters Devils Garden, 15 m. NE of Fort Rock town. But there are several approaches. Inquire at store for currently most-negotiable approach.

Fort Rock

Fort Rock is sometimes used as a way to reach the unique Lost Forest. E, *5.8 m.* Turn R. S, *10.2 m.* to Christmas Valley Rd. (See following Silver Lake, below.)

18.2 m.—from Fort Rock Jct.—**Silver Lake**, a windswept hamlet. Tourist facilities, including trailer park and garage. Since its birth in the 1880s, Silver Lake has only once made the headlines—and that because of a tragic event that wiped out about one of every five persons living in the town and within a 30-m. area around. On Christmas Eve, 1894, from 160 to 200 persons gathered in Clayton Hall, the second floor of a small, two-story, false-fronted bldg. that held one of the town's two stores, for a community party. Almost all of Silver Lake's 50 residents were there and some of the others had had to buck miles of snowdrifts and freezing winds to come in by wagon, buckboard, buggy and on horseback. As the entertainment program was nearing its end, a man who had arisen from a plank bench to cross the room, accidentally bumped his head against one of the Rochester hanging oil lamps. Immediately coal oil sloshed into the burner and the flame flared. The confusion and panic that followed is here unimportant to relate; but within two minutes the hall was an inferno. Forty persons—men, women and children—perished that night, and three more from burns within the next three months. Of those who died in the blaze, not one could be identified; even the bones crumbled on touch. The survivors placed the gathered ashes in five wooden caskets and buried them in a common grave. In 1898 a large stone monument was carted from Eugene to the small Silver Lake Cemetery, where it still stands, inscribed with the names of the 43 victims. Medical bldg. (1919) of Dr. James Thom shows the economical use made of lumber in the freight wagon days. Lumber had to be hauled in and no one could afford to build a larger structure than was absolutely needed. Original shingles were replaced in 1961. **Corum Ranchhouse** (1888), 2 m. E of town, is earliest in area.

The 20.6-m. rd. between Silver Lake and Summer Lake follows a deep, desolate valley indented and walled by volcanic, remnant hills. The highway passes Silver Lake and surmounts Picture Rock Pass, so named because of Indian petroglyphs on a stout rock long a landmark in these lonely parts. Drifting sand dunes bordering the lake constantly change formation. Here, in this stark land, dawn pours in like a cinnabar cataract, and sunset robes the distant cliffs in scarlet.

6.2 m.—from Silver Lake—turnoff to one of the foremost oddities of Oregon, Lost Forest, and other interesting sights.

* N 8 m. on county rd. to Fort Rock intersection. Turn R. 14.1 m., **Christmas Valley**, which began as a retirement community and is now drawing others. Tourist accommodations. The community is in the center of excellent trout fishing, herds of antelope, arrowhead finds and geological phenomena.

Near the settlement is **Crack-in-the-Ground**, a lava fissure 10 to 15 ft. wide at the top, narrowing downward and, in some places, as deep as 70 ft. This deep, narrow rift is open for about 2 m. and extends to the W edge of Four Craters Lava Field. There is an eerie sensation in walking between the huge, irregularly shaped walls of the crevice at its narrowest. Some of the wall outcroppings seem to be stone masks of prehistoric mammals and giant cave men, with bulging eyes staring at you. This tension fracture in basalt, as the geologists call it, was well known to the homesteaders of the area, who traveled to "The Crack" for picnics, using ice they found in the chasm's caves to make ice cream. Crack-in-the-Ground is not easily reached and only a tire trace follows it. Take rd. headed N 1 m. E of Christmas Valley Lodge.

8 m.—from lodge—Viewpoint Ranch Rd. (For an alternate—and much more rugged—way to Lost Forest. You're safest with jeep or other heavy-duty vehicle of jeep range. N 4 m. to turnoff angling NE. Follow 2 m. to **Fossil Lake** which is scarcely wet these days. Wagon loads of fossils—including primitive camels, elephants, the ancestor of the horse, birds and fish—were carted from the lake bed early in the century. Return 2 m. to rd. Continue N 4 m. Turn E. 10 m., through sand dunes, Lost Forest. Actually, prairie schooners wheeled this way, for the trace through the sand dunes is marked on BLM maps as the "Old Emigrant Road.")

10.5 m.—E from Viewpoint Ranch Rd.—Buffalo Well, now a place name without a place. The rd. to it grinds through Christmas Lake Valley, graveyard of many a homesteader dream. (At Buffalo Well, the gravel rd. continues E 25 m. to US 395.)

For Lost Forest, turn L, or N, at Buffalo Well, on dirt rd. At 5 m., sand dunes appear; 5 m. further, Lost Forest.

The 9100-acre ponderosa **Lost Forest** is "lost" because it is in a barren area, with rainfall supposedly insufficient to support it; it receives less than half the precipitation of the pine timber of the nearest national forest, more than 30 m. away. It exists in a wasteland devoid of streams or

Crack-in-the-Ground

Courtesy Oregon State Dept. of Geology and Mineral Industries
by Norman V. Peterson

springs and meted but stingy rainfall—(bring your own water). Indeed, the area is so inhospitable to life that few birds and animals are found among the trees.

Lost Forest is a remnant of the millions of acres of pine, hardwood and even palm trees that about 10,000 years ago, when the basin was lavish with "wet" lakes, covered this plateau. The survival of Lost Forest depends upon such a subtle ecological balance that the BLM, which has responsibility for the area, wants the forest and the adjacent sand dunes to be maintained as nearly as possible in their present state; that is, as a natural area. Conservation-minded people will surely approve.

From Lost Forest a dry-weather dirt rd. winds N *31 m.* to US 20.

14.4 m.—from turnoff to Christmas Valley, on O 31—Summer Lake. Tourist facilities—as much as one can expect from a dot in the grimy desert.

The road S of this point, at the base of high, crescent-shaped Winter Ridge, rims the W end of the Summer Lake Valley, with homes every m. or so. Summer Lake itself is shallow and alkali, and E of it is a Sahara-like expanse of giant sand dunes.

28.6 m.—from Summer Lake—**Paisley.** The town—population: 300, which makes it very big in these parts—retains but a lingering trace of the strong Western atmosphere which pervaded it a few decades ago. **Chewaucan Hotel,** built in the 1890s and once a famed stockman's inn, has been empty for years, but still makes for a history-pungent photo. The cattle and hay Chewaucan Valley, a lovely green basin, spreads for miles below the town. Dirt rds. spinning W and S of Paisley whorl to mtn. lakes; and other rds. lead to such intriguing places as Dairy Creek and Coffeepot Flat.

22 m., Valley Falls. Motel, store, gas. Jct., US 395.

23 m., Lakeview. (See *US 395* below.)

O 140—*Klamath Falls to Lakeview*

20.5 m., Dairy, once a thriving shipping and distributing center for a dairy region. But good rds. have built up Klamath Falls at the expense of Dairy and other rural towns. Before irrigation, the area was rightly called Alkali Valley. Jct., O 70.

* On O 70—*7 m.*, Bonanza, looking larger than its population of 250 would indicate. Before nearby springs were tapped for irrigation, the area was a treeless waste. Today Bonanza is surrounded by the green fields of lowland dairy ranches. A 41-m. loop trip around the volcanic terrain in Langrell Valley is a very pleasant rustic drive.

22 m., Beatty, long a Klamath Indian settlement—but many of the Indians have moved away. Below sagebrush hills covered in spring by the blooms

Lost Forest   *Courtesy U.S. Bureau of Land Management*

Old hotel in Paisley

of the black and yellow balsam root, Winema, "heroine of the Modoc War," was laid to rest in **Schonchin Cemetery**, Indian burial ground. Schonchin was a leader of the Modoc band who fought for their freedom and lost. Winema, niece of the Modoc's leader, Captain Jack, who with Schonchin was hanged, was married at the age of 16 to a white man. She became fluent in English and acted as an interpreter and messenger during the "Modoc War." She is credited with saving the life of Col. Meacham, at the risk of her own, during the hostilities, and was at length rewarded by the U.S. Govt. with a $25 monthly pension, which she gave to the needy on the Klamath Reservation. Over her grave the DAR placed a tablet: "Winema—the Strong Heart."

13 *m.*, Bly, an early cattle town that doesn't show it, and with no suggestion that it was once a large shipping point for sheep and wool. Cafe, station.

2 *m.*, turnoff L to **Gearhart Mtn. Wilderness.**

* A dirt and gravel rd. claws around the perimeter of the wilderness and continues through Fremont National Forest to Paisley, O 31, *41 m.* Beautiful upland scenery. No tourist facilities, but three FS CGs.

3 *m.*, on L, Sprague River FS CG, on a clear stream.

25 *m.*, Booth SP, picnic wayside in large stand of Ponderosa pine.

12 *m.*, through the lower Fremont National Forest and shining Quartz Valley, **Lakeview.** (See *US 395* below.)

US 395—US 20 to California Line

There is in every mile of this road the sense of history that has played itself out and gone to sleep, leaving in the air a chant of legend. Here, in range country of illimitable horizons, seas of sage stretch everywhere, washing against the slopes of fiery, yet soft and muted hills.

28 *m.*—from jct., US 20, at Riley—**Wagontire**, named for the 6504-ft. mtn. to the N. Cattlemen and homesteaders bitterly feuded for possession of

water holes on the mtn. Only one family lives at Wagontire. It operates the cafe-store-motel-gas pumps.

9 m., turnoff, on R, for Lost Forest, Christmas Valley, Fort Rock and Silver Lake. (See O 31 above.)

* 25 m., Buffalo Well. The rolling sagebrush country gives way to flat sagebrush plains, with alkali flats growing more numerous and eerie hills in the distance forming a wax museum of wasteland shapes. Turn N and drive 10 m. for Lost Forest. Continue W from Buffalo Well 18 m. for Christmas Valley. From Christmas Valley, Silver Lake (O 31) is 28.3 m.; Fort Rock is 28.7 m. NW.

12.8 m., Alkali Lake Station, a breath of life beside the bitter waters. Cafe-gas.

Alkali Lake State Rest Area has pit toilet but no water.

18.1 m., turnoff R for Paisley, O 31.

* A 30-m. gravel rd., touching the N end of Abert Lake, grinds through a welter of desolation to find the grasslands of Paisley.

US 395 runs along the E shore of the recessed lake, a phantom sea in a mystic basin of ghostly hills and hazy rimrock buttes and always under the eye of Abert Rim. The languid waters of **Abert Lake** reflect the desert around it so purely that it becomes a surface gallery of pastels. Some people see the marshes as green and some as purple and some as turquoise, and they are all right, because the lake is constantly shifting color. And nowhere in the state is sagebrush so varied in tint: brown, purple, red, yellow, beige, green, gray and smoke-colored.

For 19 m. **Abert Rim** hangs above the lake and rd. One of the world's great fault scarps, it rises as a wall 2000 ft. above the plateau and has an 800-ft. lava cap ending abruptly in a sheer precipice. From the summit a large chunk of south-central Oregon is laid bare. The first white party here was led by famed pathfinder John C. Fremont, of whom it was said: "From the ashes of his campfires have sprung cities."

22 m.—from Paisley turnoff—Valley Falls, at jct., O 31. Store-motel-gas.

Beyond Valley Falls the country changes in seven-league strides from sage and alkali to pine woods, fat cattle, and good-looking ranch houses. But here and there the sagebrush hangs on in tufted patches.

7 m., Chandler SP. Camp or picnic near a cheery spring in a wooded canyon.

11 m., jct., O 140. (See O 140 below.)

2.5 m., on R, Hunter's Hot Springs, with the only continuously spouting geyser in Oregon. "Old Perpetual," under the goading of stream pressure, at 200° F, flings a column of water to a height of 60 ft.

2.5 m., **Lakeview,** marketing and shipping center for some of the biggest cattle spreads in the state, and "tallest town in Oregon," because at 4800-ft. altitude it is "higher" than any other city. **Lake County Court House** has sunny, desert attractiveness. **Schminck Museum** displays relics of pioneer days. Some of Robert Ogle's magnificent Indian collection is on view in his **Indian**

Village Restaurant. Thunder eggs, agate, jasper, nodules and agatized wood are found in several areas close to town. (Inquire at Chamber of Commerce for specifics.)

14 m., turnoff R, or W, for Goose Lake Rec. Area.

* *1 m.,* SP CG, on lake shore.

Emigrant trains crossed Goose Lake when it was dry. When it evaporated again, years later, frustrated ferry boatmen found clear wagon tracks and the ashes of camp fires on the lake bed.

0.8 m., New Pine Creek, right on the border; half in Oregon; half in Calif. Modest tourist facilities.

Hart Mountain National Antelope Refuge

Lakeview is the gateway to one of the truly distinctive areas and wildlife resources of Oregon.

* **Hart Mtn. National Antelope Refuge** was established in 1936 by President Roosevelt to preserve the native antelope and other wildlife of the region. The population of the fleet-footed antelope was rapidly being decimated by "sportsmen," ranchers and homesteaders. FDR did not want these animals to go the way of the Oregon Bison, rendered extinct by indiscriminate slaughter.

The mtn. derives its name from the shape of a brand used by a foothill cattle ranch and the cowboy misspelling of "heart."

Hart Mtn., a massive volcanic ridge rising from the surrounding plain to an altitude of more than 8000 ft. above sea level, contains life zones ranging from the hot semideserts of the Upper Sonoran to the cool Canadian Zone, where on the higher ridges snow is absent only from midsummer to the first turn of autumn. Each life zone has its own species of fauna and flora, with some fauna operating on more than one level. For instance, as the desert pools dry up, the antelope climb as high as the summit for water. In spring and fall, the lakes at the W basin of the mtn. look like aviary conventions.

From below, Hart Mtn. appears monolithic, dull and barren. But it contains a large and subtle variety of geological forms and an intricate system of ecological patterns. Nodules and jasp-agate are found in the canyons and fire opal on the peaks of the W rim.

The conservation-minded Order of the Antelope, founded in 1932, holds an annual encampment on the "great oasis of the desert."

To reach Hart Mtn. National Antelope Refuge, drive N 5 *m.* on US 395 to jct., O 140. Turn E, onto O 140. The rd. sweeps through pine stands, crosses Warner Summit, rolls down into verdant Camas Prairie, and snakes between rimrock canyon walls. *15.2 m.,* jct. (Straight ahead to Adel.) Turn L, or N.

The first view of Hart Mtn., beyond the turnoff, is of a great bulky prow lying at rest in the far reaches of the deep desert sea. The first impression of Hart Lake is of a translucent pool in the amber shadows of the giant massif's rugged cliffs. But as the rd. approaches, the "pool" takes on the stretched form of a river, though it retains its luminous mistiness.

Sometimes, on this rd., you see a surging blob of cattle being turned from pasture to pasture and you hear the muffled thunder of their hooves.

17.5 m.—from turnoff toward Adel—**Plush,** a tiny hamlet that was a bustling frontier settlement before small ranches gave way to big ones and before sturdy cars and improved rds. Store-gas. Old frame house across street from store was for years the "restaurant" in Plush.

4.5 m.—from Plush—"Lone Tree," a sturdy poplar, the only tree along the road for miles. *3.5 m.*, ranch bldgs. shaded by a grove of Lombardy poplars. *2 m.*, another ranchstead, also shaded by Lombardy poplars. From here the rd. pulls *13 m.* up the side of the mtn. to **Refuge HQ**. At informal turnouts there are broad vistas of the hayfields, marshes and lakes of Warner Valley, with the grim desert in the background.

Facilities on Hart Mtn. are few and relatively primitive. (Inquire at HQ.) You can drive safely to places affording excellent views of antelope and other wildlife—but ask before you start. Some trails that appear as rds. are impassable—with dire consequences to the foolhardy.

The actual number of antelope for the area embracing Hart Mtn., the Charles Sheldon Antelope Range (in Nevada), and the 40 m. between the two HQs is less than 2000. There are also about 200 bighorn sheep and many mule deer in this same region.

From HQ, a rd. built by the Job Corps—to replace the old rocky, sagebrush monstrosity—cuts across Catlow Valley to Frenchglen, *48 m.* The

Warner Lakes below Hart Mountain

Warner Peak, Hart Mountain

old trace slithered between the corrals of Taft Miller's Ranch—the only sign of "civilization" for an awful long stretch—but the new rd., while still running through the Miller Ranch, takes a less dramatic path. Few people travel this route, but those who do, especially in jeeps or pickups, see some mighty odd and intriguing land.

(For Frenchglen, see *Eastern Oregon, US 395*.)

O 140—US 395 to Denio

15.2 m.—from US 395, 5 m. of Lakeview—turnoff to Plush and to Hart Mtn. (See *US 395*, preceding.)

12.3 m., Adel. Store-cafe-gas.

* A gravel rd. runs N *18 m.* to Plush, passing en route Crump and Pelican lakes, habitat of wild swans. *3 m.* N of turnoff, the man-made **Crump Geyser**, an oddity in the desert.

82 m., **Denio.** In this long stretch, through mystic Greaser Canyon, the playa border of grotesque Guano Valley, and the Sheldon Antelope Range, there is not a single tourist facility. So fill up at Lakeview or, at least, at Adel. About half of the rd. is in Nevada. Denio once belonged to Oregon, but the postmaster moved across the street and the town is now in Nevada. In the big cattle drive days, Denio was an important trail town on the push from Harney County to Winnemucca. An old hotel is about the last vestige of those days. Modest tourist facilities and a rock shop.

O 19—Arlington (80N) to US 26

Few visitors to E Oregon travel this road from start to finish, and many touch it not at all. Which makes the road a blessing for those who do explore the land it unlocks, because there is so much varied scenery and so many dimensions of history along O 19.

Arlington is the only place E of the Cascades where a ferryboat still operates on the Columbia. Town also has park and boat basin.

7.1 m.—after rising through a canyon to a plateau—Weatherford Historical Marker, honoring W. W. Weatherford, who came barefoot across the Oregon Trail, driving an ox team.

  * A county rd. follows the Oregon Trail W 9 m. to Rock Creek, once a modest homesteader settlement.

7.3 m., Shutler Flat. This seemingly lonely land is big business. Wheat and cattle ranches average about 5000 acres. The homes of the ranchers are as affluent as the urban rich.

Crump Geyser near Adel   *Courtsey Lake County Examiner*

1.8 m., on L, Ione Jct.

　* E *16.6 m.*, skirting Eightmile Canyon, to O 74, 3 m. N of Ione. Some days, it seems, you can drive back and forth on this rd. for hours without meeting another car.

1.2 m., on R, Olex. Store-gas. Gilliam County's oldest—and only—county school is here.

2.7 m., on R, Mikkalo Jct.

　* *1.8 m.*, Mikkalo, a meeting point in a sea of grass.

18 m., **Condon,** seat of Gilliam County. A grain elevator town, where wheat is king. Overnight camping at Burns Park, County Fairgrounds. Lovely city park at side of O 19 at S end of town makes pleasant picnic stop. **Pete's Barber Shop**, on Main (O 19) near Gilliam, has only museum in county. Condon has little more than 1000 people, but it is the biggest town on O 19.

A most interesting side trip out of Condon is to Lonerock.

　* Follow O 206 E *5 m.* and turn R. *16.6 m.*, through wheatlands and sagebrush, Lonerock. It is mystifying to see large areas of sage followed, at a higher elevation, by expanses of wheat. **Lonerock** was at the turn of the century a crackling homesteader market place; in 1970 it was down to 10 people. Still standing is the 19th-century church, a quiet companion to the great rock that gives the town its name. The pump organ was installed when the church was constructed. A block away, vacant in the toll of silence, is a two-story schoolhouse built in 1892. When Lonerock was in its prime, with children trooping in from farms up Lone Rock Creek, the upper story was the high school. An old inn and an early store, both empty, also stand, as does the city jail, which hasn't had a prisoner since the 1930s. The jail is about the only bldg. in town to have been repaired in recent years—for show purposes. The rail fence around it is relatively new. Every family has an underground shed—a relic of the early days,

Lonerock city jail built in 1891 　　　　　　Lonerock firehouse and post office

when potatoes and fruit were stored in the winter; and a wood shed, a reminder of the time when wood was the only fuel. Lonerock is still incorporated and, as a tradition, the mayor is the oldest citizen. When he or she passes on, the oldest survivor is named.

At Condon, jct., O 206—which links Condon to Heppner, another leading grain and cattle town.

* O 206 passes through sparse land, with little to show of its past and the present seen in the far-off combines, which look, enveloped in clouds of chaff, like grasshoppers stirring up puffs of stubble dust.

5 m., Lonerock Jct. So thin of settlement is this rd. that a ranch, *25 m.* beyond Lonerock Jct., appears almost as a city. *2 m.* onward, Ruggs, a store in the shadow of a grain elevator. (*10.5 m.* S of Ruggs, on O 207, the ghost town of Hardman. See this section, O 207.) *9 m.* beyond Ruggs, Heppner. (See O 74 below.)

9.5 m.—from Condon—**Dyer Wayside**, a patch of oasis along a branch of Thirty Mile Creek. Under the high rimrock of Ramsey Canyon, five generations of plainsmen have gathered in the shade of willows, cottonwoods and cherry trees to picnic with their neighbors.

3.2 m., Mayville, a once prosperous hamlet that is slowly decaying. Several old, abandoned business bldgs. on E side of rd.

7.2 m., **Fossil**, seat of Wheeler County, smallest in Oregon, with less than 2000 persons and an area of many charming, scenic and historic byways. In the entire county there are only three motels—one each in Fossil, Spray and Mitchell. Fossil was so named because of fossils found on the ranch where the town was laid out in 1867. Banks above high school football field are free-digging fossil beds. The grounds of the **Williams Home** contain fences, bldgs., gardens and fountains built of rocks from a thousand hills, and now tender memorial to the late Effie Williams.

Fossil, with a population around 500, is a shuffling, folksy, tolerant town. Almost all businesses close at 6 p.m. You can park downtown all day without getting a ticket. **Wheeler County Court House** (1901) has all the flavor of the old West. **General Mercantile Co.**, which traces its founding to 1890, is most diversified small town general store in Central Oregon. **Masonic Hall** dates back to 1880s. **Asher's Auto Museum**, in old blacksmith shop, has collection of vintage cars. **Fossil Museum** is a showcase of early Wheeler County artifacts. The aged bar came around the Horn. "**The Goose**," a rail bus which ran between Condon and Kinzua from 1929–53, is parked near center of town. Scenic float trips are conducted on the John Day River by **The Week-End**, back of Steiwer Insurance.

3.7 m.—from Fossil—Kinzua Jct.

* For a rare off-the-beaten-path small journey, try this one. It is seldom traveled by outsiders.

10.9 m.—from jct.—Kinzua, a company lumber town. The houses are all made of wood, painted the same color and look alike. *0.6 m.*, on hill

Fossil Museum, Fossil

rd., on R, overlook of a miniature mill town built by a schoolboy. Talent is everywhere. Retrace way toward O 19. At Golf Course Rd., (at RR crossing), *2 m.* W of Kinzua, turn R. *1.1 m.*, turnoff for Lonerock. (However, you can first continue straight *0.2 m.* to six-hole Kinzua golf course, only one in Wheeler County. Greens below pine hills. Return to Lonerock Rd. from golf course. Turn L.) You are apt not to meet another car on this narrow dirt rd., which slips past quiet, clear ranchspreads. From points on the plateau you can see Condon more than 20 m. away. *1.7 m.*, at forks, take R fork. *6.9 m.*, at forks, straight toward Lost Valley. *0.5 m.*, Lost Valley, a deep green basin thickly dotted with hefty cattle. *1 m.*, forks—continue straight toward Lonerock. *0.1 m.*, Wade's Lost Valley Ranch—what a real cattle ranchstead looks like. *6.6 m.*, outer farm bldgs. of Anderson's ranch, which has been in same family since 1883. All this land was originally in livestock, but when the RR reached Condon, the economy began to turn to grain. *4 m.*, Lonerock-Condon Jct. Turn R. *10.5 m.*, Lonerock. Return to Fossil by way of Condon.

7 m.—on O 19, from Kinzua Jct.—Twickenham Jct.

  * *10 m.*, Rowe Creek Reservoir, a pleasant little man-made lake cupped by juniper hills. *5.9 m.*—through breathing waves of sage—Twickenham. A white-painted schoolhouse is the last reminder of what was once a

compact settlement which almost became the seat of Wheeler County. The school hasn't operated for years. (*7.8 m.,* jct., O 207. *10 m.,* US 26.)
0.4 m., Shelton Wayside, in a smother of yellow pine.
1 m., turn L for Julia Henderson Pioneer Park.

  * *0.2 m.,* early-day picnic ground and get-together scene. Still used for reunions and other square happenings. Stage extends across a small creek and is, technically, Oregon's smallest CB.
2.6 m., turnoff L for Prairie Ranch.

  * *0.3 m.,* **Prairie Ranch,** one of the most Old West-looking ranches in the state and in as magnificent a setting as any ranch in Oregon. Immediately one is struck by the thought: Here is a perfect place to film TV's "Bonanza," so open and unblemished are the meadows, and so fair the softly contoured hills and the pine slopes of a rising range. Ranch was started in 1870 and the present house built in 1888. The two houses to the R were cowboy bunkhouses. Ranch was also a stagecoach stop on the old rd. to Mitchell.

Prairie Ranch

Old stagecoach hostelry (now unused), Spray

6.8 m., Service Creek. Store-cafe-gas. (The place was first called Sarvis Creek and the locals still use the pronunciation, though the name was changed more than 50 years ago.)

0.3 m., jct., O 207.

*6.2 m., ghost town of Richmond. (See O 207 below.)

At the jct. of O 207 the John Day River flashes into full view, and O 19 follows the lovely stream, still undammed, for several miles. Not too many years ago most of the land from Fossil to Service Creek was good for little else but grazing. But irrigation, which has taken a heavy toll of the John Day, has brought many farms into being, and this part of Wheeler County is taking on a rural atmosphere, with homes replacing clusters of sage. The rd. winds under the cropped breaks of the river—rugged, rocky bluffs that are a prism of shadows.

13.5 m., **Spray,** a small, tranquil hamlet with sagebrush hills behind it and the John Day in front, with farms along the river. Spray Hotel, vacated, is type of hostelry structure representative of stagecoach period.

3.3 m., jct., O 207—to Hardman and Heppner. (See later this section, O 207.)

0.5 m., on L, **Haystack Fossil Beds.**

9.8 m., Kimberly, at the jct. of the Middle and N forks of the John Day. Store-gas.

A county rd. leading E from Kimberly seeps between the hushed folds of multicolored formations, where early cattlemen left their mark on the land.

*1 m., Thomas orchards, largest E of the Deschutes River. Cherries, apricots and peaches grow in abundance. Efforts to persuade stockmen and wheat ranchers to diversify in favor of fruit have not been successful, but as the Thomas Orchards continue to prosper, the thinking may change. 11.7 m., **Monument,** a homespun little settlement on the N fork of the John Day. It seems every kid here has a horse and, if you wait long enough, you can get a photo of a youngster watering his or her horse in the middle of the stream. Monument has some houses dating back to the stagecoach era, including the Mattie Stubblefield home, with the sign "Roomers" on it. There are no other commercial sleeping accommodations in Monument. Several other houses of 19th-century vintage are close by, including one known as the "Old Hotel" and another occupied by Ellen Stubblefield. The store, like most cattle country general stores, carries everything from butter to saddle blankets. *9.6 m.*, on R, **Sunken Mtn.** About ¼ sq. m. of the mtn. dropped straight down and left red cliffs on all sides, with grass and timber remaining in the center. A geologic marker explains that Sunken Mtn. is a small landslide in volcanic ash bed in the lower part of the John Day Formation. *1.7 m.*, Hamilton: nothing but a few houses, very few. *11.4 m.*, US 395 and Long Creek. (See *Eastern Oregon, US 395.*)

The stretch between Kimberly and US 26, on O 19, is renowned for its fossil tombs. The highway, following the slicing stream it has kept company with since Service Creek, now companions it through a deep, winding canyon. Nestled tight against the bank are farmsteads, expanding as irrigation is developed. There are two-car garages, TV antennas and nice lawns—but the area still has a frontier feel. On the E side of the rd., sagebrush still marches to the shoulder, though irrigation is threatening to invade that wasteland. On the W side, sprinklers work furiously. The lunar-dusted sagebrush slopes mantling the

Mattie Stubblefield's rooming house, Monument

Sunken Mountain   Condon-John Day Fossil Beds

multicolored domes of the fantastically-shaped hills would seem to mark the end of where agriculture can be nourished. But even these slopes are being challenged by men, water and machinery.

The polychrome monuments of the tortured barrenlands change shape and color at every turn of the road, at every glance.

Eons ago, where these tormented hills now gasp for breath and cringe under icy rain, a low tropical jungle was spread. Its inhabitants included saber-toothed tigers, miniature horses, rhinoceroses, and the first species of bird life. They dwelt under or rested upon magnolia, fig, palm, ginkgo and redwood trees. Cataclysmic geological and meteorological changes followed. And so extinction of that life, in whatever form, with the past vaulted under the rising hills.

The fossil beds were first systematically explored by Dr. Thomas Condon, a clergyman with a geological bent, who accompanied a cavalry troop to this area in the 1860s.

9.6 m.—from Kimberly—turnoff L to **Thomas Condon-John Day Fossil Beds.**

     * *0.7 m.*, fossil beds. Remarkable finds have been discovered here. The seaweed-colored cliffs look like Egyptian tomb walls and pyramids.

2 m., view ahead of **Cathedral Rock**, a spectacular formation.

0.8 m., Johnny Kirk Springs, in the center of this most important fossil region. Rest area. Steps lead down to the river.

2.1 m., **Thomas Condon-Munro Fossil Beds.**

     * *0.1 m.*, parking area. Two trails, each about 1 m.-long, into fossil areas.

3.7 m., parking for best view of **Sheep Rock**, probably the most photographed of all places in the fossil region.

1.7 m., jct., US 26. (For US 26, preceding.)

O 74—80N to US 395

A voyage through open seas of wheat, stretching to horizons that bend against horizons.

14.6 m., Cecil. Here, coming down a bank from the E, the Old Oregon Trail crossed Willow Creek. Store, gas.

5.1 m., Morgan. Saddle Butte, to the S, was a sort of prairie beacon for the homesteaders. The first PO, established in 1882, was named "Saddle." Morgan farmers get their mail from Ione now.

8 m., Ione. Before construction of auto roads, Ione was a popular site for outdoor gatherings, because of its central plains location. With more than 300 people it's still humming, though the big doings are elsewhere now.

8.8 m., Lexington. Until a decade ago, Lexington was a close-knit town, with a far-off outlander atmosphere. But TV & better rds. and the exodus of small farmers have changed the situation. Lexington looks weary now, puffing on the plains. Store, cafe, station.

Jct., O 207. (See O 207 below.)

9.1 m., **Heppner.** Dominating the town is the **Morrow County Court House,** built in 1902 of native stone dug up on nearby Balm Fork. Fine museum in salmon-colored brick city library bldg.

Beyond Heppner the rd. spins as a darkling thread round & round the rising ridges of a hill humping high above a silent empire of Wheatlandia. The country is hilly, silent and spacious, with few ranches and fewer dwellings.

16 m.—from Heppner—Little Butter Creek. There was once a PO here, named Lena. It was closed long ago. In the early days, before rural delivery and the exodus of small farmers, the plains were dotted with small POs.

21 m., jct., US 395. (See *Eastern Oregon, US 395.*)

O 207—US 730 to US 26

This road begins in E Oregon but curves so far inland that, for all practical considerations, it belongs in this section, on Central Oregon.

7 m., Hermiston, burgeoning commercial center of large irrigation farming area. Excellent petroglyph rubbings in Inland Empire Bank.

Jct., O 32.

* *5.8 m.,* on O 32, Stanfield, a plains settlement that still wears some garb from the homesteader days.

(S of Stanfield on a county rd., *2.7 m.* to Echo, small and folksy. The county rd. W of Echo, *8 m.* to Echo Jct., parallels the old Oregon Trail.)

6 m.—from Hermiston—80N.

4.8 m.—on O 207—**Echo Jct.** Past the Gaylord Madison house here the gravel rd. W winds 2 m. up a long slope to ruts of the Oregon Trail.

S, O 207 drifts up Butter Creek and across Sand Hollow. The terrain is broken by ravines and distorted by scablands, making good hideouts for the cattle and horse thieves of the 1880s.

27 m.—from Echo Jct.—Lexington. *9 m.,* **Heppner.** (For both, see O 74, preceding.)

9.5 m., Ruggs. Store. *10.5 m.,* **Hardman,** a ghost town so ghostly it almost makes you shudder. All of the bldgs. on O 207, which was Main St., are empty; so are almost all the bldgs. off the road. A windmill leans against the roof of a weary barn, houses sleep deep in beds of weeds, no hand is on the water pump. There was much more to Hardman when the land around held many small farms.

7 m., Anson Wright County Park. CG. Fishing, rockhounding.

10 m., turnoff L for Bull Prairie FS CG (trailers)—*3 m.* Fishing and swimming in pine-fringed reservoir.

0.5 m., turnoff L for Fairview FS CG—*0.5 m.* Small area whose main attraction is scenic: far-reaching panoramas of varied landforms.

16.6 m., Spray. *13.5 m.,* Service Creek Jct. (For both, see this section, O 19.)

5.5 m., Richmond Jct.

* L off 207. *0.7 m.,* **Richmond,** deserted village. At one time it had a population of several hundred. Still standing are the school, general store bldg., church and some houses. These are of the past. The present is manifest in heaps of garbage. One more lovely place profaned. *13 m.,* Waterman. Only a stagecoach barn remains of a one-time town. *11 m.,* US 26.

1.4 m.—on O 207—on L, Waldron Community Hall. The last salute of a gusty horse-and-buggy settlement.

Oregon Trail ruts near Echo Junction

Abandoned general store, Hardman

Old lodge hall, Hardman

The road climbs up a grade which reveals gorgeous views of the painted uplands—great place for dramatic photography in color.

7.6 m., Twickenham Jct. Up the gravel rd. to the R the land was settled in the 1880s by homesteaders. Twickenham (*7.8 m.*—see O 19, this section) was founded and things looked good. But crops failed and the farmers left. For years the land lay sullen. Irrigation is now doing what the homesteaders without water could not do.

10 m.—bending around Sutton Mt.—US 26. (See US 26, this section.)

Eastern Oregon

Eastern Oregon calls to mind the furor and pageantry of gold strikes, roaring camps, gunfire between red men and white men, bloody feuds which pitted stockmen against homesteaders and turned cattlemen and sheepmen into deadly antagonists, legends which have grown tall under the big sky, and the mystery of lost men, lost mines, lost rivers and lost settlements—swallowed and hidden by and in the vast wastelands and gone forever from sight in hills and mountains seldom seen up-close and rarely explored.

All the stuff that makes for solid, gripping Western story-telling is here, long after the actors departed from a scene none of them really understood.

There is enough truth in the lore of Eastern Oregon to provide anyone with dramatic material enough to last a lifetime. The bloated myths that are arising, as vultures to feed on facts laid low, demean the land and those who lived and dreamed and won and lost on it. (Few won.) In this sparsely-settled country, the past is present only in suggestion—but how wide each touch of verity opens the gates of honest history!

Int. 80N-US 30—Jct., O 74 to Idaho Line

16.9 m., Boardman, major highway stop. Complete tourist facilities.

3.7 m., jct., US 730.

* 15 m., **Umatilla**, farm mart. Eastons Restaurant has small but impressive display of Western Americana. 1 m., Columbia River bridge. (Short cut to Wash. cities of Kennewick, Pasco and Richland.) 2 m., **McNary Dam.** 5.8 m., jct., O 207. (See *Central Oregon*, O 207.) 0.5 m., **Hat Rock SP**, on the banks of Lake Wallula, created by McNary Dam. Boat ramp, bathhouse, fishing. 1.5 m., jct., US 395. (See later this section, US 395.) 10 m., Wash. line.

7.6 m.—from jct., US 730—Umatilla Army Depot. Those brown mounds on the L hold deadly chemicals.

5 m., Hermiston Jct.

* 6 m., Hermiston. (See *Central Oregon*, O 207.)

2.4 m., jct., O 207. Another road to McNary Dam.

6.1 m., jct., O 32. Turnoff for Stanfield. (See *Central Oregon*, O 207.)

4.6 m., Echo Rd. Turnoff to placid village on site of old Oregon Trail and Ft. Henrietta (1855).

13.9 m., **Pendleton**, largest city in E Oregon and home of the great four-day **Pendleton Round-Up**, held each Sept. Historical display in Umatilla County Courthouse.

Jct., O 11.

* In spring and fall, particularly fall, this 42-m. rd. between Pendleton and Walla Walla, Wash., is as exciting in color as it always is in contour. In Sept. and Oct., after the pea and wheat harvests, the rhythmically undulating fields are rubbed by the chemistry of the turning season to rich autumnal tones.

At Weston Jct., 22.5 m. from Pendleton, O 204 branches off O 11. O 204 climbs E into the Blue Mtns. and reconnoiters through crisp woods to Elgin, 41.5 m. The mtns. to the S roll away in one hazy ridge after another. 15.5 m., Woodward FS CG. 0.5 m., Tollgate FS PG. 25.5 m., Elgin. (For Elgin, see 80N below.)

2.3 m.—from 80N-Pendleton city center exit—jct., US 395. (See US 395 below.)

6.6 m., Mission-Gibbon Jct.

* This road, following the Umatilla River through the unprosperous Umatilla Indian Res., also parallels the old Oregon Trail for about 8 m. 9.8 m. from 80N—Cayuse, a dusty hamlet. 10.8 m., Gibbon, named for (of all people!) a general who won his reputation fighting Indians. 10.1 m., Bingham Springs, an early warm sulphur springs spa in the Blue Mtns. Nearby, on a dude ranch, is a two-story log bldg. that was constructed as a hotel and stagecoach station. 3.4 m., Umatilla Forks FS CG. 18 m.—on a ridge of the Blue Mtns.—Emigrant Park-Meacham turnoff.

* 0.5 m., **Emigrant Springs SP.** This, because of the spring, was a favorite rest area for the Oregon Trail wagoners. The old rd. leads 3.3 m. to Meacham, a tourist facility stop. 4.6 m., Meacham-Kamela turnoff.

* 0.6 m., Meacham.

14.3 m., jct., O 244. (See US 395 below.) Hilgard Jct. SP. CG.

8.5 m., **La Grande,** market center of the table flat Grande Ronde Valley, which the covered wagon emigrants found so pleasurable. **Pierce Museum** at **Eastern Oregon College** has relics of regional Indians and Union County pioneers. But La Grande ought to be best known for the four-day, annual, mid-June **Indian Festival of Arts,** a flowering of individual skills of males and females from many tribes. Mt. Emily Scenic Route winds 10 m. to top of Mt. Emily, 3000 ft. above Grande Ronde Valley.

Jct., O 82.

* 2.5 m., Island City, agricultural suburb of La Grande.

(Jct., O 237. 13.6 m.—on O 237—Cove, in a far corner of the Grande Ronde Valley, overhung by the Wallowa Mtns. The houses, cherry orchards and green plots on the glistening rises of the dew-washed vale NE of Cove comprise one of the prettiest pictures of bucolic Oregon. From Cove you can see clear across the valley to the W—a shallow saucer upon which sunlight spills wonders. Cove's business district is shabby; it ought to be an artist's colony; lots of empty bldgs. available. 8.6 m., Union. [See O 203 below as part of 80N-US 30.] 11.1 m., **Marie Dorion Marker.** Here—or at least in this vicinity—on Dec. 30, 1811, a day nagged by snow and cold rain, 25-year-old Marie Dorion gave birth. Although she was Indian and her husband part-Indian, it is commonly held that the baby was the "first white child born in the Oregon Country." On this genetic basis, it is probable that some results of the Lewis and Clark expedition have prior claim to that distinction. The wife of Pierre Dorion, Sioux-French scout with the Wilson Price Hunt-Astoria party, Marie Dorion was as brave and as competent as any man in the group. She was, later, one of the first Willamette Valley settlers, and her championship of the Indians was widely recognized. She is buried in St. Louis, Ore. [See *The Great Heartland.*] *4 m.*, North Powder, a declining town which time has passed by. The tall tales of the old-timers grow reedier as their companions straggle to the grave. *1 m.*, jct., US 30. *20 m.*, Baker.)

9.7 m.—from Island City, on O 82—Imbler, which calls itself "Grass Seed Center of the World." A sagging town on the fertile flat plain. There were once many apple orchards around Imbler, but they were all uprooted. PO is in old mercantile store bldg. of the last century. Red wooden bldg. on L was livery stable. (Turn at Brooks Lane, at N end of Imbler, *0.5 m.* from PO. *1.2 m.*, on L, **Brooks House**, handsome structure built in the 1890s. Return to start of Brooks Lane. Turn R to Summerville Rd. *3.1 m.*, Summerville, a tattered fragment of its false-front stage coach and homesteader days. Less than 100 people now. Store, gas. Just beyond store, take gravel rd. on L. *1.8 m.*, McKenzie ranch, which has been in same family since 1868. Setting, with full-girthed barns and lawn-shaded house, is a bit of Iowa.) *7.9 m.*, **Elgin**. City Hall and Rex Theater have been in same bldg. since construction in 1911—probably nothing

Adminstrative and cultural center of Elgin; movie house inside city hall

Wright house, Union

like it anywhere else in the U.S. Two-story white house to R of LDS church and bldg. housing drug store date back to mid-1890s. Red brick bldg. diagonally across street from city hall was hotel when put up at turn of century.

2.8 m.—from La Grande, on US 30—jct., O 203.

  * *10.4 m.*, jct., O 237. (See *80N-US 30* preceding.) *0.5 m.*, **Union**, founded in 1862 by Union sympathizers. Some of the museum-piece stores appear almost as old as the town. Union has more distinctive Victorian homes than any city in E Oregon. Most prominent: **Wright House** (1882), 429 N Bellwood. Large brick Italianate villa, with gazebo (which served as summer house), marble fireplace, and tall wooden water tower, with servant's quarters on main floor. **Thompson House** (1873), 475 N Main. Cottage with octagonal tower. **Eaton House** (1907), 464 N Main. Brick-walled, with square tower, wrought-iron railing and mansard roof. Said by locals to be last mansard-type house built in America. **Townley House** (1894), 782 5th. Modified Queen Anne, with narrow Tudor chimneys, oak-paneled and soft-colored tile fireplaces, stained glass window on stairwell, and original copper doorknobs. **Rustic House** (1882), 612 S Main. Small cottage notable for its gable trim. Porch was added in 1890s. **Wildwood** (1869), in park-like grounds at Main & Bryan. Wooden Gothic mansion with octagonal tower and many gables and finials. Methodist Church (1905), on N Main, has flavor of Union in its prime. Gravestones in Union Cemetery go back to 1867. *7.6 m.*—from Union, on O 203—turnoff R for Catherine Creek SP. CG. Fishing. *12.2 m.*, Medical Springs, where aching settlers came for the hot sulphur springs. *22.2 m.*, jct., O 86. (See O 86 on *80N* below.) *2 m.*, Baker.

20.8 m.—on US 30, from jct., O 203—Anthony Lakes Jct.

  * *21 m.*, **Anthony Lakes**, a prime recreation area 7100 ft. high in the Elkhorn Range of the Blue Mtns. Lakes are headwaters of Grande

Wildwood, Union

Ronde, North Powder and N Fork of the John Day Rivers. One of the fastest growing ski areas in Oregon. Resort. Three FS CGs. Good reputation for Eastern brook trout and rainbows; no motorboats.

1 m., jct., O 237. (See O 237 on *80N-US 30* preceding.)

7.1 m., Haines. **Eastern Oregon Museum** (four blocks N of US 30) has surrey with fringe on top, buggies, horse-drawn sleighs that carried mail, a complete blacksmith shop, and much more of the memorabilia of E Oregon. **Radium Hot Springs**, popular spa since the late 1890s, has largest natural warm water pool in state. CG. (N of US 30 *0.8 m*; turn E *0.4 m.*)

12.4 m., **Baker,** a key passage on the Old Oregon Trail. Born of the gold rush in the 1860s, Baker managed to survive the death of a hundred boom camps by becoming the county seat, a freighting center and a RR center. Ten-story Baker Hotel is tallest bldg. E of Cascades. It has had more owners than a poker chip at an all-night game. State's largest gold display in **U.S. National Bank**, 2001 Main.

There are two important historical and scenic side trips out of Baker: Hells Canyon and the Ghost Gold Town Country.

Hells Canyon

The swift, relentless Snake River has cut the deepest gorge on the continent, between the Wallowa Mtns. of Oregon and the Seven Devils of Idaho. From the 9235-ft. summit of He Devil Peak, Hells Canyon reaches a depth of 7900 ft. Inside the heart of the twilight chasm, the black, beetling walls erupt 2000 ft., reach a bench, then soar 2000 feet to a second bench.

Before Idaho Power Co. removed the Snake's fangs by construction of three dams (Brownlee, Oxbow and Hells Canyon), the stream, traveling up to 15 m. per hour, created some of the most vicious white water in America. Further dam construction is seriously opposed by conservationists, who are deeply concerned about the survival of the Snake as a living river.

Once seen, this view of Hells Canyon leaves a lasting impression: the somber hue of the rock-faced lava walls, the endless gorges slicing into the awful trench, the barren and impassable hills, and the directionless sea of mtns., all combining to form an overpowering portrait suggestive of Dante's inferno.

Few men have failed to be terrified or shaken by the steep chasm. The Nez Perce made long detours around it. Explorer Robert Stuart, viewing the Wallowas, wrote: "Mountains appear here as if piled on mountains." French-Canadian trappers, coming upon the Snake, called it *"la maudite riviere enragee,"* and fled the gorge. The brutal days some of the Wilson Price Hunt party experienced here had ravaging effects. In 1843, Fremont, with rare understatement, described the mtns. the Snake flowed through as "rocky and impracticable." Those emigrants who left the Oregon Trail to seek a short cut by following the Snake as it disappeared into its long defile were lucky to stagger back, though near-naked and half alive. Some never came out.

Take O 86 from Baker.

41 m., Richland, with the last 22 m. following Powder River through a sparkling, serene valley. The Wallowas in the background seem miniature Himalayas and one has the feeling that if he surmounts the snow coifs he will find Shangri-La. Richland has general store, cafe, garage, station.

New Bridge-Sparta Jct.

* 3 m., Eagle Valley hamlet of New Bridge. Store-gas. 7 m., Eagle Forks FS CG. Fishing in a forest stream. *5.4 m.*, molding remains of Sparta, which flourished briefly as a gold mining town.

Huntington Jct.

* 40 m.—via all-weather county rd.—Huntington, on 80N. Most of the distance is along the recreational Brownlee Reservoir of the Snake.

* 3 m. E of Richland, Hewitt County Park. PG, swimming, fishing.

11.4 m.—on O 86, from Richland—**Halfway**, a picturesque, cheerful village of about 600. Modest tourist accommodations.

* 11 m. N of Halfway, the tottering, crumbling remains of **Cornucopia**, out of whose 30 m. of underground workings came more than half of Oregon's gold output. Founded in 1885, town was going strong until Oct. 31, 1941, when mines were suddenly closed. Within 24 hours, practically all the 700 inhabitants pulled out. Despite its disintegrating, Cornucopia is still the largest gold ghost town in Oregon. Camp under the pines on the banks of Pine Creek and fish in the bouncy stream.

17 m.—from Halfway—Oxbow, at Oxbow Dam. Here was the site of wicked Copperfield, whose sinfulness prompted Gov. Oswald West in 1914 to send out an "invasion force" of six men and led by the governor's private secretary, Miss Fern Hobbs. The saloons were shut down and a few months later Copperfield burned to the ground, and was never rebuilt. Trailer-camper CG near by. Store-PO.

* 12.5 m. S of Oxbow Dam, skirting Oxbow Reservoir, Brownlee Dam. Trailer-camper CG near by. A bridge connects to Idaho 71. 29 m., Cambridge, Idaho, US 95.

3.9 m. N of Oxbow Dam, Homestead. Before dam construction, it was one of the smallest and most isolated settlements in Oregon. Nothing left at the townsite but a few old bldgs. *1.8 m.*, Ballard Landing, end of all roads on the Oregon side of the Snake. Before the dams were built the bridge at Ballard Landing was the only fixed crossing of the Snake for about 200 m. Odd as it may seem, there was a PO here early in the century.

From Oxbow there are two land ways to see the tumultuous formations of Hells Canyon. The first is little known and is much the more difficult.

     * Cross the Snake and corkscrew *9 m.* uphill to Cuprum, Idaho. Store-cafe-gas. A *10-m.*, steep, narrow forest rd. weaves to Kinney Point. This is the view: the basaltic walls, the mtn. peaks, the folded hills, the far-off murky blue hanging over the high ranges, patches of forest, dagger-pointed rifts knifing through the cliffs, the gnarled wastelands, the Snake twisting around a burnished column and unfolding in its dark pit. All integrate into one supremely grotesque mosaic. *2.5 m.*, an even more awesome view from Sheep Rock, an overhanging shelf. Across the gulf of space is the peaked roof of the Wallowas, the white-tipped summits impaled in a cloudless sky. The heights descend in purple shadows to a green-fringed mesa, and for a moment all seems serene. But below the mesa, the spiny-tinged brown hills flare out, zooming downward at a terrifying angle. And there is the Snake, a wiggling eel from this eagle's nest. The other land route is at river level, or on a shelf above the stream.

     * Instead of taking the gravel grade, continue on the paved rd. *22 m.*, Hells Canyon Dam, at the gateway to the "real" or "box" chasm. Hells Canyon Park, on the reservoir en route to the dam, has trailer-camper hookups with water and electricity. Also, flush toilets, picnic tables, boat ramps, dock.

Jet boats, shooting the boiling rapids, penetrate the canyon for 7 m. below the dam. The most spectacular "looking up" scenery is in this section. For boat arrangements, write: Jim Zanelli, PO Box 145, Oxbow, Ore.

Gold Country Towns

One of the most persistent and intriguing Oregon legends is the tale of the "Blue Bucket Mine." There are many versions, all of which speak of the finding of gold nuggets somewhere between the Snake and Deschutes rivers by one or more members of the numb and disoriented Meek's Cutoff Party of 1845, which was seeking a "short cut" to the Willamette Valley.

The California Gold Rush brought nuggets into Oregon and these breathed new and more-vigorous-than-ever life into the wanly smoldering legend of "lost gold," with the sparks fanned by every promoter who could find an audience and a bankroll.

Hundreds of men, including some who had been in the Meek party, made tracks for E Oregon, scouring every river and creek they could find. In the search, gold was accidentally discovered, in 1861, near the present site of Baker. In every direction, a host of camps overnight arose. Like Roman candles, they peaked quickly and sputtered out. Nobody now knows their exact locations.

Hells Canyon from Sheep Rock, Idaho

The placer diggings, worked clean, gave way to lode mining. About a dozen hard rock towns developed. In time, they, too, ran downhill. All but a few have either settled back to earth or are completely deserted, their dilapidated ruins staring blindly at grass-grown trails.

At Baker, take O 7.

2.3 m., Griffin Creek, where gold was discovered on Oct. 31, 1861, setting off the era of boom towns.

5 m., dirt rd. turnoff.

* W 4 m. to approximate location of Auburn, which in 1862 had 5000 population and was second biggest town in Oregon. But in 1864 the PO was discontinued; not enough people. Today, all that was Auburn has been obliterated.

2 m., jct., O 220.

* On O 7: 4.5 m., Dooley Mtn. State Rest Area. Views to the W of the hills where many gold camps stood. 11.5 m., Bridgeport Jct. (5.2 m., Bridgeport. In the 1860s it was a terminal supply point for placer gold camp several m. SE. Store-gas. 10.8 m.—on O 7 from Bridgeport Jct.— Hereford. In 1885 it was location of largest horse outfit in Oregon. Store, gas 4.7 m., turnoff for Whitney—17 m. (See Gold Country Towns below.)

2.5 m., Unity Lake SP. CG, fishing. *3.2 m.,* jct., US 26. (See this section, US 26.)

8.8 m.—on O 220, from jct., O 7—well-developed **Union Creek**, FS CG, on large reservoir, behind Mason Dam. Fishing, boat ramp.

The CG is in the heart of the wide green meadows of Sumpter Valley, spread out toward the snow crests of the Elkhorn Range of the Blue Mtns. in breath-taking panoramas. Within the past decade, land values in Sumpter Valley have doubled and tripled, a direct product of the "open West" hunger of claustrophobiac, affluent Californians. Houses are going up everywhere and there is talk of Sumpter Valley becoming another Jackson Hole.

11.2 m., **Sumpter.** It wasn't more than a huddle of crude log cabins until 1896, when the narrow-gauge RR out of Baker reached the camp. Then Sumpter boomed as a hard rock, deep shaft mining town. It had 3000 persons, three newspapers, twice as many churches, four times as many saloons, sidewalks, electric lights and a brewery. It erected an opera house which, for some reason, barred sheepmen. Twelve m. of tunnel were simultaneously in operation. In 1902 a local paper asked in rhetoric ecstasy: "Sumpter, golden Sumpter, what glorious future awaits thee?"

The evidence is not hard to find. Even before the devastating fire of 1917, Sumpter had fallen on hard times. The truth is, there was not as much gold in the mines as had been anticipated. All that stands now of a business section that once was a crowded seven blocks long could be spread out in a single block—and the population is little more than 100. The only remains of the town's euphoria days is an 1899 vault of the Bank of Sumpter, many years extinct. Old mining dredge is tourist attraction. Store, cafe, gas.

From Sumpter, roads reach out to the hard rock mining camps of yore.

* N, *6.3 m.,* **Bourne,** below the green-masted prow of 8330-ft. Ireland Mtn. The gravel road clings to the bank of Cracker Creek, a loud-

Ore mill at Bourne   Bourne

mouthed stream that tumbles out of the high pine country. Back of the road, sometimes partially hidden by trees, are several ancient cabins and an old brick stamp mill bldg. Started in the 1870s as the whoop-it-up camp of Cracker, most of Bourne's people left in 1906, when almost all the active mines shut down. By then, Bourne had acquired considerable notoriety for its shameless wild-cat ventures. The biggest mining swindles in the state emanated from here, and before they were halted by federal authorities, many hundreds of persons had been heavily defrauded through promotions which promised huge profits in nonexistent "rich strikes" and "sensational" mining activities. Bourne today is a seedy scatter of scarecrow houses strewn over the hills and flats, with loose boards flapping in the banshee winds.

* W, *4.8 m.,* McCully Forks FS CG. Fishing. *11.3 m.,* **Granite.** Settled on July 4, 1862, by Calif. prospectors, the place was first called Independence; changed to present name in 1878. Granite profited as much from being a trading, distributing and shipping center as from its mines. Drummers who came in buggies to peddle their wares stayed at the three-story, 30-room Grand Hotel. Granite has a fair number of elderly bldgs.: city hall, general store, dance hall, tavern. Summer sees an influx of vacationers. Store-cafe-tavern-gas. In 1970 a dirt road was cut between Granite and Greenhorn (see below.)

* S *10.6 m.,* Whitney. A sawmill and freighting village that supplied the Greenhorn mining area, Whitney was a bold-letter point on the Sumpter Valley Railway. But it never had more than 200 people. A small boxcar, turned into a trail horse stall, is a memento of the RR days—and that's all that is left of Whitney, though scavengers hunt high and low for garbage dumps, as they do at all ghost towns. *9 m.,* the first half along the N Fork of Burnt River, Bonanza, the richest gold producer of the region. Little left but the rubble of a stamp ore mill and the trace of a mine that was worked to a depth of 1250 ft. *5.2 m.,* **Greenhorn,** which around the turn of the century had 2000 people, two hotels, several stores, and its share of saloons. And now of yore—a battered cabin here and there. Greenhorn is one of the state's prime rockhound areas, mainly for the jasper-hard, easily polished Greenhorn fern. Beyond Greenhorn a primitive trace—for jeeps and pickups—winds *16 m.,* past several abandoned mines, to 8131-ft. Vinegar Hill, formerly called Greenhorn Peak. The entire Greenhorn region is aswarm with long-forgotten mines, many of them reachable only by trail. (Don't go alone—and always let someone staying behind know where you're going.)

Resume 80N at Baker.

23 m., Durkee. Store, gas. Here the Burnt River enters from the W and flows S to Huntington. The wracked and wretched wastelands of the Burnt River Canyon constituted one of the most agonizing sections of the Old Oregon Trail.

18.5 m., Huntington turnoff.

*1.8 m., **Huntington,** a desert town started as a stagecoach tavern in 1862. In 1884 it became a RR division point. Construction of the freeway, good rds. to Ontario, Weiser and Baker, and the closing of the roundhouse took all the fat off Huntington—and a lot of the lean flesh, too. The broken, dusty glass above the cobwebbed door of the IOOF Hall reflects the condition of the town.

Huntington is the terminal of a county rd. which follows Brownlee Reservoir of the Snake River to Richland, O 86, and Hells Canyon. (See *Hells Canyon, 80N-US 30* preceding.)

6.2 m., **Farewell Bend SP,** on Brownlee Reservoir. At this point the wagon trains left the Snake in their trek to the W. CG, boat ramp, swimming.

4.1 m., jct., US 30N.

* The rd. follows the Snake through pretty hay and orchard lands to Weiser, Idaho, 15 m.

19.2 m., turnoff to Ontario.

* 2 m., **Ontario,** a modern city with excellent accommodations.

2.4 m., Idaho line.

US 395—Washington Line to US 20

This is the great high country cattle road of Oregon, touching only three cities with poulations of more than 3000 in its almost 400-m. journey.

10 m., Hat Rock SP. (See *80N-US 30,* preceding.)

31 m., **Pendleton,** the biggest city on the route. From here on, it is 197 m. to the next town of more than 2000 persons. (For Pendleton, see *80N-US 30,* preceding.)

14.5 m.—past McKay Creek National Wildlife Refuge—Pilot Rock, a mill town satellite of Pendleton.

7.8 m., jct., O 74. (See *Central Oregon.*)

17.1 m., **Battle Mtn. SP,** in prismatic pine woodland. The last gun battle between white and red men was fought here, in 1878.

9 m., jct., O 244.

* 0.8 m., Ukiah, an old cattle town that has followed the unfenced herds over the hills. Store-cafe-gas. 10 m., Lane Creek FS CG. (1 m., Bear Wallow Creek FS CG.) Fishing on Camas Creek. Profoundly moving woods. 6.3 m., turnoff for **Lehman Springs.** (1.5 m. S. Since the 1880s, the hot sulphur springs has been a popular spa. Located on a high ridge of the Blue Mtns., facing slopes of yellow and lodgepole pine.) 1.6 m., turnoff for Frazier FS CG. (1.4 m. S. Fishing on Frazier Creek.) 22.1 m., Red Bridge SP, in the bosom of a forest waving over the Grande Ronde River. 7.4 m., 80N (8.5 m., La Grande.)

2.5 m.—on US 395, from jct., O 244—turnoff to Ukiah-Dale Forest Wayside, scenic forest canyon extending along Camas Creek.

The rd. follows a narrow canyon of Camas Creek and 3 m. of the N Fork of the John Day before spiraling up a grade flanked by yellow pine. The 4127-ft. summit—18.5 m. from the turnoff to the forest wayside—is the divide between the drainage of the Middle and N forks of the John Day.

7 m. beyond summit, Ritter Jct.

* W, *11.5 m.*, Ritter Hot Springs, often mentioned in the annals of the early settlers.

13.1 m., Long Creek, a small cattleman's town living in the past. Store, cafe, station. Gateway to Galena-Susanville mining area—(*26 m.* NE).

Hamilton Jct. (See *Central Oregon, O 19.*)

9 m., Fox. Abandoned church at S end of town typifies the falling-apart village that seems to hang on despite itself. Store-gas.

The rd. runs through Fox Valley, a green and yellow sink, with scarcely a tree.

6.5 m., Beech Creek FS CG, a shady spot in the Malheur National Forest.

17 m., Mt. Vernon. Jct., US 26—to W. (See *Central Oregon, US 26.*)

8.6 m., **John Day**. (See *Central Oregon, US 26.*)

Jct., US 26—to E. (See *US 26*, below.)

2 m., **Canyon City**, the throbbing gray ghost of a golden era.

One day in 1862, some tired prospectors, in weary search of the "Blue Bucket Mine," stretched out on Whiskey Flat. Billy Aldred, spotting some interesting-looking dirt across Canyon Creek, waded over. Having no sluice pan at hand, he stripped, knotted the sleeves and legs of his underwear, filled the longjohns with dirt, recrossed the creek, and fell to washing dirt. Within hours, Canyon City, first town in Grant County, was born.

In its prime, Canyon City had 10,000 more people than its present 650. Pack trains bulging with supplies choked its narrow streets. The Pony Express galloped into town from The Dalles. Unionist Oregon miners stormed up a hill on July 4, 1863, as the battle of Gettysburg was being decided across the continent, to tear down a Confederate flag hoisted by California Johnny Rebs.

Into this churning, zesty carnival rode young Cincinnatus Heiner (Joaquin) Miller, whose gusty ego was matched only by the grandeur of the Blue Mtns. A few weeks after arriving in 1866, he was elected first judge of Grant County, serving until 1870, when he left the burly gold camp to blaze literary fame as the bard of a loftier range—"Poet of the Sierra."

Canyon City is still traced by narrow, hairpin Main St., on which stands St. Thomas Episcopal Church, built in 1876. But the paramount attraction is the **Herman and Eliza Oliver Historical Museum**, one of the finest regional museums anywhere in the NW.

Adjacent to the museum is the Joaquin Miller cabin, with some of his belongings still inside, and the old Greenhorn jail. The jail, which had been located 75 m. away, in the Baker gold country, "suddenly appeared" on the museum grounds on June 17, 1963. Across the highway, on sagebrush hills, are the debris of early "diggins."

14 m., turn R to Starr FS CG.

1.6 m., turnoff for Paulina, Post and Prineville. (See *Central Oregon, US 26.*)

8 m., Seneca, an old, yellow-pine logging town in Bear Valley.

* In the early 1900s the soil E along Bear Creek was soaked with the blood of men and animals slain in a ruthless range war. Rd. 162 today is a scene of peace, though sometimes of a peace which has paid a heavy toll. From Seneca, *11 m.* to Parish Cabin FS CG, an enchanting glade on Bear Creek. (Good arrowhead hunting N of road.)

For an exciting journey to the breathless scenery of **Strawberry Mtn. Wilderness,** continue *3.8 m.* past Parish Cabin FS CG to Shoestring Glade. Turn L. *11 m.,* High Lake Viewpoint. *1 m.,* stop and climb to top of ridge (100 ft.) for look down into Wilderness Area. Magnificent view.

0.5 m., Roads End. *2.4 m.,* by Skyline Trail No. 375, top of 9038-ft. Strawberry Mtn.

*9.8 m.—*on US 395—Silvies, portal to **Pons Ranch,** which has largest buffalo herd in NW as well as various exotic animals, including unusual cross-bred species. Area, *5.5 m.* W of Silvies, is fenced off, and visitors are not permitted access without escort. Inquire at HQ bldg. in Silvies.

17.2 m., Joaquin Miller FS CG. *2.1 m.,* Idlewild FS CG. *12.9 m.,* jct., US 20. (See this section, US 20.)

3.1 m., Burns. *27 m.,* Riley. Store-cafe-station.

(For US 395 from Riley to Calif. line, see *Central Oregon, US 395.*)

Burns, an up-to-date town of 3800 persons, is the largest city between Pendleton and Susanville, Calif., a distance of more than 500 m. Harney County Historical Society Museum adjacent to Chamber of Commerce.

The town was once the hub of a vast cattle domain. Of the many great names in cattle ranching associated with Burns, the most famous is that of Pete French, a short, dark-complexioned, intense autocrat of the range. Because of the way he lived and died, he is the most colorful legend of the sprawling cattle country.

Pete French came into the Blitzen Valley, S of Burns, in 1872, driving a herd of cattle, and proceeded to build, by disputatious means, a far-reaching cattle kingdom. His gunfire encounters with Indians and his even more bitter clashes with homesteaders, for possession of the land, constitute dramatic chapters of rimrock lore. His cowboys adored him; the homesteaders cursed him.

The day after Christmas, in 1897, homesteader Ed Oliver, long at personal odds with French, put a bullet in the cattle king's head. A homesteader jury in Burns speedily acquitted Oliver—and French's great P-Ranch was on its way to dissolution.

For a journey to be long remembered, explore the land S of Burns. This is "Big Sky" country, roomy and remote, anchored by the mighty bulk of Steens Mtn., stretching N and S for 50 m., and rising to a height of 9670 ft. It is a land where distances become beautiful and nothingness takes on a haunted quality; a land of the past and of timelessness; of the unexpected in a sea of expectancy; of rimrock canyons, water-color hills, safranine hazes, ser-rulated cliffs, Zane Grey hamlets, and far-flung cattle spreads.

Big Sky Country

From Burns, follow O 78 for *2 m.* to jct., O 205. Take O 205.

1 m., ranch founded by William Hanley, last of the cattle barons. Hanley, born in the gold town of Jacksonville, came to E Oregon in 1879 "as a kid hazing a bunch of horses across the sagebrush." He selected Harney Valley because he wanted "a big country for a big man." His great ranch was the Double O, SW of here. It had 17,000 acres, and Hanley's house was 8 m. from the front gate. Later, Hanley moved to his Bell A Ranch—this site—a 7000-acre spread. He died in 1935.

Hanley and his wife lived in a nine-room frame dwelling built at the turn of the century. He had his office in a blockhouse-shaped bldg., its top story encircled by a veranda, and the structure shaded by Chinese elms.

Near the willow-lined Silvies River, which runs the length of the ranch, are many structures built in the early 1900s: old-fashioned windmill, corrals, horse barn, granary, bunkhouse, cookhouse, blacksmith shop, slaughter house, dwellings.

S of the ranch for *6 m.*, a lovely valley, where the grass is green all summer and small ranchsteads bloom. Then sage flats, washing around little grass islands. Then—*21.1 m.* from the former Hanley Ranch—turnoff W to the Double O unit of Malheur National Wildlife Refuge. (*17 m.* to the former Hanley ranch, now harboring large flocks of snow geese and lesser numbers of Canada geese, Ross's geese, whistling swans, sandhill cranes, and many species of ducks—as well as dowitchers, avocets and other shore birds.) Then—continuing on O 205—the Narrows, a thong of land bound to Harney and Malheur Lakes. Malheur, on the E, is fresh and sweet; Harney is alkaline.

3 m. from last turnoff, turnoff to **Malheur National Wildlife Refuge.**

For a most rewarding nature excursion, visit the refuge. This natural wonderland is habitat and waystop for some 230 species of birds, ranging from lordly Trumpeter Swans to tiny Audubon's Warblers. There are also about 50 species of mammals, including deer, antelope, muskrats, mink, raccoons and coyotes. Dirt roads reach out along the canals, where most bird life—especially waterfowl—is found. But inquire first at HQ; some rds. may be impassable. The sod house site, at HQ, *6 m.* E of O 205, was locale of Pete French slaying. An excellent museum at HQ features displays of birds and mammals native to this area.

(A gravel rd. continues through the refuge to Princeton, on O 78, *15 m.* from HQ.)

16.5 m.—from Refuge HQ turnoff—Diamond Valley Jct.

* E, *6 m.*, **Diamond Craters**, 20 craters in a 35-sq.m. area of recent volcanic activity. The rd. forks here. S fork goes *5.5 m.* to pioneer cattle hamlet of Diamond and then *13.5 m.* N, where it joins the other fork, which has traveled *9.7 m.* through Diamond Valley. Near the joining is the round barn of Pete French, built to hold horses for saddle breaking. Rd. continues *14.2 m.* to Princeton, O 78.

Snowy egret nest in Malheur marsh   *Courtesy Malheur National Wildlife Refuge*

17.6 m.—from Diamond Valley Jct.—**Frenchglen,** named after Pete French and Dr. Hugh Glen, his Calif. partner.

Frenchglen, with a population which has hovered around 20 for the past two or three decades, is the biggest settlement in an area of at least 10,000 sq. m. Frenchglen Hotel (1916), as frontier as an old cattle brand, has eight rooms, none with bath, but all comfortable, and a family-style dining room. Coffee, served in giant mugs, is free to all, any time of day or night. (Fruit drinks free to kids.) Almost everyone driving through Frenchglen pauses here —and many take photos of the row of branding irons displayed outside the inn. Frenchglen also has a colorful general store, with gas pumps.

Frenchglen is the portal to one of the most scenically exciting round-trip mtn. drives in the state—into **Steens Mtn.**

The mtn., say geologists, is unusual in that it is a block fault; "a 30-mile rip in the earth's surface caused when the basaltic crust was thrust skyward along the fault line, to form the rugged face east. The west slope rises more gradually from Harney Valley to meet the east rim at 9670 feet, a cool mile above the surrounding grass and sagebrush-covered plains."

Frenchglen Hotel

From sageland to aspen-bordered meadows, the mtn. is rich in dramatically contoured and placed slopes, ridges, streams and lakes. Plant life is as varied as it is plentiful. Quail and chukar are thick, and sage grouse are observed with some frequency. The lower slopes are roamed by pronghorn antelope, mule deer continue up the west-facing slopes until winter snows force them downhill, and bighorn sheep are at home on the upper ridges.

The 52-m **Steens Mtn. Summit Rd.** has been designed for outdoor lovers. Along the way are four CGs and two PGs, all maintained by the BLM. In addition, there are several viewpoints, each offering a different panorama and all stunning. All CG and PG sites have fireplaces, toilets and garbage disposal units, but there are no trailer hookups, showers or electricity.

The largest and most popular CGs are at Page Spring, *3 m.* from Frenchglen, and 7000-ft.-high Fish Lake, *13 m.* from Page Spring. (The lake is stocked with rainbow trout.) The Summit Rd. passes, at *18 m.* from Frenchglen, the entrance to the P Ranch HQ of Pete French. Only the "long barn" remains.

Resume S on O 205 at Frenchglen.

6.8 m., turnoff R to Hart Mtn. trail. (See *Central Oregon, US 395.*)

3 m., S end of Steens Mtn. Summit Rd. *5.1 m.*, Roaring Springs Ranch. *8.2 m.*, Home Springs Ranch. *3 m.*, Three Mile Ranch. (All these ranches are large cattle spreads.)

26 m., **Fields,** an old stagecoach and freighting station at the E end of a parched valley separating Steens Mtn. from the 8545-ft.-high Pueblo Mtns. Its most prosperous days were in the 1890s and the first few years of the 1900s, when borax operations in nearby Alvord Valley were at peak level. The "mining" consisted of Chinese laborers scooping up crude borax from the dry lake beds. After being refined and crystallized, the pure borax was sacked and

Kiger Gorge, Steens Mountain
Courtesy U.S. Bureau of Land Managem

Wildhorse Lake, Steens Mountain
Courtesy U.S. Bureau of Land Management

loaded onto wagons. Borax trains of five wagons drawn by 20 mules were common sights in Fields, Denio and all along the way to Winnemucca, Nev., the rail shipping point. (The remains of the borax works, on the W side of hot Borax Lake, is reachable by taking a twisty, sand-gritty, sagebrush rd. *4 m.* N of Fields, on the route to Andrews, and following for *3 m.* A sod house, near the skeleton of the evaporating works, was built by the Chinese. Before embarking on this safari, inquire at Fields for rd. conditions.)

Fields is a most interesting scene: general store, cafe, four-unit motel, 1-room schoolhouse, stagecoach stable of local rock materials, PO in a trailer, sod house, sagebrush cemetery, windmill and airfield. Planes taxi down the dusty street to park, a rather unusual sight but typical of the frontier character of this deep hinterland village, which receives mail only twice a week.

* Fields is at the S end of the 250-m. Loop Trip from Burns to Burns, and omitting all side trips, including the Refuge. *15 m.*—from Fields—and through a borax region, the virtually ghost hamlet of Andrews, on the edge of forbidding Alvord Desert. *15 m.*, historic **Alvord Ranch**, an oasis in the desert. First white men here were troopers of the First Oregon Cavalry, in 1864. Ranch, which dates back to the 1870s, is at base of 5000-ft. fault, to top of Steens Mtn. Scene bceomes more awesome when viewed in perspective: the steep scarp soaring to the white summit and, on the other side, the inferno sink of the Alvord Desert and the purplish slopes of Wildhorse Mtns. *35 m.*, past wasteland, rangeland and unpredictable lakes, O 78. *70 m.*, Burns.

Resume S at Fields.

8 m., turnoff for Whitehorse Ranch.

* The dusty, rough, rock-bottomed road was not meant for fast travel. Tires in this wasteland are short-lived and rock puncturing of gas tanks is not rare. But an easy pace and caution will get you through. *20 m.*, **Whitehorse Ranch,** one of the oldest and most remote cattle spreads in Oregon. In 1969 it celebrated its 100th anniversary. A shady rest stop in an aura of historic charm. *21 m.*, US 95.

13 m.—from turnoff for Whitehorse Ranch—**Denio.** PO in Nevada. A paved road begins here to Winnemucca, Nev., 93 m. Modest tourist facilities. Jct., O 140. (See *Central Oregon.*)

US 26—*John Day to Idaho line*

13 m.—from John Day—**Prairie City.** Little of its old livestock and mining atmosphere has lingered on—apart from being artifacted in **DeWitt Museum**—but the picturesque foothills in which the town is nestled are as lovely as ever. Tourist facilities.

* A FS rd. from Prairie City leads *11.5 m.* to Strawberry FS CG. *1 m.* beyond, by trail, Strawberry Lake, one of five lakes in **Strawberry Mtn. Wilderness.** Lavish varieties of mammals, birds and flora. In July and Aug. the meadows and hillsides seem to burn with the bright colors of blooming wildflowers and bushes. Trail to top of 9038-ft. Strawberry Mtn.

Strawberry Lake   Courtesy U.S. Forest Service

* 1 m. from Prairie City on Strawberry Lakes rd., paved turnoff L. Follow 11 m. to Blue Mtn. Hot Springs, cradled by deep forests in a glossy fold of the snow-dappled range.

8.1 m.—from Prairie City, on US 26—Dixie FS CG. 7.7 m., Bates Jct.

* 1 m., Bates. Store-gas. A gravel rd. winds NW to an old mining district. (17 m., at forks, gravel rd. R goes 2.4 m. to Susanville, a gold camp started in 1862. It perished quite a while back, but people still come, questing for the "souvenir gold" of antiques. They cart out the miners' junk and leave their own. Straight from turn to Susanville, 2.1 m. to Galena, another defunct camp. Beyond Galena a graded rd. follows the Middle Fork of the John Day 21 m. to US 395, at Ritter Jct. At the Galena-Susanville Jct., a gravel rd. S cuts through woods for 23 m. to US 26, 4 m. W of Prairie City.) 1.9 m. past Bates, Austin, site of a once-renowned stagecoach hostelry.

3 m., turnoff for "back entrance" to Gold Country ghosts of Greenhorn, Granite and Whitney. (See this section, 80N-US 30, *Gold Country Towns.*)

5.5 m., Oregon FS CG. 2 m., Yellow Pine FS CG. 9 m., jct,. O 7. (See this section, 80N-US 30, *Gold Country Towns.*) 2 m., Unity. Store, cafe, station.

18.2 m., Ironside, looking across a vale to 7820-ft. Ironside Mtn., so named because its rocks look like iron.

US 26, which has left the mtns. and descended to a high plain, often barren of everything but juniper and sagebrush and the occasional shack of a "blowed out, dried out" homesteader, begins to find fertile land. Farms and orchards appear.

23 m., Brogan. Store-gas. Here Willow Creek meets the road and companions it. As the stream broadens, settlements and fertility increase. At Vale, Willow Creek is captured by the Malheur River.

24 m.—from Brogan—**Vale,** a burly market place of a large, very productive irrigated area. During the covered wagon days, the hot springs, at the E edge of town, and the adjacent wild ryegrass, were a boon to the weary emigrants, who had come through grimy, stock-hungry country. The springs were frequently mentioned in pioneer diaries; each wagon train must have washed tons of clothes here. Ruts of the Oregon Trail are observable S of town, off the N half of a county rd. leading to O 201. Old stone house (1872), near city park, is one of oldest bldgs. in Malheur County.

16.4 m., **Ontario,** largest and most modern city on the E Oregon border. *2.4 m.,* Idaho line.

US 20—Burns to Ontario

The land through which this road silently unfolds has known so much sorrow and bitter disappointment that it could be called "Homesteader's Heartbreak." The high desert, bleak, treeless, arid and desolate, drove off with the wrath of denial the throngs of naive settlers who sought to break the desert to their will. The land is still stingy, is still driving away people. In this harsh region, the largest settlement for more than 100 m. is less than 100 persons. Most people driving the road see little more than a chaotic hemisphere of washes, ridges, canyons and sagebrush—barren and repelling. Few are aware that, in reality, the desert is alive and exciting, with its own vivid wildlife and ecology. But to understand that, you have to leave the paved road, trek into the desert, and be patient.

12.6 m.—from Burns—turnoff L to site of Ft. Harney.

* *2 m.,* the almost vacant location of Harney City, which was partially built from the structures of Ft. Harney and which, for a spell, was a crackling settlement. But the town was no match for the desert. *2 m.,* site of Ft. Harney, built in 1867 and abandoned in 1880. All that remains of the post is a small cemetery.

29.4 m., on L, Drewsey Jct.

* *2.5 m.,* **Drewsey,** which dates back to 1883 and in the early days was also called Gouge Eye, because of the style of fighting employed when things got wild. Sequestered among splayed sagelands, which in true Western mystique spread to the gossamer swales of the breathing hills, Drewsey is genuine leather, sweat-stained and wind-scarred. In the last 30 years its population has fallen from 66 to 40; the old Catholic Church stands empty, as does the IOOF Hall, put up in 1900. Apart from the gas station, there is only one business in town, the Porter Sitz Co., a general store started before 1885 and in the same family since 1909. It is the most general general store in Oregon, an old-fashioned mercantile establish-

Old lodge hall, Drewsey   Rock formations on road to Westfall

ment which has retained its horse-and-buggy character while adding modern wares. The goods are piled to the rafters, hung from the rafters, jammed on counters, overflowed on shelves and heaped in corners.

16 m., **Juntura**, the major stop between Burns and Vale. With 90 people and even modest tourist facilities, it seems like a metropolis on the desert.

34 m., on L, Harper Jct.

* 1.2 m., **Harper**, which boomed when the RR came through in 1912 and declined when the RR eliminated Harper as a stop. No billboards, parking meters, sidewalks, traffic lights or air pollution. Store, garage, cafe-tavern, PO and three churches, one of which (Church of Christ) is in old RR depot, moved two blocks to present site. 0.5 m. N is Don Gregg Apiary, one of largest bee-keeping operations in NW.

11.8 m., **Westfall.** Between Harper and Westfall the lonely road passes spectacular rock formations and a choppy sea of sageland, over which Meek's Cutoff Party strained and gasped in 1845. Westfall is the only PO in Oregon—and perhaps in all the U.S.—which doesn't have a single resident. (Postmaster lives outside town.) Westfall was founded in the 1880s, when homesteaders began pouring into the valley. It prospered in the early 1900s, when it was a freight stage station on the road from Burns to Vale. The town then had about 40 homes, a schoolhouse with about 100 students, two general stores, blacksmith shop, two hotels, three saloons, a telephone system, barber shop, church and dance hall. The whole town looked up to the grandeur of the two-story house Mose Hart had built in the 1890s. It was the residential showplace of the valley. And settlers drove many miles to shop at the Jones and Company store, opened in 1889. Today, the Mose Hart house, formidable—and eerie—as it seems from a distance, is hollow and banshee-ridden, all of it but the stone peeling and rotting. The Jones and Co. store has been closed since 1964; little remains inside but an iron pot-bellied stove, an old scale, and a few items of yesteryear. The PO, which occupies part of the store bldg., has only 24 boxes, for ranchers who drive many miles to pick up or deposit mail, and is open only two hours a day. In the surrounding wind-scoured valley, where once there had been barns and horses and corrals and sheds, there is now only stock range. Even the town is grazing land. Westfall would have failed anyway, because the settlers couldn't make it on small farms, and sold out to large livestock companies. The immediate reason for its decline was that the RR decided to lay its tracks through Harper. After that came the exodus.

22 m.—from Harper Jct.—**Vale,** a principal market place in the rich Malheur Valley.

16.4 m., **Ontario,** the glittering showcase of Oregon's Snake River country.

Ontario is a popular jumpoff point for Owyhee (O-wy-hee) Lake, one of the foremost tourist attractions of E Oregon. The lake is a dammed product of the river, which was originally named Sandwich Island River, "so called," explained Peter Skene Ogden, "owing to two of them murdered by Snake Indians in 1819." The two men, employees of Hudson's Bay Co., came from the Hawaiian—or Owyhee—Islands, which our early Englishman friend, Capt. Cook (see *Oregon Coast*) had "discovered" and "honored" with the name of the first lord of the Admiralty, the Earl of Sandwich. The name of the river was later changed from Sandwich Island to Owyhee.

* Take O 201 (which is also US 26-US 20) from Ontario. (The road to the lake is well marked.) *12.5 m.,* where US 26-US 20 turns L to go into Nyssa (a sugarbeet and potato town with good tourist facilities) O 201 turns R. Follow it. *7.9 m.,* Owyhee Jct. Store, cafe, stations, garage. *22.7 m.*—through brilliantly colored butte and canyon country which elsewhere would be a much-heralded scenic drive—**Owyhee Dam.**

The dam was built as an integral part of the Vale-Owyhee Irrigation Project, largest in Oregon. When it was completed in 1932, rising 405 ft. from bedrock, the dam was second highest in the world.

Rising in several widespread branches in N Nevada, the Owyhee flows 250 m., through one of the most feral desert regions in the U.S., to join the Snake 20 m. below Ontario. Rarely does it come within sight of a habitation, let alone a hamlet. Where the dam now stands the river poured through a narrow basaltic gorge, impervious to cries for water from parched land and hungry homesteaders.

Behind the dam is the man-made lake, 1–7 m. wide and 53 m. long. In recent years it has become popular for motor boating and has gained regional attention for boat racing. It is also popular for its bass and crappie fishing.

2.4 m.—beyond dam—entrance to **Lake Owyhee SP.** CG, PGs, boat ramps. *2.2 m.,* resort: store-cafe-cabins-boat rentals.

Owyhee Lake winds stealthily through a silent, barren, contorted plateau endowed with the lavish coloring and stunning formations of the Grand Canyon country. Newcomers are caught unaware by each new configuration: fluted cliffs, redstone pinnacles, jagged rocks that look like ghostly ships, high-spired towers that appear in the distance as Arabian

"The Cathedral," Lake Owyhee

castles, blood-red battlements, and bottom slope swellings that conjure up the image of elephant feet in motion. The massive cliffs across the lake from the resort are pockmarked with grottos, into which boats slip with ease. Inside the cool, dark cavities, one feels a long way from the blistering desert.

Hot as the day is, night is cool and crisp at the lake. Sunset is always a miracle of redemption. The night sky is so prodigal of its stars it could lose a thousand in a night and still be a complete crystal dome. Dawn splashes on the hills and sunset paints in fresco.

Some of the painted buttes and horned hills along the lake look like giant murals bearing the Promethean strokes of a Diego Rivera or an Orozco. But the most spectacular scenery is in **Leslie Gulch,** 27 m. from the resort and reached at the W end by boat. Some travelers hold that the gulch is even more dazzling than Utah's Bryce Canyon. You can camp at the lake and hike down the gulch.

The Southeastern Corner

The least known part of Oregon is its SE corner. In these many thousands of sq. m., the largest community has less than 200 population, and no other settlement can count 50 persons within its boundaries. This area is so remote that in the 101 m. between Jordan Valley and McDermitt there are only two motels, and in the 147 m. between Burns and McDermitt, only one motel is available.

In this thinly populated land, side roads are relatively few, and ranchers who find tourists at their gates are apt to exclaim: "How in thunder did you ever get here?"

Yet, for all—or because of—its copious silence, its haunted hills, its ghostly rimrock canyons, its vast basins of sagebrush, and its mystic playa, SE Oregon is really a land for exploration by camper, or jeep. It isn't really inviting when traveling either of the two main roads at high speed. But off the highways, there is a topographical life spirit and a compelling ecological relationship that leaves its spell upon the wanderer.

SE Oregon is really a land for exploration by camper, or jeep, but there are enough passable roads for trailers and passenger cars to make sure that everyone who ventures off the pavement will be rubbed with a bit of magic.

The heart of SE Oregon is Jordan Valley, though it is pressed against the Idaho border. Actually, only one road reaches Jordan Valley, US 95; but from Burns to US 95, the only paved road is O 78.

O 78—Burns to Jordan Valley

16.6 m.—from Burns—Lawen. Store-gas.

* W 1 m., site of old Lawen, reduced to a one-room schoolhouse (1891) and a few scattered dwellings. In 1910, Lawen had hotel, bank, dance hall, livery, shops, "fancy woman house," and saloon, which also served as high school. Only traces of streets and bldg. foundations remain.

10.8 m., Crane Jct.

* 0.8 m., **Crane,** which has the only boarding high school in the state. Students come from distances up to 120 m. Almost every student is a good horserider. At one time Crane was a big cattle shipping point and had a right smart business section. But a series of fires in 1920 and the removal of the RR terminal to Burns in 1924 doomed the town. Sagebrush covers the sidewalks.

9.4 m., Princeton. Store-gas. A cheerful news exchange and meeting place for the ranch families of the area.

Lawen schoolhouse

Jct. for Malheur National Wildlife Refuge, Diamond Craters and Frenchglen. (See *Eastern Oregon, US 395*.)

3.7 m., on L, abandoned homestead with stark windmill, such as were common on the high desert many years ago.

9.6 m., on L, turnoff for **Malheur Cave**.

3.6 m. Local ranchers call this lava bubble or dome a "sinkhole." Cave wide and high with no side paths. Underground lake, about 800 ft. from entrance, is 30 ft. deep, cold, and not recommended for swimming. The road goes on 9 m. to the site of Venator, on the S Fork of the Malheur. Here the road branches. W, 16 m. to Crane; N, 20 m. to Riverside, where white plume agate is abundant. 18 m. more, past Warm Springs Res. (trout, bass, catfish), to Juntura, US 20. (See *Eastern Oregon, US 20*.)

14.1 m.—from Malheur Cave turnoff—turnoff L for Duck Pond Ridge.

* This road is suggested only for the hardy who have jeeps or sturdy campers. The first 26 m., to the site of Crowley, (where there was once a settlement, founded in the 1870s), is gravel. After that the rd. is, as the highway engineers say with twinkling euphemism, unimproved. 17 m. beyond Crowley, to the NE, the rd. forks. N, 38 m. to Harper Jct., US 20, with thunder eggs and obsidian found along Dry Creek, 11 m. above the forks. E, 66 m. to US 20, 4 m. W of Vale. Both trails are lonely, seeing only a few ranches, but explore an area not many have the time, tenacity and gumption to probe.

Turnoff R for Alvord Ranch, Andrews and Fields. (See *Eastern Oregon,* US 395.)

7 m., to E, Saddle Butte Lava Tube Area.

(In 1967, a series of caves were rediscovered in this region and received widespread news coverage. The chain of tubes in this 82-sq.-m. lava field are reachable only by trucks, four-wheel-drive units, helicopter, horseback or on foot. However, all of the caves are unsafe and, whatever your sense of adventure, do not risk your life in investigating the tubes.)

19 m., **Burns Jct.** Motel-cafe-station.

* S *25 m.—*on US 95—Basque Station, a state highway maintenance community. The only sign of life on this windswept plateau for many miles.

30 m., **McDermitt.** Oregon ends a few yards from the PO, putting McDermitt in Nevada. The state line cuts through some bldgs., the White Horse Inn, for one. Slot machines, forbidden in Oregon, are on the Nevada side. So, you gamble in Nevada and you sleep in Oregon— under the same roof. The dusty hamlet is lively and hot in summer; quiet and freezing in winter. Colorful general store is shopping and social center of vast sagebrush basin. Modest tourist facilities.

*5.8 m.—*E of Burns Jct., on US 95—**Crooked Creek State Rest Area.** Here are sandstone formations of brilliant greens and yellows deeply steeped in history. Through this land the Bannock Indians, seeking a safe land, passed in 1878. But they were soon crushed. (Snakeskin agate found in area.)

7.2 m., **Rome,** so named because rock formations 2 m. NW, rising from the desert plain, suggested the ruined temples of Rome. Modest tourist facilities.

* At Rome a dirt rd. takes off SE for the Owyhee canyon lands. On this safari are encountered fossil-bearing clay formations which assume a multitude of weird shapes, including solitary blocks up to 100 ft. high. Dusk casts these formations as monsters of a werewolf world but moonlight transforms them into a fairyland setting. Just drive an hour or so and then turn back.

5.6 m., Arock Jct.

* *4.5 m.,* the ranching hamlet of **Arock** (A'-rock), given this name because of the nearness of a massive rock inscribed with Indian pictographs. The rd. brings into view several interesting rock formations. Store-gas. Also, W. W. Jones School, honoring pioneer doctor of Jordan Valley. Take rd. that turns to the L, then heads N, and follow it *5 m.* to ranch with large modern house built on hill adjacent to rd. To L of rd., view of **Sheep Ranch House,** completed in 1868 as stage station on the rd. between Idaho gold fields and Calif. It was also a telegraph station. House, with portholes for defense, ought to be museumized. Sheep Ranch House is at the S boundary of the lava beds of Jordan Crater. The dirt rd. continues *12 m.,* skirting the lava beds, to the edge of the craters. It then forks. For a something special trip—with the proper vehicle—turn L. 8

Sheep Ranch house north of Arock

Ruby Ranch barn at site of old Danner (built circa 1865); stagecoach
rebuilt by Jordan Valley rancher Mike Hanley   *Courtesy Mike Hanley*

GRAVE OF JEAN BAPTISTE CHARBONNEAU. FEBRUARY 11, 1805

BORN TO SACAJAWEA AND TOUSSANT CHARBONNEAU
INTERPRETERS FOR THE LEWIS AND CLARK EXPEDITION.

GUIDE, TRAPPER, MINER, WORLD TRAVELLER, SCHOLAR, AND
POLITICIAN.
IN THE SPRING OF 1866 HE SET OUT FOR THE MINES OF MON-
TANA, CONTACTED PNEUMONIA AND DIED HERE,
INSKIP'S RANCH, MAY 16, 1866.

J.V. COMMERCIAL CLUB

Supposed grave of Charbonneau   **Courtesy Mike Hanley**

m., Owyhee Canyon, replete with jolting configurations. The rd. follows S along the canyon for *4 m.* before pulling E. It then slithers over rocky mesas and up and down yellow-green-brown-purple-ocher hills before reaching Arock, *22 m.* Quite a trip if you have the stamina.

10 m.—from Arock Jct.—Danner Jct.

* 4 m., site of a no longer existent homesteader settlement, Ruby Ranch. Remains of the **Inskip** (or **Inskeep**) **Rock House**, built in 1860s,

largely of native lava, as a fortified stagecoach station and dwelling. Barn is of same vintage. Immediately N is old cemetery. One of the graves is claimed to contain the remains of Jean Baptiste Charbonneau, the son of Sacajawea. "Pomp" was carried on his mother's back the entire route trekked by the Lewis and Clark expedition from Ft. Mandan. Whether it is really Charbonneau who is buried here is open to question. Supposedly, according to those who believe it is Charbonneau, he died here in 1866 of mountain fever, or pneumonia, while on his way from Calif. to the Montana gold fields. From the Ruby Ranch it is possible to reach Jordan Crater, *10 m.* distant, by jeep. But the going is rough.

11.5 m., turnoff L for Cow Lakes and Jordan Crater.

* *13.7 m.*, **Cow Lakes,** created by the eruption resulting in the nearby lava formations. Cow Lakes BLM CG. (No trailers.) Good fishing. *4.3 m.*, the outrim of **Jordan Crater,** a mammoth black hole that is the hollow obituary of a mtn. which burned itself out, in frantic spasms, about the time Columbus was landing in the New World. The eruption not only covered miles of the flat land with lava of various shapes and strengths but created many tubes and tunnels. Many of the blowholes are deep, with rock prongs at the bottom, so approach gingerly, because the overhanging crust is sometimes treacherously thin.

5.5 m., **Jordan Valley.** The first known white men to come here, in 1863, were prospectors. One of them was Michael Jordan, who was slain by Indians the following year. The town, on the banks of Jordan Creek, was chiefly a supply and way station for Idaho miners until the late 1860s, when Con Shea drove in two herds of Texas longhorns. The colorful Shea made his HQ at Sheaville. He and other ranchers ran large herds of cattle until the disastrous "double winter" of 1888–89 killed most of the cattle. Then sheep were introduced and Jordan Valley gained recognition as a great sheep center. To tend the developing flocks, Basques were imported. During the first decade of this century they arrived in large numbers, and Jordan Valley took the name, "Home of the Basques." The sheep, which once covered the hills in numbers of up to 150,000, are just about all gone. Livestock wealth is almost all cattle

Jordan Crater   **Courtesy Sid King**

now. The Basques have assimilated; only among the elders is the "native" tongue spoken, and Basque dress is seen only at rare festivals. In the town center stands the Pelota Frontone, the handball court of the Basques, built in 1915. The Catholic Church, a striking example of desert architecture, was built in 1912, of native stone. So, about the same year, were a number of other structures. Just browse around; you can cover the town in an easy walk. Jordan Valley Gift Shop, a drug store for half a century, contains one of the largest collections of period pharmaceutical equipment and medicine bottles in the NW.

Pelota Frontone, Jordan Valley   *Courtesy Mike Hanley*

0.5 m. E of Jordan Valley, on R, **Hanley Ranch.** Mike Hanley restored the stagecoach and wagons parked in the barnyard and uses them to follow where wagon wheels bounced a century ago.

Much of the area belongs to the Owyhee River, some of whose water has turned the desert into strips of greenery. Generally, the wastelands engulf the river but here and there, below a burnished hill, the stream, cool and rippling, flows through an oasis of handsome ranches.

* S & N of US 95 the Owyhee has cut through the colorful substrata chasms as deep as 2000 ft. These canyons, sometimes called "breaks," are seldom visited; they are little known and generally reachable only on poor dirt roads. Spectacular formations abound, and many of the views are overwhelming, but motorists ought to be prepared for gruelling stretches. At Three Forks, no more than a dot on the map, the wild, rugged canyon of the Owyhee begins to reach maturity. Beyond this confluence, where the forks of the river unite, the canyon deepens and grows more forbidding and richer in saffrons and purples as the Owyhee flows toward the Snake.

From Jordan Valley to **Three Forks,** *37 m.* The rd., partly in Idaho, and about half of it gravel and the remainder dirt, does not approach the Owyhee except at Three Forks. About the only signs of life along the parched rd. are the few crossroad mailboxes, several corrals made of sagebrush sticks, a cattle-loading chute, and a log cabin that some early cowhand used for range quarters. The view—looking down at the confluence of the forks from the edge of the plateau—is awesome. Some people who reach Three Forks, via a trace that snakes down a cliff, go wading up the N Fork, which is generally shallow, but most people first start snapping pictures of the sheer rock walls which thunder above the stream. The return to Jordan Valley may be made by backtracking *5 m.* from Three Forks and taking a *30-m.* dirt rd. which runs W to the Owyhee Canyon and then N, emerging at US 95, 1 m. E of Danner Jct.

US 95—Ontario to Jordan Valley

From Ontario, in the N, there are several approaches to Jordan Valley. The most popular, most comfortable and swiftest is US 95 all the way. (All other approaches eventually work into US 95.)

For US 95, take 80N at Ontario. *8 m.,* in Idaho, US 95. *13 m.,* Parma, a pleasant farming town. Complete tourist facilities. *13 m.,* Homedale, another agricultural hub.

* Some travelers prefer to drive to Nyssa, *13 m.* S of Ontario and turn E *2 m.* to US 95. (*6 m.,* Parma.)

* Still another way is to follow O 201 *32 m. to* Homedale Jct. and turn E *5 m.* to Homedale, US 95.

Below Homedale, US 95 serpentines the rims of arid hills, trudges melancholy badlands and riffles through wasteland draws.

36.5 m.—from Homedale—Malloy Ranch, once a way station on a freight wagon rd. It is in run-down condition. The old house would make a pretty picture if it were fixed up.

  * The most scenic route to Oregon's SE corner is via the 38-m. gravel stretch between Homedale Jct. and Malloy Ranch. Years ago this road was part of the main pike—and was the only "prime" road from any part of Oregon to Jordan Valley.

  14 m., **Succor Creek State Recreation Area,** in the heart of Succor Creek Canyon. A deep box chasm cut into solid lava rock, the canyon is best known to knowledgable rockhounds—for its thunder eggs, jaspers and petrified woods. (Good findings all the way S to Rockville.) In the inner gorge of the canyon, walls shoot up 300 ft. and then slope skyward another 700 ft. to culminate in a remarkable gallery of pinnacles, towers, mounds, cones, spires, faces, silhouettes, monuments and monoliths, gorgeously dyed with free-wheeling reds, greens and yellows.

  9 m., jct., old rd. to **Leslie Gulch.** Some sophisticated travelers regard this narrow canyon, which extends *9.5 m.* W to Owyhee Lake, as containing the most gorgeous and incredible scenery in all Oregon. The

Succor Creek Canyon from south end   *Courtesy Sid King*

Leslie Gulch   Courtesy Sid King

gulch varies in width from about 20 ft. at Succor Creek to about 300 ft. at the lake.

Red is the dominant color of Leslie's towering spires and sheer rock walls: red, from the fiery brick-red of Bryce Canyon through filtering shades of red-browns to dark red. The rock pinnacles, which soar up to heights of 2000 ft. above the dry stream bed of the canyon floor, are set against a background of cliffs ranging in colors through beiges, yellows and oranges, with sandwiched strata of pastel greens and violet. Variations in moisture on the rock surfaces and the constant shifting quality of light render a kaleidoscopic character to the cliffs and pinnacles.

7.5 m.—from old Leslie Gulch Jct.—Rockville. Only a grade school for children of nearby ranches.

3.5 m., new rd. to Leslie Gulch. A grade winds through thorny desert, slowly climbs the Mahogany Mtns., and zigzags down to Leslie Gulch. The rd. is dusty and there are many stretches without turnouts. But the scenery—including occasional views of wild horses and bighorn sheep—is grand.

4 m., Malloy Ranch, at US 95.

10 m.—on US 95, from Malloy Ranch—turnoff R for Cow Lakes and Jordan Crater.

* *19 m.*, **Cow Lakes BLM CG.** Trails and traces lead to lava beds and Jordan Crater.

8 m., **Jordan Valley.** Adequate tourist facilities.

The Wallowa Highlands

Here are the "shining mountains" of Oregon, the Wallowas, a half-moon-shaped range, 80 m. long and 25 m. at its widest. Here are pristine rifts, saltant rivers, cloud lakes and songbird meadows that glow with freshness—a pure and immense outdoors land with much ruggedness and few pretty touches.

This historic Nez Perce "Valley-of-the-Winding-Waters" produced the greatest saga in the state's history—a struggle for freedom, epitomized by the leadership of Chief Joseph.

It is a bit ironic to note that Chief Joseph, or 'Young Joseph,' as he was sometimes called, was regarded as a bloodthirsty savage by the grandfathers of men who now extoll his deeds and who exploit his name for tourism.

The speeches and quoted thoughts of Chief Joseph reveal him as a humanistic philosopher, gifted with a wisdom that bespoke the tongue of nature and the longing for justice.

To his people, a band of the *Numipu*, he was *Hin-ham-too-yah-lat-kekht*, interpreted as "Thunder-rolling-in-the-mountains" or "Thunder-strikes-out-from-the-water." His white man's name was derived from his father, Old (Chief) Joseph, who had been given the Christian title by Rev. H. H. Spalding at the Lapwai Mission, where the elder Joseph was one of Spalding's first two converts.

What happened to the Nez Perce was an old story. First the U.S. Govt. set aside land—in this case, the Wallowa and Grande Ronde valleys—for the Indians. Then, as word of good land spread, whites violated the treaty and occupied the valleys. Elsewhere this system had worked—so why not in NE Oregon as well. Always the troops would be sent in to protect white lives; always the soldiers would be hailed throughout the nation as saviors.

In some places, where treaties were violated, the Indians fought back, but the people of Chief Joseph did not. They appealed for protection to the govt., which had given its solemn word. Then the govt. duped or bribed some chiefs into signing a treaty which surrendered the Wallowa and Grande Ronde valleys to the whites. It was an old story.

Old Joseph refused to sign the treaty, and as he lay in his lodge, aged and sightless, he summoned his erect, handsome son, then 31 summers old.

The scene was described some years later by Chief Joseph: ". . . my father sent for me. I saw he was dying. I took his hand in mine. He said: 'My son, my body is returning to my mother earth, and my spirit is going very soon to see the Great Spirit Chief. When I am gone, think of your country. You are the chief of these people. They look to you to guide them. Always remember that your father never sold his country. You must stop your ears whenever you are asked to sign a treaty selling your home. A few years more, and white men will be all around you. They have their eyes on this land. My son, never forget my dying words. This country holds your father's body. Never sell the bones of your father and your mother.' I pressed my father's hand and told him I would protect his grave with my life. My father smiled and passed away to the spirit-land.

"I buried him in that beautiful valley of winding waters. I love that land more than all the rest of the world. A man who would not love his father's grave is worse than a wild animal."

In 1877 the govt. ordered Chief Joseph's people to quit their valley within 30 days for the Lapwai (Idaho) Reservation. Crossing the Snake into Idaho, they joined with other bands of Nez Perce. One of these, in retaliation against white outrages, had razed the homes of some white settlers and left blood on the land.

A strong body of troops was dispatched to punish the Indians, but at White Bird Canyon, Idaho, the pursuers were repulsed. Then Joseph and his chiefs devised a grand strategy which would take the Indians—women, children and the aged, too—to Canada. There, as every Indian knew, treaties were respected.

The retreat—of 2000 miles through enemy country—lasted four long and terrible months. The Nez Perce, with never more than 300 defenders, were opposed by 5000 soldiers and perhaps almost as many civilians. The Indians traveled without a supply train and they did not leave their wounded behind, yet again and again they fought their way past far superior forces, inflicting defeats upon famous generals and colonels. A dozen times they broke out of traps. When the soldiers had the Indians cornered at night, empty campfires were the only prizes of dawn. At the battle of Big Hole, in Montana, the Indians were attacked as they slept, but they rallied, drove back the soldiers, and captured a howitzer. The Nez Perce took no scalps, let women go free, harmed no children. It cannot be said the soldiers were as courtly.

The fighting retreat, conducted with extraordinary skill and courage, was carried on through Idaho, Wyoming and Montana. There, only 30 miles from Canada and freedom, the emaciated Indians were surrounded by fresh troops. A few Nez Perce stole through the lines and reached Canada, but most surrendered.

"Hear me, my chiefs," vowed Joseph in surrender. "My heart is sick and sad. From where the sun now stands, I will fight no more, forever."

Surrender terms guaranteed that the Nez Perce would be taken to Lapwai. Instead, they were herded to Oklahoma, an alien land. It was 16 years before Joseph saw the NW again, at the Colville (Wash.) Reservation, where he is buried. Not many miles from his grave a great dam bearing his name arises to confront the mighty Columbia. But the only monument he ever wanted, he said, was that 'all men should live as brothers.'

Only two roads enter the Wallowa Highlands.

The first is O 3, which begins in Clarkston, Wash., as W 129. Clarkston sits across the Snake River from Lewiston, Ida. At Lewiston, jet boats make two-day, overnight cruises 100 m. up the Snake to Willow Creek, deep in the canyonlands. (Write: Hells Canyon Excursions, PO Box 368, Lewiston, Ida.)

O 3—Clarkston, Wash., to Enterprise

31 m. S of Clarkston the rd. begins to climb down the Grande Ronde River Canyon. The hairpin descent is *10 m.*, with many beautiful views. At the canyon bottom, near the state line, the gossamer-like Grande Ronde is flanked by green fields—a portrait of nature's magic. Then the rd. climbs for *10 m.* At every turn, with the canyon deepening and more hills swimming into view, the spread of scenery is glorious. At the top it is heart catching.

1 m. from S end of Grande Ronde Canyon, turnoff R for Flora and Troy.

* *1.4 m.*, on gravel rd., Flora.

1 m., another turnoff to Flora.

* *3 m.*, on paved rd., Flora. Store-gas. From Flora, W *13 m.* to **Troy**, on banks of Grande Ronde and Wenaha Rivers. As a sawmill town, Troy once had 100 persons. Today, whatever there is exists for hunters and fishermen. Store-cabins-cafe-gas. Pack trips organized here for several areas of Wallowa Highlands.

A hairpinny dirt rd. out of Troy clings for *18 m.* to the canyon of the Grande Ronde, the rd. emerging at Anatone, Wash., 25 m. N of the first Flora turnoff. Close-up views of the river reveal white water rapids, beaver, otter, quail, ducks, elk, mule deer, falcons, ospreys and sparrow hawks. And, of course, there is the clownish chukar, who is everywhere— tantalizing and mocking. Long may the chukar survive!

Troy is the gateway to the **Wenaha Backcountry Area**, a 11,200-acre tract embracing the crest of the N Blue Mtns. and set aside for all available forms of undeveloped outdoor recreation. Motorized travel prohibited; trail use limited to horse and foot travel. Deep canyons slope sharply from trout streams to rugged basaltic ranges which afford sweeping vistas of the area's grandeur. The variety of timber should be pleasing to tree lovers: Douglas, white and alpine fir; ponderosa and lodgepole pine; Engelmann spruce; and western larch. A virgin white pine stand in the upper Butte Creek drainage features one white pine 66 inches in diameter and another 130 ft. tall.

4.8 m.—from S turnoff to Flora—**Joseph Canyon Viewpoint**, one of the least known and most exciting overlooks in Oregon.

11.3 m., on R, **Sled Springs**, a forest conservation trail that seems to provide particular enjoyment to children of grade school age.

18.2 m., **Enterprise**.

O 82—Elgin to Joseph

The other road to the Wallowa Highlands is O 82. This rd. begins at La Grande, 80N. (See *Eastern Oregon, 80N-US 30.*) 20 m., Elgin.

Elgin is also reached from Pendleton, 80N, via Weston Jct., O 11. *64 m.,* Elgin. (See *Eastern Oregon, 80N-US 30.*)

Elgin, a neat little town with moderate tourist facilities, is another portico to Troy's rich game country.

    * An all-weather gravel rd. follows the Grande Ronde for 17 m. before entering heavy woodlands. *38 m.*—from Elgin—Bear Canyon FS CG. *4.5 m.,* Elk Flats FS CG. *5.1 m.,* Mosier Spring FS CG. *15.4 m.,* Troy. *13.5 m.,* Minam, at the confluence of the Minam and Wallowa rivers.

    * Turnoff for Minam SP—*2 m.*

    * No rd. follows the Minam River and its sometimes rugged canyon S of here. Within 8 m. the river enters the Wallowa-Whitman National Forest and penetrates an area of magnificent woods and mtns. Relatively unknown, it is nature's purest bliss to those who pack in. Rising in the Eagle Cap Wilderness high in the Wallowa Range, the Minam River flows NW 45 m. to join the Wallowa River at Minam, and somehow it is fitting that there is very little of anything at the "town" of Minam. The last unroaded major river valley in Oregon, the Minam is home range of large herds of mule deer and elk. The river is copious with native rainbow trout and is the spawning grounds of steelhead and salmon.

The road E of Minam follows the Wallowa River, a crystal clear rippling stream, first through a canyon and then through a shallow trough below green

Bridge across Wallowa River

hills. There are few houses on its banks and a rustic pioneer atmosphere back of it. This country is so fair to the eye that even those things one sees elsewhere, stock and barns and houses and fences, seem to take on a special meaning here, as though touched by the spirit of enchantment.

12.3 m., Wallowa, farming and logging town with modest tourist facilities. Tick Hill, just N of town, with its stark basaltic formations, forms an odd contrast to the pine, birch and larch hills.

7.7 m., Lostine, a small sawmill town near the river of its name. Store, cafe, station.

* A rd. follows the Lostine River for almost 19 m. up a scenic canyon that leads to jumpoff points for the Eagle Cap Wilderness. The FS calls this route: "Following the retreat of the ancient Lostine Glacier." It explains: "Nearly one million years ago, the earth's climate became colder, causing more snow than rain to fall, and forming a large ice field in the center of the Wallowa Mountains." The large grassy mounds observed from the rd. are moraines, formations of dirt and rock carried down by the glacier from the higher rises of the canyon. Basing their estimates on the heights of the moraines, geologists believe the thickness of ice in the Wallowas was once 400 ft. *2.5 m.*, moraines. *1.1 m.*, more moraines. *5.8 m.*, **Lostine Gorge Overlook.** Short trail from parking area to impressive view of Lostine River below. *1.7 m.*, Williamson FS CG. Chinook salmon complete their life cycle here, spawning in the sand bars. *0.7 m.*, Lake Creek FS CG. Two fascinating points rolled into one: a plummeting creek and a hanging valley. *0.3 m.*, Hunter Falls Trail. (*0.3 m.*, Lake Creek flings itself with a cry of abandon into Lostine Canyon.) *0.2 m.*, Lostine Guard Station. From here on, the rd. is generally rough and narrow. Between the guard station and the end of the rd., at Two Pan Trailhead, *6.6 m.*, there are five FS CGs and a dude ranch, which specializes in Wallowa pack trips.

Trails from Two Pan Trailhead lead up both forks of Lostine Canyon into the **Eagle Cap Wilderness**, where no less than 45 mtn. lakes are accessible to hikers. The more than 220,000-acre area actually contains almost 75 lakes, snowfields, residual glaciers and alpine waterfalls—all under the great snowpeaks of the Wallowas, topped by 10,004-ft. Matterhorn and 10,033-ft. Sacajawea Peak. The Matterhorn, so named because it resembles the Matterhorn of th Swiss Alps, is the most striking peak: its sheer, blue-white marble soars above the spruce-fringed meadows of Hurricane Creek Canyon. Sacajawea Peak, which honors the young Shoshone mother who was the only female on the Lewis and Clark expedition, is a reddish conglomerate 1 m. N of Matterhorn. In a deep cirque to the E of these two peaks is 7100-ft. Ice Lake, dotted with floating "icebergs" even in summer.

10 m.—from Lostine—**Enterprise**, seat of Wallowa County and its largest community. Complete facilities. The mtn. scenery provides an exhilarating lustre to what would otherwise be an ordinary-looking town. Wal-

Old bank in Joseph, now Chief Joseph Museum   Imnaha River Canyon

Iowa County Courthouse, built in early 1900s of native rock, resembles an English gaol. Bowlby Bldg. (1889) was constructed of same material.

Jct., O 3—to Troy and Lewiston. (See O 3, preceding.)

6.7 m., **Joseph.**

* A more scenic route than the highway here is a paved rd. to the W of it. 7.6 m., Enterprise to Joseph. This rd. also leads to **Hurricane Creek Canyon,** looking up to the Matterhorn. Rd. dead-ends 4 m. from canyon entrance at Hurricane Creek FS CG.

Joseph has the stagecoach trappings of a leathery cow town. Its many old bldgs. include the Methodist Church (1909) and the house across the street. Kooch's Pioneer Museum has objects dating back to homestead days. **Chief Joseph Museum** is in 1902 bank which occupies a unique place in Oregon history. One of three men who robbed the bank later became president of it. Variety store is in 1908 bank bldg. Large brown house across from Indian Lodge Motel was put up at turn of century. For short side trip: turn L on Hurricane Creek Rd. 0.2 m., Chief Joseph Rodeo Grounds. Chief Joseph Days, with the grandest backdrop of any rodeo in the state, is held in late July. 0.2 m., on L, Hayes House, built in 1907. To L of it, hidden behind a willow, is house built in 1880, one of oldest in this part of state. 1.8 m., Hurricane Creek Jct. L to Hurricane Creek Canyon.

There are two prize off-the-beaten-path trips out of Joseph. Actually, they can be combined as a good (but hard driving) one-day trip.

* 30 m., through delightful highland meadows and sinuous canyons, **Imnaha,** a colorful outpost. General store, cafe, station. At Imnaha, the rd. forks. One branch goes up the Imnaha River; the other takes off for Hat Point.

First, the rd. to Hat Point. It is dirt and gravel, rough and dusty. Make sure you have good tires and plenty of gas in your tank. And drive cautiously. The first 6 m. wind up a steep grade; use low gear to prevent overheating.

5.2 m., **Five Mile Viewpoint.** A splendid panorama of the wild Imnaha River Canyon, with the white roof of the Wallowas in the background. The gracefully contoured patches of green in the coves of the bare-boned amphitheater, as seen from the uphill drive, seem out of place. But there are more than a score of cattle ranches along the Imnaha, with most of the herds large by any Oregon standard. Those rolling bunch-grass hills you see from the viewpoint are prime grazing lands. *6.2 m.,* Viewpoint. Imnaha Canyon on the R, Horse Creek Canyon on the L. *0.2 m.,* Horse Creek Viewpoint. *7.2 m.,* Saddle Creek Viewpoint. Picnic area; fireplaces & toilets; no water. The view overlooks Hells Canyon, with the Seven Devils of Idaho in the background. *2.2 m.,* Two Buck

Hells Canyon from Hat Point lookout tower   *Ralph Friedman*

Saddle, overlooking Snake River. *3 m.*, rd. forks. (To L, *0.5 m.*, Saca-jawea Springs FS CG. Drinking water and primitive overnight camping facilities.) *0.1 m.*, Hat Point FS CG. No water. *0.1 m.*, **Hat Point Look-out Tower.** Visitors welcome—but keep a very tight rein on children. 97 steps to the 12-by-12-ft. platform, with an 18-inch-wide walk around the lookout. Hat Point is at altitude of 6982 ft., 5706 ft. above the Snake, which looks like a blue trough twisted in a maze of eroded hills.

Return to Imnaha. If you're feeling up to it, drive back to Joseph via the Upper Imnaha River Canyon. It will be a memorable and cleansing experience. The Upper Imnaha was until recently little known to out-siders, apart from some hunters. Now tourists, including trailerists, are filtering into the area. The high, rock-ribbed mtns., with their precipitous rimrock, are among the most rugged and magnificent in Oregon. Between Imnaha and Joseph, 67 m., there is not a store or gas station. The ranchers, most of them off the rd., are friendly but there are sometimes long distances between ranches. However, there are a group of FS CGs about midway between Imnaha and Joseph. From Imnaha, follow N-111 *31 m.* to jct. with S-393, the Wallowa Mtn. Loop Route. (To reach O 86, 10 m. NE of Halfway, follow S-393 S for *24 m.* For Halfway, gateway to Hells Canyon, see *Eastern Oregon, 80N-US 30.*) For Joseph, from jct., follow S-393 W and then N for *27 m.* to paved rd., O 350. Turn L. Joseph, *9 m.*

From Joseph, merely reverse directions. *9 m.*, turn R onto S-393. *27 m.*, jct., N-111. Take N-111. *31 m.*, Imnaha. Apart from Lick Creek FS CG, 24 m. from Joseph, the other FS CGs—half a dozen—are clustered within a 9-m. stretch along the Upper Imnaha, the closest of these CGs being 34 m. from Joseph.

O 82 runs out at Joseph, but a good paved rd. continues S to one of Oregon's top scenic lakes.

1.3 m.—from Joseph—on R, **Chief Joseph Monument.** Here sleeps Old Joseph. He died in 1871 or 1872 and was first buried 4 m. N of Lostine. The grave is at N end of Wallowa Lake.

4.5 m., past **Wallowa Lake**, Wallowa Lake SP, on S end of lake. A com-plete recreational CG in pleasant wooded area.

Wallowa Lake is a precious emerald reflecting snow-capped peaks—unless the summer is abnormally dry. For sheer beauty of color, the lake is surpassed only by Crater Lake. For the grandeur of its environs, it has few peers.

Riding horses available near park. Wranglers guide horse parties into the mtns. Ice Lake, 8 m. away, at 7100 ft., is popular trip. Pack-in trips can be arranged here or at Enterprise or Joseph. Trails from Wallowa Lake lead to glorious alps scenery and high lakes. Resorts and dude ranches near some high lakes.

1 m. S of SP, High Wallowas Gondola Lift. Gondolas rise 3700 vertical ft. to 8020-ft. Mt. Howard in 15 minutes. Trails from tramway terminal on

TO THE MEMORY
OF CHIEF
OLD JOSEPH
DIED 1870

Grave of Chief Joseph at north end of Wallowa Lake

Wallowa Lake

Mt. Howard lead to viewpoints which show the many faces of the Wallowa Mtns. and Wallowa Valley. (Bring field glasses and lunch.)

This Oregon, as we have said again and again, is a beautiful land, but it has suffered at the hands of the careless, callous and selfish, who in small or large ways have despoiled one square foot or many square miles. This we must never forget: the land is ours only temporarily: we keep it in trust for those who follow—if there is a time for following. To paraphrase Woody Guthrie:

> This land is your land, this land is my land;
> From the redwood forest to the Wallowa highland.
> From Jordan Valley to the Western Sea,
> This land belongs to you and me.

Index